✓ **How to Pass**

HIGHER
Biology
for CfE

Billy Dickson and Graham Moffat

HODDER
GIBSON
AN HACHETTE UK COMPANY

The Publishers would like to thank the following for permission to reproduce copyright material:

Every effort has been made to trace all copyright holders, but if any have been inadvertently overlooked the Publishers will be pleased to make the necessary arrangements at the first opportunity.

Although every effort has been made to ensure that website addresses are correct at time of going to press, Hodder Gibson cannot be held responsible for the content of any website mentioned in this book. It is sometimes possible to find a relocated web page by typing in the address of the home page for a website in the URL window of your browser.

Orders: please contact Bookpoint Ltd, 130 Park Drive, Abingdon, Oxon OX14 4SE. Telephone: (44) 01235 827720.
Fax: (44) 01235 400454. Lines are open 9.00–5.00, Monday to Saturday, with a 24-hour message answering service. Visit our website at www.hoddereducation.co.uk. Hodder Gibson can be contacted direct on: Tel: 0141 848 1609; Fax: 0141 889 6315;
email: hoddergibson@hodder.co.uk

First published in 2014 by
Hodder Gibson, an imprint of Hodder Education,
An Hachette UK Company,
2a Christie Street
Paisley PA1 1NB

Impression number   5 4 3 2 1

Year   2018 2017 2016 2015 2014

Cover photo © anna - Fotolia
Illustrations by Aptara, Inc.
Typeset in India
Printed in Spain
A catalogue record for this title is available from the British Library
ISBN: 978 1444 18200 2

Contents

General introduction

Welcome to *How To Pass Higher Biology for CfE*!

The fact that you have opened this book and are reading it shows that you want to pass your SQA Higher Biology course. This is excellent because that type of attitude is needed in order to pass and pass well. It also shows you are getting down to the revision that is *essential* to pass and get the best grade possible.

The idea behind the book is to help you to pass, and if you are already on track to pass, it can help improve your grade. It can help boost a D into a C, a C into a B or a B into an A. It cannot do the work for you, but it can guide you in how best to use your limited time.

In producing this book we have assumed that you have followed an SQA Higher Biology course at school or college this year and that you have probably, but not necessarily, already studied National 5 Biology.

We recommend that you download and print a copy of the Higher Biology Course Assessment Specification from the SQA website at www.sqa.org.uk.

You should note that in your exam only the material included in the Mandatory Course Key Areas can be examined. Skills of scientific inquiry, described on pages 48–51 of the Notes, are also examined. You should get copies of any specimen or past papers that are available on the SQA website.

We have tried to keep the language simple and easy to understand and we have used the language of SQA Higher support materials. This is the language used in the setting of the exam papers.

Although we have covered the entire Higher course within these materials, we have tried to emphasise those areas that cause most difficulty for students. We have concentrated on support for the examination element of the course assessment, which is worth about 83% of your final grade. The other 17% is covered in your assignment and you will have support for this from school or college, although we have provided some material in the short chapter on pages 168–172.

We suggest that you use this book throughout your course. Use it at the end of each Key Area covered in class, at the end of each Unit in preparation for Unit assessment, before your preliminary examination and, finally, to revise the whole course in the lead up to your final examination.

There is a grid on page x that you can use to record and evaluate your progress as you finish each Unit.

Course assessment outline

The Higher Biology course is assessed in three parts: the National Units, an assignment and a course examination. It is necessary to pass *all* assessments to achieve a course award. The grading of the course award (A, B, C or D) comes from the assignment and course exam marks.

National Units

Each of the three National Units is assessed at your school or college on a pass or fail basis. There are different methods of Unit assessment. Each school or college will have its own approach but all students have to pass a test in each Unit and write up an experiment they have carried out. Your school or college will assess the Units and you will probably have a chance to try Unit assessments again if you need to. You must pass all three Units.

Assignment (20 marks)

The assignment is an open-book task that is based on some research that you have carried out in class time. The investigation will be supervised by teachers, and you will have to write up the work in the form of a report during a controlled assessment. During the write-up you will have access to your research material and notes.

The assignment has several stages:
1 Selecting a topic
2 Planning the investigation
3 Identifying resources
4 Carrying out the investigation
5 Selecting and gathering relevant information
6 Writing up an investigation report in a controlled assessment

The write-up is marked out of 20 marks, with some of the marks being for scientific inquiry skills and some for the application of knowledge:

	Marks available
Skills	15
Knowledge and understanding	5
Total	**20**

The marks are allocated as follows:

Skills, knowledge and understanding	Mark allocation
Aim	1
Applying knowledge and understanding of biology	5
Selecting information	2
Processing and presenting data/information	4
Analysing data/information	2
Conclusion(s)	1
Evaluation	3
Presentation	2

The assignment is marked by the SQA and contributes 17% of the overall grade for the course. We have provided a grid on page xi that will allow you to check that you are prepared for the controlled assessment.

Course examination (100 marks)

The Higher examination is a single paper consisting of a booklet of questions in two sections:

- **Section A** contains 20 multiple-choice questions for 1 mark each.
- **Section B** contains a mixture of restricted- and extended-response questions for a total of 80 marks. The extended-response questions range from 2 to 9 marks and the higher-mark allocation questions offer a choice.

The majority of the marks test knowledge, with an emphasis on the application of knowledge. The remainder test the application of scientific inquiry, analysis and problem-solving skills. There will usually be an opportunity to comment on, or suggest modifications to, an experimental situation.

The course examination is marked by SQA and contributes 83% to the overall grade for the course.

The various components of the Higher assessment system are as follows:

Higher Biology	Assessment	Who does the assessing?
Units (pass or fail)	Unit 1 tests	School staff
	Unit 2 tests	School staff
	Unit 3 tests	School staff
Course (graded A–D)	Assignment (worth 17% of grade)	Marked by SQA out of 20 marks
	Examination (worth 83% of grade) 20 multiple-choice marks and 80 restricted- and extended-response marks	Marked by SQA out of 100 marks

About this book

The course content section is split into three chapters, which cover the three Units of Higher Biology. Each chapter is divided into Key Areas. Each Key Area has four features.

Key points !

These list and expand the content statements from the SQA specification using words and phrases needed to answer examination questions. Where a key term appears for the first time it is in **bold** and you will find it listed in the Glossary on pages 176–186. It is essential to read the Glossary definitions when working with the key points. After having worked on a Key Area, the key points should be easy to understand. You might want to use the boxes to show progress. We suggest marking like this – if you are having difficulty, like this + if you have done further work and are more comfortable and this * if you are confident you have learned a particular idea. Alternatively you could traffic light them using coloured dots – red for 'not understood', orange for 'more work needed' and green for 'fully understood'.

Summary notes

These give a summary of the knowledge required in each Key Area. You must read these carefully. You could use a highlighter pen to emphasise certain words or phrases and you might want to add your own notes in the margin in pencil. In these summary notes we have tried to give examples of the biology from life situations. There are diagrams to illustrate many of the key learning ideas. Some areas contain separate boxes to show selected links to other Key Areas in the course or sometimes to emphasise ethical issues raised by modern biology.

Questions ?

These are designed to help you assess your knowledge and understanding of the key points and should be attempted on separate paper. Mark your own work using the answers provided towards the end of each Unit. Good performance in these tests is a sign of learning and progress in the course. The questions are in two parts:

Restricted response

This part has a set of restricted-response questions. Those worth 1 mark are usually straightforward and start with *name, state* or *give*. They can usually be answered quickly with a word or two. Those worth 2 marks are often more complex and require a description or explanation. They usually require two- or three-part answers.

Extended response

This part includes extended-response questions worth between 4 and 9 marks. These questions require detailed answers. In your exam each will usually offer a choice of questions.

Hints & tips ★

Where we offer a tip to help learning it is boxed like this. These tips can be very general or can be specific to the content of the Key Area. Many tips alert you to topics that are linked to other areas in the course and where you can read more. The tips are suggestions — don't feel you need to use them all.

Practice course assessment

Schools can have widely differing ways of assessing Units.

Although the practice assessment is designed to test *Units*, it can also give you an idea of your overall progress in the *course*. We have designed the assessments to be like mini course exams, with multiple-choice, restricted-response and extended-response questions.

We have included a practice assessment linked to each Unit. The questions are intended to replicate the types to expect in the course exam. They allow you to judge how you are doing overall. There is a combination of questions testing knowledge and its application and some testing scientific inquiry skills. The questions are provided in roughly the same proportion as in your final exam.

Give yourself a maximum of 60 minutes to complete each test, but don't worry if you go over this suggested time. Your timing will improve with further revision and practice.

Mark your own work using the answers provided at the end of each Unit. Although Units are not graded, you could grade your work as you go along to give you an idea of how well you are doing in the course. The table below shows a suggested grading system:

Mark out of 50	Grade
20–24 marks	D
25–30 marks	C
31–35 marks	B
36+ marks	A

Skills of scientific inquiry: three approaches

This science skills section offers three different approaches to revising and improving your skills of scientific inquiry. In the first, we offer some tips and hints for tackling exam questions. The second approach involves four practice questions in which all the individual skills have been identified for you so that you can work to your strengths and improve weaker areas. The third approach focuses on one investigation and provides questions about the thinking that should go into experimental design. Most students should use all three sections.

Your assignment

We give an introduction to the assignment, some suggestions for suitable topics and some information, with hints, to help you complete the task. On page xi is a grid on which to record evidence for your controlled assessment.

Your exam

We give some hints on approaches to your final exams in general, as well as more specific tips for your Higher Biology exam.

Glossary

We have given the meanings of the special terms that occur in the Assessment Specification for Higher Biology in the context of the Key Areas where they first appear in the book. You could use the Glossary to make flash cards. A flash card has the term on one side and the definition on the other. Get together with a friend and use these cards to test each other.

Answers

Short answers are provided for all of the questions in this book. These are intended to replicate SQA standard answers but we have tried to keep the answers short, and any instructions simple, to make them easier to use – there will be other acceptable answers.

Record of progress and self-evaluation

Use the grid below to record and evaluate your progress as you finish each of the three Units.

Feature	As an indicator of progress, I have...	Unit 1	Unit 2	Unit 3
Key points	used the minus (−), plus (+), star (*) system to identify areas of strength and areas requiring further attention for each of the key points sections			
Summary notes	read and thought about the summary notes for each Key Area and used highlighters to pick out the main points			
Hints & tips	read and thought about the hints and tips and exam technique advice for each Unit			
Questions	answered, marked and corrected the restricted-response questions at the end of each Key Area of each Unit			
	answered, marked and corrected the extended-response questions at the end of each Key Area of each Unit			
Practice course assessment	answered and marked Section A of the practice course assessment (10 multiple-choice marks for each Unit)			
	answered and marked Section B of the practice course assessment (40 restricted- and extended-response marks for each Unit)			
Skills of scientific inquiry	read and thought about the tips given for each of the skills for each Unit			
	answered, marked and corrected the skills questions in each Unit			
	gone through and thought about the skills areas in approach 3 and looked at the answers to these			
Glossary	used the Glossary terms and definitions to create a set of flash cards for each Unit			

Assignment evidence checklist

Your preparation for the communication stage of your assignment should allow you to produce a report that has evidence of the following assessment points.

Assessment point	Evidence	Check
Topic	My topic is related to a Key Area of Higher Biology	
Aim	My aim(s) have been clearly stated and I have described what is to be investigated	
Applying knowledge and understanding of biology	I have clearly explained the topic I have researched, using correct biological terms and key ideas	
Selecting information	My information has been selected from a variety of sources	
	This information includes some of the following: raw data from an experiment/ practical activity, extracted tables, graphs, diagrams and text	
	The information sources I have selected are relevant, reliable and could give similar or different perspectives to each other and I have stated why	
Processing and presenting information	My information is processed and presented in a variety of forms, using calculations and units where appropriate and raw data has been included	
	This processing includes performing calculations, plotting graphs from tables, populating a table from other sources and/or summarising referenced text	
	I have made it clear where my raw or extracted data/information came from	
	My presentation of processed data/information includes appropriate formats from the following: summary, graph, table, chart or diagram (at least one is a graph, table, chart or diagram)	
	I have used suitable scales, units, headings and labels	
Analysing data/ information	My analysis includes the interpretation of data/information used in the report in order to identify relationships	
Concluding	My conclusion(s) are clearly stated and relate to the aim(s); they are supported by what I have found out	
Evaluating	I have included an evaluation of my individual sources and an evaluation of the investigation as a whole	
	My judgements of the investigation are based on criteria, which may include the following: ● reliability of data/information ● validity of sources ● evaluation of experimental procedures.	
Presentation	My report has an appropriate structure, with an informative title and headings	
	I have given references to at least two sources used in the report in sufficient detail to allow someone else to find them again as shown: ● reference to text books, including title, author, page number and either ISBN or version/edition number ● reference to journals must include title, author, volume and page number ● reference to websites must give complete URL address.	

DNA and the genome

The structure of DNA

Key points !

1 Genetic information is inherited. ☐
2 **DNA** is a substance that encodes the genetic information of heredity in a chemical language. ☐
3 DNA is a very long double-stranded molecule in the shape of a **double helix**. ☐
4 Each strand is made up from chemical units called **nucleotides**. ☐
5 A nucleotide is made up of three parts: a **deoxyribose** sugar, a **phosphate** and a **base**. ☐
6 Deoxyribose molecules have five carbon atoms, which are numbered 1 to 5. ☐
7 The phosphate of one nucleotide is joined to carbon 5 (5') of its sugar and linked to carbon 3 (3') of the sugar of the next nucleotide in the strand to form a 3'–5' sugar–phosphate backbone. ☐
8 There are four different bases called **adenine** (A), **guanine** (G), **thymine** (T) and **cytosine** (C). ☐
9 Genetic information is encoded in the sequence of bases along the length of one of the strands of a DNA molecule. ☐
10 The nucleotides of one strand of DNA are linked to the nucleotides on the second strand through their bases – the bases form pairs joining the strands. ☐
11 Bases pair in a complementary way – adenine always pairs with thymine and guanine always pairs with cytosine. ☐
12 Base pairs are held together by **hydrogen bonds**. ☐
13 Each strand has a **sugar–phosphate backbone** with a 3' end that starts with a deoxyribose molecule and a 5' end that finishes with a phosphate. ☐
14 The two strands of a DNA molecule run in opposite directions and are said to be **antiparallel** to each other. ☐
15 Molecules of DNA can be linear or circular. ☐
16 **Prokaryotic** cells do not have a distinct nucleus and their DNA is organised into circular **chromosomes** and **plasmids**. ☐
17 **Eukaryotic** cells have nuclei containing their DNA in linear chromosomes. ☐
18 Linear chromosomes in eukaryotic cells have very tightly coiled DNA, which is packaged with associated **proteins**. ☐
19 Yeast cells have nuclei in which their DNA is found but some species also have circular plasmids. ☐
20 **Mitochondria** and **chloroplasts** in eukaryotic cells have DNA in circular chromosomes. ☐

Summary notes
Function of DNA

Genetic information is coded into the chemical language of DNA (deoxyribonucleic acid). This genetic information gives cells the ability to synthesise specific proteins that determine the cell's structure and allow it to control metabolism. Copies of a cell's genetic information are inherited by daughter cells when it divides.

Structure of DNA

Each DNA molecule is very long and has two strands coiled into the shape of a double helix. Each strand of the double helix is made up from nucleotides. Figure 1.1 shows a single DNA nucleotide made up of a deoxyribose sugar to which a phosphate group and a nitrogenous base are attached. The carbon atoms of the deoxyribose sugar are numbered from 1 to 5, as shown in the diagram.

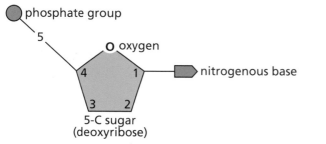

Figure 1.1 One nucleotide of DNA with the carbon atoms of the deoxyribose sugar numbered

Nucleotides are linked by their deoxyribose sugars and phosphates to form a strand with a sugar–phosphate backbone, as shown in Figure 1.2.

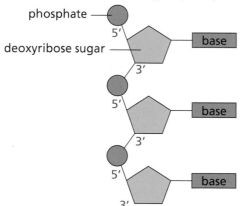

Figure 1.2 Short strand of DNA showing three nucleotides linked by a 3'–5' sugar–phosphate backbone

Two strands are connected by hydrogen bonding between complementary pairs of bases. The base adenine (A) always pairs with thymine (T) and guanine (G) always pairs with cytosine (C) making the two strands complementary to each other, as shown in Figure 1.3. Note that the strands run in opposite directions (antiparallel) depending on the bonding through the carbon atoms of the sugar–phosphate backbone. One strand has deoxyribose (3') at one end of the molecule, but its complementary strand has a phosphate group (5') at the same end of the molecule.

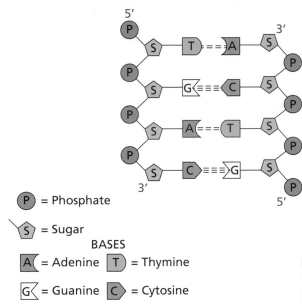

P = Phosphate

S = Sugar

BASES

A = Adenine   T = Thymine

G = Guanine   C = Cytosine

Figure 1.3 Short double strand of DNA showing complementary base pairing and its antiparallel structure

Figure 1.4 summarises the structural features of a DNA molecule.

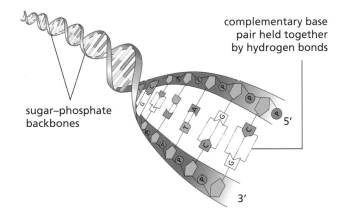

complementary base pair held together by hydrogen bonds

sugar–phosphate backbones

5′

3′

Figure 1.4 DNA showing double helix, sugar–phosphate backbones, complementary bases pairing and the antiparallel strands

Organisation of DNA in cells

DNA is organised into structures within cells.

Prokaryotic cells

In prokaryotic cells such as bacteria there is no distinct nucleus and the DNA is organised into circular chromosomes and plasmids, as shown in Figure 1.5.

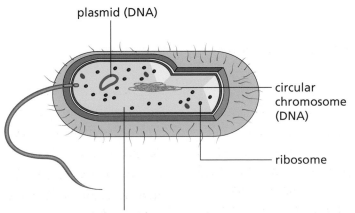

plasmid (DNA)

circular chromosome (DNA)

ribosome

cytoplasm

Figure 1.5 Main structures in a prokaryotic bacterial cell, showing circular chromosome and plasmids

Hints & tips

There are a number of features of DNA molecules that you should note for your exam:

✓ double helix shape
✓ sugar–phosphate backbones
✓ antiparallel strands
✓ hydrogen bonds linking strands
✓ complementary base pairing rules applied to nucleotides.

Hints & tips

There is more about prokaryotic cells and DNA in Key Area 2.7 (page 88).

Eukaryotic cells

In the nuclei of eukaryotic cells, the DNA is found tightly coiled into linear chromosomes and associated with proteins that help to keep the DNA strands untangled, as shown in Figure 1.6.

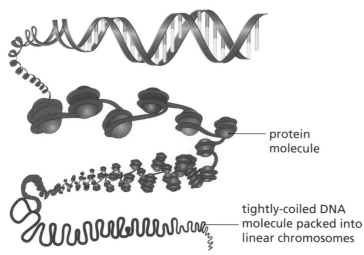

protein molecule

tightly-coiled DNA molecule packed into linear chromosomes

Figure 1.6 Organisation of DNA in eukaryote chromosomes

Eukaryotes also have small circular chromosomes within their mitochondria and within their chloroplasts in the case of plant cells, as shown in Figure 1.7.

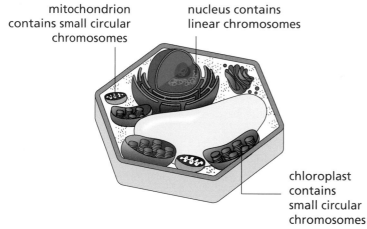

mitochondrion contains small circular chromosomes

nucleus contains linear chromosomes

chloroplast contains small circular chromosomes

Figure 1.7 Organisation of DNA in a eukaryotic plant cell

In yeast cells the DNA is also tightly coiled into linear chromosomes within the nucleus but some yeast species also have plasmids in their cytoplasm. The following table provides a summary of the organisation of DNA in cells.

Organism	Cell type	Organisation of DNA		
		Linear chromosomes	Circular chromosomes	Plasmids
Bacteria	Prokaryotic	Not present	In cytoplasm	Yes
Animals	Eukaryotic	Within nucleus	Within mitochondria	No
Green plants	Eukaryotic	Within nucleus	Within mitochondria and chloroplasts	No
Some yeasts	Eukaryotic	Within nucleus	Within mitochondria	Yes

Key words

Adenine (A) – base that pairs with thymine in DNA (and uracil in RNA – see page 13)
Antiparallel – parallel strands in DNA running in opposite directions
Base – nitrogenous substance that is a component of a DNA nucleotide
Chloroplast – organelle in which the chemical reactions of photosynthesis occur
Chromosome – structure that contains the genetic material of an organism encoded into DNA
Cytosine (C) – base that pairs with guanine in DNA
Deoxyribose – pentose sugar that is a component of a DNA nucleotide
DNA – deoxyribonucleic acid; a molecule that holds the genetic code in living organisms
Double helix – three-dimensional shape of a DNA molecule
Eukaryotic – cell with a discrete nucleus
Guanine (G) – base that pairs with cytosine in DNA
Hydrogen bond – weak chemical link joining complementary base pairs in DNA
Mitochondria – cell organelles in which the aerobic stages of respiration occur (*sing.* mitochondrion)
Nucleotide – component of DNA consisting of a deoxyribose sugar, a phosphate group and a base
Phosphate – component of a DNA nucleotide that is derived from phosphoric acid, H_2PO_4
Plasmid – circular loop of genetic material found in prokaryotic organisms and some yeasts
Prokaryotic – cell that has no discrete nucleus
Protein – large molecule made up from a chain of amino acids linked by peptide bonds
Sugar–phosphate backbone – strongly bonded strand of DNA
Thymine (T) – base that pairs with adenine in DNA

Questions ?

Restricted response (structured in 1- or 2-mark parts)

1 DNA is a complex double-stranded molecule made up from nucleotide units.
   a) Describe the shape of a DNA molecule. (1)
   b) Describe how the two strands of DNA are held together. (2)
   c) Name the **three** components that make up a nucleotide. (2)
   d) Explain what is meant by the following terms as applied to DNA structure:
      (i) complementary (2)
      (ii) antiparallel (2)
2 Cells can be classified as prokaryotic or eukaryotic. Describe the organisation and distribution of DNA in the following cell types:
   a) a prokaryotic bacterium (2)
   b) a eukaryotic plant cell (2)

Extended response (4–9 marks each)

3 Describe the function of DNA and give an account of the structure of a DNA molecule. (7)

Answers are on page 39.

Key Area 1.2
Replication of DNA

Key points ❗

1. **Replication** is the process by which DNA molecules can direct the synthesis of identical copies of themselves. ☐
2. DNA molecules replicate prior to cell division. ☐
3. DNA unwinds and unzips to form two **template strands**. ☐
4. Replication starts at several places along the DNA molecule at the same time. ☐
5. The enzyme **DNA polymerase** adds complementary DNA nucleotides to the 3' end of a DNA strand. ☐
6. DNA polymerase requires **primers** to start replication. ☐
7. Primers are short complementary sequences of nucleotides that allow binding of DNA polymerase. ☐
8. The **3'–5' lead strand** is replicated continuously in the direction from its 3' end towards its 5' end. ☐
9. Nucleotides are added as fragments on the **lagging strand**. ☐
10. The replicated fragments on the lagging strand are joined together by a **ligase** enzyme. ☐
11. The **polymerase chain reaction (PCR)** is a laboratory technique for the amplification of DNA. ☐
12. PCR uses primers complementary to specific target sequences at the two ends of a DNA region to be amplified. ☐
13. In PCR, heating separates the two strands of the DNA to be amplified. ☐
14. The separated strands are cooled to allow primers to bind to target sequences. ☐
15. **Heat-tolerant DNA polymerase** (Taq polymerase) replicates the region of DNA that has been primed. ☐
16. A cycle of PCR doubles the number of copies of a region of DNA. ☐
17. Repeated cycles of heating and cooling amplify the region of DNA. ☐
18. Practical applications of PCR include forensics and studies in evolution. ☐

Summary notes

Replication of DNA

DNA is the hereditary material of cells. It can make identical copies of itself by a process called replication. DNA replicates before cell division and copies are passed to daughter cells.

Figure 1.8 shows a cell with four linear chromosomes before and after their DNA

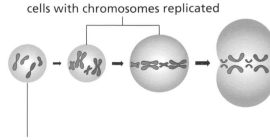
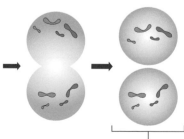

cells with chromosomes replicated

mother cell with four chromosomes

daughter cells with identical copies of the mother cell chromosomes

Figure 1.8 Chromosomes being replicated during mitosis

has replicated and how the chromosomes then move to form daughter cells.

Stages in replication of DNA

The double helix of DNA is unwound by an enzyme and the hydrogen bonds that connect the two strands are unzipped. The unwinding and unzipping form a replication fork.

Primers are short complementary sequences of nucleotides that allow DNA polymerase to bind. A primer joins the 3′ end of the 3′–5′ lead template strand and DNA polymerase adds free complementary DNA nucleotides to synthesise a complementary strand continuously.

On the lagging strand, primers are added one by one into the replication fork as it widens. DNA nucleotides are added in fragments. These fragments are then joined by DNA ligase to form a complete complementary strand. The process requires energy, which is supplied by ATP produced by the cell's respiration. The replication process is summarised in Figure 1.9.

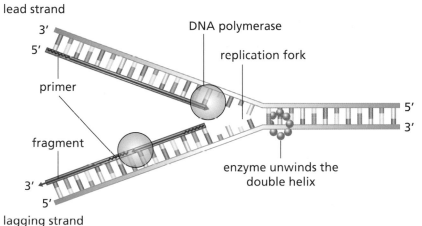

Figure 1.9 Replication of DNA

Importance of DNA replication

When the DNA in a chromosome is being replicated, many replication forks are formed at the same time. As a result, the DNA of whole chromosomes is replicated quickly and precisely, as shown in Figure 1.10.

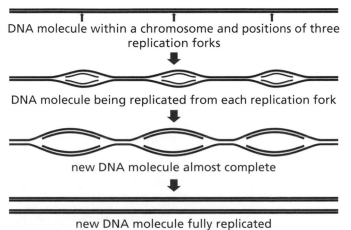

Figure 1.10 Multi-replication forks

DNA replication is important because it ensures that identical copies of the genetic information of a species are passed on from cell to cell and from generation to generation, as shown in Figure 1.11.

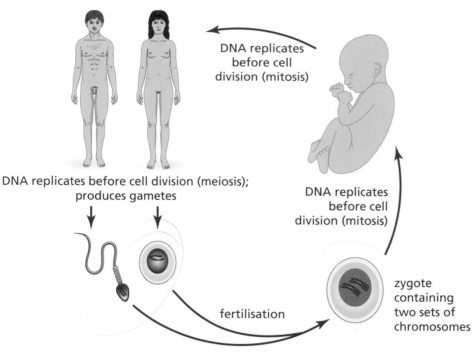

Figure 1.11 Importance of DNA replication in the human life cycle

Polymerase chain reaction

The polymerase chain reaction (PCR) is a laboratory technique that is used to produce billions of copies of specific target sequences of DNA. The technique is carried out *in vitro*, which means that it happens outside the body of the organism in laboratory apparatus, and involves cycles of heating and cooling, as shown in Figure 1.12.

PCR involves exposing DNA to a series of temperature changes known as thermal cycling. Firstly the DNA is denatured at 90°C, which separates the strands. Cooling to below 60°C then allows complementary primers to bind to specific target sequences. The temperature is then raised to over 70°C, when heat-tolerant DNA polymerase is used to synthesise new strands from free DNA nucleotides. These stages can be automated in a thermal cycling machine.

Many repeated thermal cycles allow billions of copies of the target sequence to be produced.

Hints & tips

Figure 1.11 illustrates the idea of vertical inheritance of genetic information from parents to offspring. There is more about inheritance patterns in Key Area 1.7 (pages 28–29).

Hints & tips

In vitro means outside the body of an organism – the opposite of in vivo, which means inside the body. DNA replication is in vivo but PCR is in vitro.

Hints & tips

In PCR, the primers locate a specific sequence of DNA, which is a bit like looking for a needle in a haystack. Once the DNA 'needle' has been found it can be amplified to make its own 'haystack' of copies.

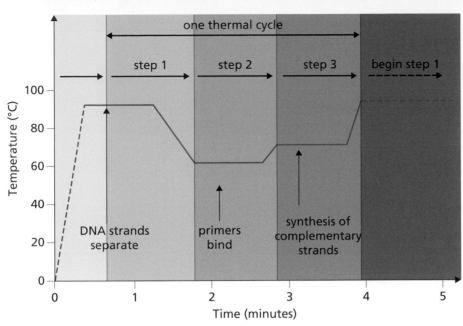

Figure 1.12 A summary of the events in the polymerase chain reaction

Hints & tips ⭐

You should be able to calculate the number of DNA molecules present after a number of cycles in a PCR machine. Remember that after one cycle there are two molecules and the number doubles after every further cycle.

Hints & tips ⭐

Heat-tolerant DNA polymerase comes from extremophile bacteria that live in hot springs. Their enzymes are adapted to work at high temperatures. There is more about extremophiles in Key Area 2.5 on page 79.

Figure 1.13 shows the pattern of amplification of a target sequence of DNA by the PCR process.

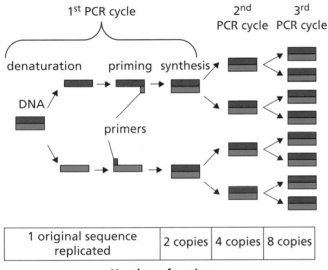

1 original sequence replicated	2 copies	4 copies	8 copies

Number of copies

Figure 1.13 Amplification of a target sequence of DNA by PCR

Applications of PCR

PCR has a variety of applications. In forensics it can be used to amplify tiny quantities of DNA from biological sources such as blood or semen. This allows confirmation of the presence of individuals at crime scenes from small samples of biological material.

Another common application is in amplifying DNA in studies of related species to show their true place in evolution.

Key words

3'–5' – strand of nucleic acid running from a sugar to a phosphate
DNA polymerase – enzyme that adds free complementary DNA nucleotides during replication of DNA
Heat-tolerant DNA polymerase – enzyme from hot-spring bacteria, used in PCR
Lagging strand – DNA strand that is replicated in fragments
Lead strand – DNA strand that is replicated continuously
Ligase – enzyme that joins DNA fragments to make the lagging strand
Polymerase chain reaction (PCR) – method of amplifying sequences of DNA *in vitro*
Primer – short complementary strand of DNA
Replication – formation of identical copies of DNA molecules
Template strand – DNA strand on which a complementary copy is made

Questions ?

Restricted response (structured in 1- or 2-mark parts)

1 The flow chart below shows temperature changes during steps in the polymerase chain reaction (PCR) procedure.

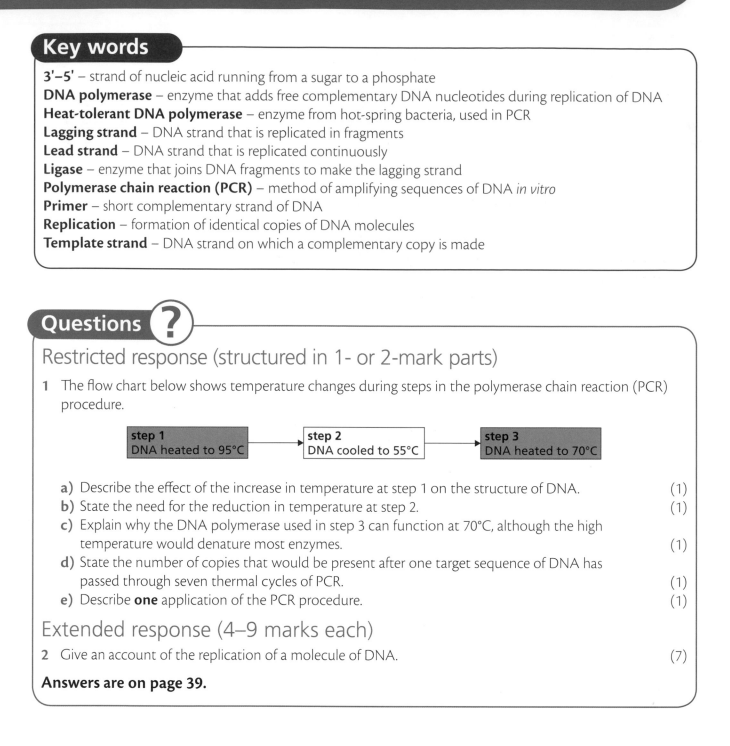

step 1	step 2	step 3
DNA heated to 95°C	DNA cooled to 55°C	DNA heated to 70°C

   a) Describe the effect of the increase in temperature at step 1 on the structure of DNA. (1)
   b) State the need for the reduction in temperature at step 2. (1)
   c) Explain why the DNA polymerase used in step 3 can function at 70°C, although the high temperature would denature most enzymes. (1)
   d) State the number of copies that would be present after one target sequence of DNA has passed through seven thermal cycles of PCR. (1)
   e) Describe **one** application of the PCR procedure. (1)

Extended response (4–9 marks each)

2 Give an account of the replication of a molecule of DNA. (7)

Answers are on page 39.

Key Area 1.3
Control of gene expression

Key points (!)

1 Genes are encoded into DNA and the genetic code is found in all forms of life. ☐

2 Eukaryotic genes have **introns** (non-coding regions) and **exons** (coding regions). ☐

3 Genes are transcribed and translated during gene expression. ☐

4 **Gene expression** is controlled by the regulation of **transcription** and **translation**. ☐

5 Gene expression can be influenced by intracellular and extracellular environmental factors. ☐

6 Genes are expressed to produce proteins. ☐

7 Gene expression results in proteins which determine the **phenotype** of an individual organism. ☐

8 Proteins have a variety of structures and molecular shapes, which allows a wide range of functions. ☐

9 Proteins are formed from **polypeptides**, which are chains of amino acids held together by **peptide bonds** and folded in various ways. ☐

10 The chains are held in their folds by hydrogen bonds and other **molecular interactions** between individual **amino acids**. ☐

11 Protein function depends on the three-dimensional shape of its molecules. ☐

12 Protein functions include acting as structural components of cells, enzymes, some hormones and antibodies. ☐

13 Only a fraction of the genes in a cell are expressed. ☐

14 Gene expression involves three types of **RNA**. This is similar to DNA but it is single-stranded, its nucleotides contain ribose instead of deoxyribose and the base **uracil** replaces the thymine found in DNA. ☐

15 DNA in the nucleus is transcribed to produce **messenger RNA (mRNA)**, which carries a copy of the genetic code. ☐

16 In transcription, **RNA polymerase** moves along DNA, unwinding the double helix and aligning RNA nucleotides by complementary base pairing to form a **primary transcript**. ☐

17 Introns are removed from the primary transcript and the exons spliced to form a mature mRNA transcript. ☐

18 Alternative **RNA splicing** allows different mRNAs to be formed from the same primary transcript depending on which RNA segments are treated as exons and introns. ☐

19 Triplets of bases on mRNA are called **codons**. ☐

20 Translation of mRNA results in the production of a polypeptide. ☐

21 Most codons code for specific amino acids but there are also start and stop codons, which start and stop **translation**. ☐

22 **Ribosomes** are made from **ribosomal RNA (rRNA)** and proteins. ☐

23 mRNA carries a copy of the DNA code from the nucleus to the ribosomes, where it is translated. ☐

⇨

⇨

24 **Transfer RNA (tRNA)** folds because of base pairing and forms a triplet **anticodon** site and an attachment site for a specific amino acid. ☐

25 Amino acids are carried by specific tRNA molecules. ☐

26 tRNA anticodons align with their complementary codons on mRNA. ☐

27 tRNA molecules deliver amino acids in sequence, which are then joined together by peptide bonds to form polypeptides. ☐

28 Following polypeptide formation, tRNA exits the ribosome to collect further amino acids. ☐

29 **Post-translational modification** allows different proteins to be created by cutting and combining polypeptide chains or by adding phosphate or carbohydrate groups to the protein. ☐

30 As a result of alternative RNA splicing and post-translational modification, one gene can express many proteins. ☐

Summary notes

The genetic code

The base sequence of DNA forms the genetic code. This code is found in all forms of life, which suggests that all life originated from a common ancestor.

Genes are the units of genetic code that make up the genotype of an organism. These are expressed to produce proteins, which form the structure and control the functions of the organism. The phenotype of an individual organism is determined by the proteins produced by the expression of its genes. Only a fraction of the genes in a cell are expressed depending on the proteins required by that cell.

Figure 1.14 summarises how the genetic code results in the phenotype of an organism.

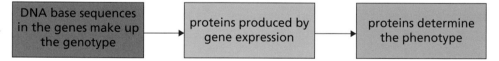

Figure 1.14 Flow chart showing how the genetic code determines the phenotype

Gene expression can be influenced by intracellular and extracellular environmental factors.

Structure and function of protein

Protein molecules are polypeptide chains. A polypeptide is a chain of amino acids held together by peptide bonds. The polypeptide is folded to give a protein with a three-dimensional shape held in place by hydrogen bonds and other interactions between individual amino acids. The shape of a protein is linked to its function.

Functions include structural components of cells, enzymes, certain hormones and antibodies, as shown in the following table.

> **Hints & tips**
>
> There is more about the idea of common ancestors in Key Area 1.8 (page 36).

> **Hints & tips**
>
> There is more about which genes in a cell are expressed in Key Area 1.4 on page 18.

Protein group	Function	Example
Structural components of cells	Building blocks of cell structure	Actin and myosin form structural fibres in muscle cells that allow contraction
Enzymes	Speed up the rate of chemical reactions	Pepsin speeds up the breakdown of protein in the stomach during digestion
Hormones	Chemical messengers involved in regulation	Insulin is involved in the regulation of sugar levels in blood
Antibodies	Defensive substances that give immunity against specific diseases	Measles immunoglobulin specifically recognises measles antigens and renders them inactive

Stages of gene expression

Genes are expressed in two main stages, transcription and translation. In transcription a copy of the gene in the form of a molecule called mRNA is created. In translation, a specific sequence of amino acids is built up using the mRNA code. These stages are shown in Figure 1.15. In eukaryotes, post-translational modifications produce the final structure of the protein.

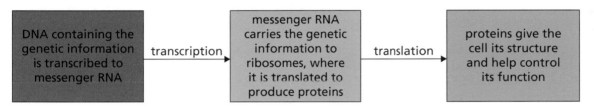

Figure 1.15 Relationships between the substances involved in gene expression

Ribonucleic acid (RNA)

Gene expression relies on various forms of RNA. RNA is very similar to DNA but has differences mainly in the nucleotides that make it up. DNA nucleotides have deoxyribose sugar but RNA nucleotides have ribose. DNA nucleotide bases are adenine, thymine, guanine and cytosine. In RNA, the base uracil (U) replaces thymine. Uracil also pairs with adenine in complementary base pairing. RNA is single stranded although there can be some base pairing of nucleotides. RNA nucleotides are shown in Figure 1.16.

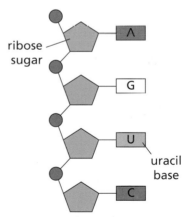

Figure 1.16 RNA nucleotides linked into a single strand, and showing the differences from DNA nucleotides

There are three types of RNA. Messenger RNA (mRNA) carries a complementary copy of the genetic code from the DNA in the nucleus to the ribosomes in the cytoplasm. Transfer RNA (tRNA) carries specific amino acids to ribosomes, where they can be assembled to form polypeptide chains. Ribosomal RNA (rRNA) is combined with proteins to make up the structure of ribosomes.

Transcription

In the first step, the enzyme RNA polymerase unwinds and unzips the double helix of the gene to be expressed and aligns free RNA nucleotides against the exposed DNA nucleotides of the template strand.

Complementary base pairing ensures correct positioning of RNA nucleotides, which are then joined to form a primary transcript. The primary transcript is a complementary copy of the gene made up of groups of three bases called codons, as shown in Figure 1.17.

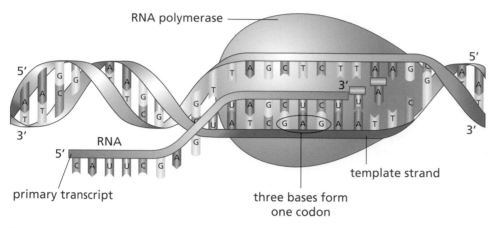

Figure 1.17 Formation of a primary transcript

Each transcript has introns and exons. Introns are non-coding regions and are removed from the primary transcript, leaving coding regions known as exons. The exons are then spliced together to form a mature mRNA transcript, as shown in Figure 1.18.

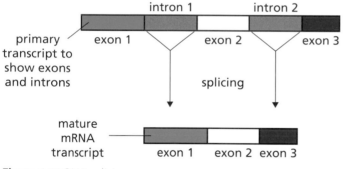

Figure 1.18 RNA splicing

Alternative splicing allows a primary transcript to form different mature mRNA molecules depending on which sequences are treated as introns and which as exons.

Ribosomes and translation

In eukaryotes mRNA molecules move from the nucleus to the ribosomes to be translated.

Ribosomes made of rRNA and protein are found free in the cytoplasm of cells or bound to the membranes of its endoplasmic reticulum (ER). A mature mRNA molecule binds onto a ribosome. mRNA carries a start codon, which starts translation, and a stop codon, which causes translation to finish when the polypeptide is complete.

The folded tRNA molecules, held by complementary base pairs, have a triplet of three bases called an anticodon and an attachment site to transport a specific amino acid to mRNA on the ribosomes, as shown in Figure 1.19. They are recognised and align with the mRNA according to their anticodons, which are complementary to the codons of mRNA. The amino acids that have been lined up bind through peptide bonds to form polypeptides. The polypeptide folds to form a protein, which is held together by hydrogen bonds and other molecular interactions between amino acids.

Translation is summarised in Figure 1.19.

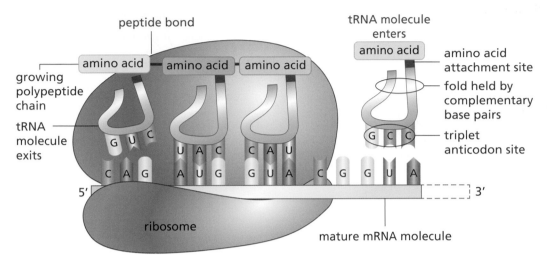

Figure 1.19 Translation of mRNA to form a polypeptide chain

Post-translational modification completes the formation of the protein by making changes to the chemical structure of the polypeptide chain. Figure 1.20 shows how the polypeptide chain of insulin is modified by the combining and cutting of the chain.

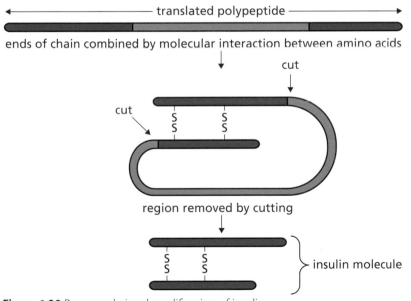

Figure 1.20 Post-translational modification of insulin

Other post-translational modifications include the addition of phosphate or carbohydrate groups to a polypeptide chain.

One gene, many proteins

Different proteins can be expressed from the same gene due to alternative RNA splicing and the various types of post-translational modification that can occur. This idea is summarised in Figure 1.21.

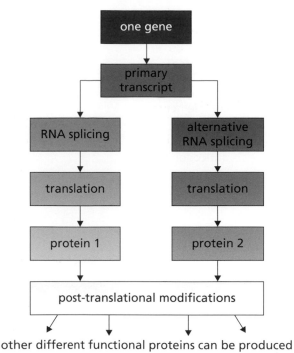

Figure 1.21 Production of different proteins from one gene

Key words

Amino acid – unit of polypeptide structure

Anticodon – sequence of three bases on tRNA that specifies an amino acid

Codon – sequence of three bases on mRNA that specifies an amino acid

Exon – sequence of DNA that codes for a protein

Gene expression – transcription and translation

Intron – non-coding sequence of DNA

Mature messenger RNA (mRNA) – carries a copy of the DNA code to a ribosome

Molecular interactions – various chemical links joining amino acids and giving protein molecules their shape

Peptide bonds – strong chemical links in the primary structure of polypeptides

Phenotype – outward appearance of an organism

Polypeptide – short strand of amino acids

Post-translational modification – changes made to polypeptides following translation

Primary transcript – molecule made when DNA is transcribed

Ribosomal RNA (rRNA) – type of RNA that makes up ribosomes

Ribosome – site of protein synthesis; composed of rRNA and protein

RNA – ribonucleic acid, which occurs in several forms in cells

RNA polymerase – enzyme involved in synthesis of primary transcripts from DNA

RNA splicing – joining of exons following the removal of introns from a primary transcript

Transcription – copying of a DNA sequence to make a primary transcript

Transfer RNA (tRNA) – transfers specific amino acids to the mRNA on the ribosomes

Translation – production of a polypeptide using sequences of mRNA

Uracil – RNA base not found in DNA

Questions ?

Restricted response (structured in 1- or 2-mark parts)

1 Proteins are chains of amino acids folded into three-dimensional shapes.
   a) Name the bonds that hold the amino acids together in sequence. (1)
   b) Describe how the chains of amino acids are held in their three-dimensional shape. (1)
   c) Explain the importance of the three-dimensional shape of a protein molecule. (1)
2 Give **two** ways in which the expression of a single gene can result in different proteins being produced. (2)
3 Eukaryotic genes are made up from base sequences known as introns and exons. State how introns and exons differ. (1)
4 Describe **two** post-translational modifications of polypeptides produced by eukaryotic cells. (2)

Extended response (4–9 marks each)

5 Give an account of gene expression in eukaryotic cells under the following headings:
   a) transcription of DNA (4)
   b) translation of mature mRNA. (4)

Answers are on page 40. (total = 8)

Key Area 1.4
Cellular differentiation

Key points ❗

1 Cellular **differentiation** is a process in which a cell develops more specialised functions. ☐
2 Specialised cells express the genes to produce proteins characteristic of that type of cell. ☐
3 **Meristems** are regions of unspecialised cells in plants. ☐
4 Meristem cells can continue to divide and differentiate into specialised cells. ☐
5 **Stem cells** are relatively unspecialised cells in animals that can continue to divide and differentiate into specialised cells. ☐
6 In the very early mammal embryo, **embryonic stem cells** can divide and differentiate into all of the cell types that make up the organism. ☐
7 **Tissue (adult) stem cells** replenish differentiated cells that need to be replaced following damage or disease. ☐
8 Tissue stem cells can divide to give rise to a more limited range of cell types than embryonic stem cells. ☐
9 Stem cell research provides information on how cell processes such as cell growth, differentiation and gene regulation work. ☐
10 Stem cells are used **therapeutically** in the repair of damaged or diseased organs or tissues. ☐
11 Stem cells can be used as model cells to study how diseases develop or for drug testing. ☐
12 Stem cell use and its regulation raise ethical issues. ☐

Summary notes

Cellular differentiation

Differentiation is a process by which unspecialised cells become specialised for a specific function in the body of a living organism. The process depends on the control of gene expression. Specialised cells express the genes characteristic of that cell type. A mammalian muscle cell expresses mammalian muscle cell genes and so on. Therefore mammalian muscle cells produce mammalian muscle cell proteins. This idea is shown in Figure 1.22.

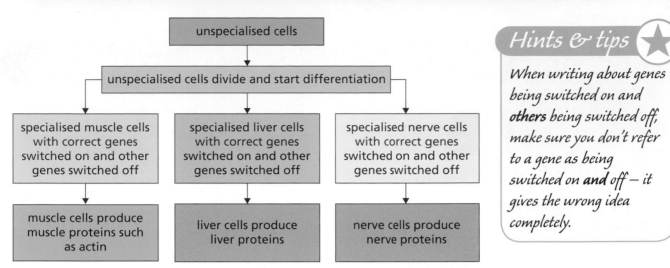

Figure 1.22 Differentiation

Meristems

Regions in plants containing unspecialised cells are called meristems. Meristem cells are capable of cell division and produce new cells that can then differentiate to produce permanent tissues. The meristems of a flowering plant are shown in Figure 1.23.

Stem cells

Stem cells are relatively unspecialised cells in animals. They can divide to produce cells that can then differentiate into various cell types and more stem cells. In early embryos, embryonic stem cells differentiate into all the cell types that make up the adult organism, as shown in Figure 1.24.

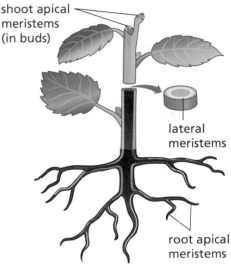

Figure 1.23 Plant seedling, showing the positions of meristems

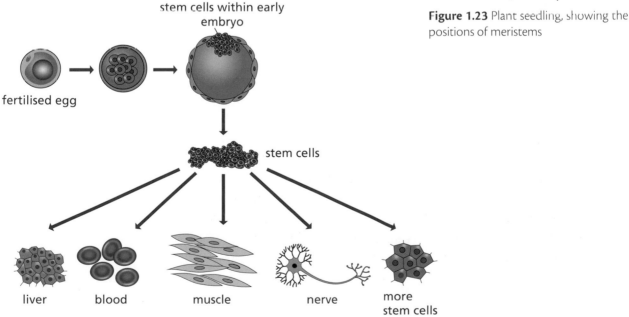

Various differentiated cells can be produced following the division of stem cells.

Figure 1.24 Embryonic stem cells

In adults, stem cells within tissues differentiate to replace damaged cells of the type in those tissues, as shown in Figure 1.25.

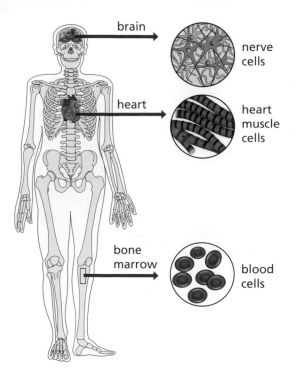

Figure 1.25 Adult stem cells

Stem cell research

Stem cell research provides information on how cell processes such as growth, differentiation and gene regulation work. Stem cells can be used therapeutically to repair damaged or diseased organs and tissue. They can also be used as model cells to study how diseases develop or for drug testing. There are various ethical issues raised by stem cell research and there is strict regulation of this activity. The following table summarises some of these issues.

Ethical question	Notes
Is the prevention of suffering more important than the duty to preserve human life?	Embryonic stem cell research gives us a moral dilemma. It forces us to choose between two moral principles important to humans: our duty to prevent or ease suffering and our duty to respect the value of human life. Which is more important?
Is there a possibility of stem cells being used eugenically?	Embryonic stem cells might be used to change the body characteristics of already healthy and well individuals. Should this be allowed?
Could stem cells become part of an illegal trade in biological material?	It is possible that stem cells might be bought and sold illegally and treatment could become subject to the ability of an individual to pay. Should this be allowed?

Embryonic stem cell research could lead to new medical treatments, which could save human lives and relieve human suffering. On the other hand, to obtain embryonic stem cells, an early-stage embryo has to be destroyed, meaning the loss of a potential human life. Which moral principle should be followed in this situation? Does the answer lie in our attitude to the embryo? Does it have the status of a person? What do you think about this issue?

Key words

Differentiation – changes to cells involving switching on certain genes and switching off others

Embryonic stem cell – stem cell from an embryo that can divide and become any type of cell

Meristem – region in a plant in which mitosis occurs

Stem cell – cell that can divide and then differentiate in animals

Therapeutic – used as part of medical therapy

Tissue (adult) stem cell – stem cell from tissue that can divide and differentiate to become cells of that tissue

Questions ?

Restricted response (structured in 1- or 2-mark parts)

1 Describe how an embryonic stem cell differs from an adult stem cell. (2)
2 Describe the importance of adult stem cells in the human body. (2)

Extended response (4–9 marks each)

3 Give an account of the process of cellular differentiation in animals and the function of meristems in plants. (4)
4 Give an account of ethical issues related to stem cell use. (4)

Answers are on page 40.

Structure of the genome and mutation

Key points !

1. The **genome** of an organism is the genetic information encoded into its DNA that can be inherited by its offspring. ☐
2. DNA sequences that code for protein are known as genes. ☐
3. A genome is defined as the genes that code for protein and other DNA sequences that do not code for proteins. ☐
4. Most of the genome in eukaryotic species consists of **non-coding sequences**. ☐
5. Non-coding sequences include those that regulate transcription and those that are transcribed into mRNA but are not translated. ☐
6. Some non-coding DNA sequences have no known function. ☐
7. **Mutations** are random changes in the genome. ☐
8. Mutations can alter genes, gene expression or chromosomes. ☐
9. Mutations of genes result in no protein or an altered protein being expressed. ☐
10. Single gene mutations affect DNA nucleotide sequences and include **deletion**, **insertion** and **substitution** of nucleotides. ☐
11. Single nucleotide substitutions include missense, nonsense and **splice-site mutations**. ☐
12. Nucleotide insertions or deletions result in frame-shift mutations. ☐
13. Nucleotide insertions may lead to expansion of nucleotide sequence repeats. ☐
14. Mutations are important in evolution. ☐
15. Splice-site mutations can alter post-transcription processing. ☐
16. Chromosome mutations that involve alterations to the structure of a chromosome include **duplication**, **deletion**, **inversion** and **translocation**. ☐
17. Duplication is important in evolution. ☐
18. Errors can occur during the separation of chromosomes during cell division, which can result in cells with whole-genome duplications. ☐
19. An organism with genome duplication is known as **polyploid**. ☐
20. Polyploidy is important in evolution and in the development of cultivated crop plants. ☐

Summary notes

Structure of the genome

The genome of an organism is the total genetic information encoded into the base sequence of its DNA. The genome contains those sequences that code for protein (genes) and those that do not. The non-coding sequences include those that regulate transcription, those that are transcribed into RNA but not translated and some non-coding DNA sequences that have no known function. The following table summarises genome structure.

Part of genome	Function of sequences
Coding sequences (genes)	Code for amino acid sequences in proteins
Non-coding sequences	Regulate transcription by turning genes on or off
	Transcribed but not translated (e.g. rRNA, tRNA)
	No known function

Organisms pass copies of their genome to their offspring.

Mutation

Mutations are rare, random changes to DNA sequences. The following table shows different types of mutation and their effects.

Mutation	Effect
...of single genes	Changes the amino acid sequence of the protein coded for
...of regulatory sequences	Alters the way in which genes are expressed in the phenotype
...at splice sites	Can cause introns to be left in mature mRNA, leading to an altered protein
...of chromosomes	Affects structure or number of chromosomes present in cells

Hints & tips

Remember **ROLF** — mutations are of *random* occurrence and low frequency.

Single gene mutations

Single gene mutations occur within genes and involve alterations of a DNA nucleotide sequence. Gene mutations result in no protein or an altered protein being expressed, as shown in the following table.

Hints & tips

Single gene mutations are a bit like spelling errors in the genetic code.

Hints & tips

Remember **DIGS**—
Deletion
Insertion
Gene mutation
Substitution

Single gene mutation	Description	Example of nucleotide base sequence changes	Impact on protein structure
Substitution	A single nucleotide removed from a DNA sequence and replaced by another with a different base	Normal sequence: ...ATGTCCATG... Following mutation: ATG**G**CCATG...	Minor impact, since there is a maximum of one amino acid changed in the protein structure – called missense Major impact could result if mutation results in production or loss of a stop codon – called nonsense
Insertion	Additional nucleotide added into a DNA sequence	Normal sequence: ...ATGTCCATG... Following mutation: ...ATGT**G**CCATG...	Major effect on protein likely since all amino acids coded for after the mutation could be affected Sometimes called frame-shift mutations Some insertions lead to expansion of nucleotide sequence repeats
Deletion	Nucleotide removed from a DNA sequence but not replaced with another	Normal sequence: ...ATGTCCATG... Following mutation: ...ATGTC_ATG...	

Mutation in nucleotide sequence repeats

Nucleotide sequence repeats occur throughout the human genome and consist of multiple copies of sequences of nucleotides of various lengths, from one nucleotide to many. Insertion can cause expansion of a sequence repeat and some of these can cause phenotypic effects.

> ### Example
>
> Fragile X Syndrome is caused by expansion of the CGG DNA triplet repeat in a gene found on the X chromosome. Fragile X causes intellectual disability, especially in boys.
>
> Huntington's disease (HD) is caused by expansion of a CAG DNA triplet repeat in a gene which codes for a protein whose absence can lead to the neurological degeneration linked to HD in humans.

Splice-site mutation

A single gene mutation at a splice site could result in an intron being left in the mature mRNA and so contributing to protein structure. This could result in an altered protein that would not function normally, as shown in Figure 1.26.

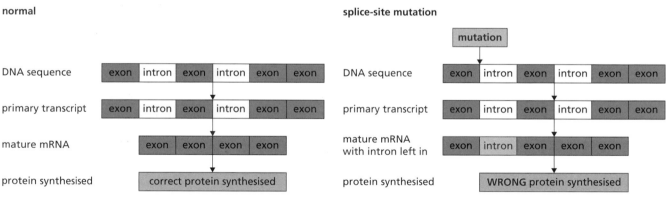

Figure 1.26 Effect of a splice-site mutation on a protein

Significance of gene mutation in evolution

Mutation provides the only source of new variation for living organisms and so has had vital importance in evolution. An example involving a single gene mutation of the gene for human haemoglobin is outlined in the following example box.

Example 🚩

Sickle cell disease

Haemoglobin is a protein that carries oxygen in the blood. Each person has two copies of the haemoglobin gene, each of which codes for half of their haemoglobin.

About 5000 years ago, a single gene mutation of the gene is thought to have arisen in Africa. This involved a substitution, which resulted in a form of haemoglobin with one amino acid different from the normal form. This abnormal haemoglobin leads to the collapsing of the red blood cells that contain it when conditions become acidic during exercise. The collapsed cells stick in narrow blood vessels, causing sickle cell disease.

Individuals with two copies of the mutation have a seriously debilitating condition called sickle cell anaemia. Individuals with one copy of the normal gene and one copy of the mutated gene have sickle cell trait and show less severe symptoms of the disease. In some parts of Africa, it is an advantage to have sickle cell trait because it protects individuals from malaria parasites. The parasites live inside red blood cells and their acidic waste products cause cells to collapse, which targets them for destruction by white blood cells. The mutation is now common in parts of Africa and demonstrates the importance of mutation in evolution.

Hints & tips ⭐

There is more about selection pressure in Key Area 1.7 (page 28) and parasites in Key Area 3.5 (page 126).

Chromosome mutations

Some mutations affect the structure or number of chromosomes present in the cells of living organisms, as shown in the following table. Those affecting the structure arise when pieces of one chromosome break off and are lost or join back into the chromosome complement in a different way.

Hints & tips ⭐

Remember **DICTD** —
Deletion
Inversion
Chromosome mutation
Translocation
Duplication

Chromosome mutation	Description	Diagram	Example or effect
Duplication	A set of genes from one chromosome becomes attached to its matching chromosome, leading to repeated genes	A B C D E F G H → duplication → A B C B C D E F G H	Some duplications can be highly detrimental; others can be important in evolution
Deletion	Detached genes are lost completely	A B C D E F G H → deletion → A B C E F G H	Cri du chat syndrome in humans involves a loss of part of chromosome 5
Translocation	Detached genes become attached to a different chromosome in the complement	A B C D E F G H / M N O P Q R → translocation → M N O C D E F G H / A B P Q R	One type of Down syndrome in humans is caused in this way

Chromosome mutation	Description	Diagram	Example or effect
Inversion	Chromosome breaks in two places and a set of genes rotates through 180°	A B C D E F G H inversion → A D C B E F G H ↻180°	Unable to produce gametes, leading to infertility
Complete non-disjunction	Spindle fibre failure during cell division leads to extra sets of chromosomes in a cell	Can produce an organism with extra sets of chromosomes in its cells (whole genome duplications)	Polyploidy in human food crops

Chromosome mutations and evolution

It is thought that duplicated genes can undergo single gene mutations without affecting the functioning of the original copy of the gene. A new gene could then appear, giving an organism a selective advantage without any effect on the functioning of the original gene.

One example is found in some coldwater fish. They have an antifreeze protein in their blood that has allowed colonisation of extremely cold water. The gene that encodes this protein seems to have been formed by the mutation of a gene coding for a vital digestive enzyme but, because of duplication, the modern fish retains its digestive enzyme as well as having the antifreeze.

> **Hints & tips** ★
> There is more about food security in Key Area 3.1a (page 105).

Polyploidy and evolution

Many plants are polyploid, suggesting that polyploidy has been important in evolution, as shown in Figure 1.27.

Step 1 Two wild ancestors of modern bread wheat hybridised naturally to produce a hybrid that had selective advantage but was sterile.

Step 2 A chromosome mutation involving complete spindle failure during cell division doubled the chromosome number of the hybrid, making it fertile.

Step 3 The fertile hybrid hybridised yet again with another wild grass. The offspring had selective advantage but were sterile.

Step 4 Again, complete non-disjunction made the hybrid into the modern fertile bread wheat *Triticum vulgare*, which is so important for food security in many countries today.

Polyploid human food crops

Polyploid plants are often larger, stronger and more productive than their diploid ancestors. This has led to humans bringing these species into cultivation. Examples include tomato and strawberry. Breeders have hybridised different species of the wild ancestors to produce polyploid crop plants with vigorous growth and high yields. Examples include banana and potato.

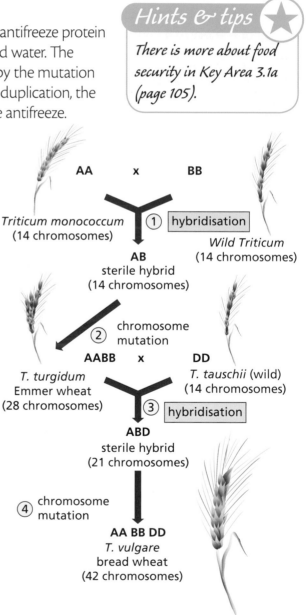

Figure 1.27 Four steps in the evolution of modern bread wheat

Key words

Deletion of genes – chromosome mutation in which a sequence of genes is lost from a chromosome
Deletion of nucleotides – single gene mutation involving removal of a nucleotide from a sequence
Duplication – chromosome mutation in which a sequence of genes is repeated on a chromosome
Genome – total genetic material present in an organism
Insertion – single gene mutation in which an additional nucleotide is placed into a sequence
Inversion – chromosome mutation in which a set of genes rotates through 180°
Mutations – random changes to DNA sequences
Non-coding sequence – DNA sequence that does not encode protein
Polyploidy – possession of extra sets of chromosomes
Splice-site mutation – mutation at a point where coding and non-coding regions meet in a section of DNA
Substitution – single gene mutation in which one nucleotide is replaced by another
Translocation – mutation in which part of a chromosome becomes attached to another

Questions ?

Restricted response (structured in 1- or 2-mark parts)

1 The table below shows the effects of some gene mutations on base sequences in DNA.

Original base sequence of gene	Number	Effect of mutation on base sequence
...TTACGCTAC...	1	...TACGCTAC...
	2	...TTACGGCTAC...
	3	...TGACGCTAC...

    a) Name mutations 1–3. (2)
    b) Describe the effects of mutations 1 and 3 on the structure of the polypeptide coded for by the original gene. (2)
2 Describe the importance of single gene mutation in evolution. (2)
3 Give the meaning of the following types of mutation:
    a) regulatory sequence mutation (1)
    b) splice-site mutation. (1)

Extended response (4–9 marks each)

4 Name and describe the types of structural mutation of chromosomes. (4)
5 Give an account of duplication and polyploidy and their importance in evolution. (6)

Answers are on page 41.

Key Area 1.7
Evolution

Key points (!)

1   **Evolution** is the result of changes in organisms over generations as a result of genomic variations. ☐
2   In **vertical inheritance**, genetic sequences pass from parent to offspring as a result of sexual or asexual reproduction. ☐
3   Prokaryotes can exchange genetic material by **horizontal inheritance**, resulting in rapid evolutionary change. ☐
4   Prokaryotes and **viruses** can transfer sequences horizontally into the genomes of eukaryotes. ☐
5   **Natural selection** is the non-random increase in the frequency of DNA sequences that increase survival. ☐
6   **Sexual selection** is the non-random increase in the frequency of DNA sequences that increase reproductive success. ☐
7   **Deleterious sequences** decrease the chances of survival and are reduced non-randomly. ☐
8   Selection can be **stabilising**, **directional** or **disruptive**. ☐
9   **Genetic drift** is the random increase or decrease in frequency of DNA sequences, particularly in small populations. ☐
10 Genetic drift can occur as a result of neutral mutation or founder effects. ☐
11 **Speciation** is the generation of new **biological species** by evolution, as a result of isolation, mutation and natural selection. ☐
12 A species is a group of organisms capable of interbreeding to produce fertile offspring and which does not normally breed with other groups. ☐
13 **Geographical barriers** prevent gene flow in **allopatric speciation**. ☐
14 **Behavioural** and **ecological barriers** prevent gene flow in **sympatric speciation**. ☐
15 **Hybrid zones** form when closely related species meet and attempt to breed. ☐

Summary notes
Inheritance

Genomic sequences are inherited vertically. This means that the genetic material is passed from parent to offspring either sexually or asexually when a species reproduces, as shown in Figure 1.28.

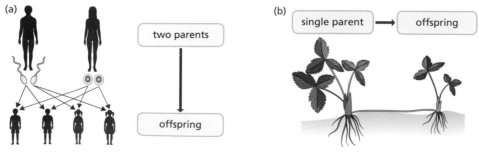

Figure 1.28 Vertical inheritance **(a)** Sexual – genetic sequences passed from male and female parents to offspring **(b)** Asexual – genetic sequences passed from single parent to offspring

Some prokaryotes and viruses can exchange genetic material horizontally, as shown in Figure 1.29.

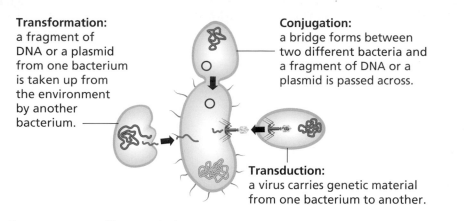

Transformation: a fragment of DNA or a plasmid from one bacterium is taken up from the environment by another bacterium.

Conjugation: a bridge forms between two different bacteria and a fragment of DNA or a plasmid is passed across.

Transduction: a virus carries genetic material from one bacterium to another.

Figure 1.29 Types of horizontal inheritance

Some can also transfer genetic material horizontally into the genomes of eukaryotic species, as shown in Figure 1.30.

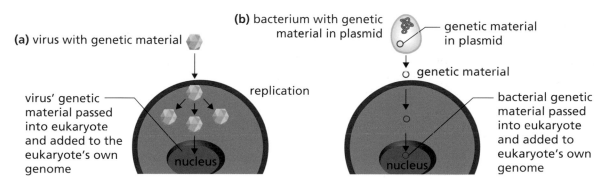

(a) virus with genetic material

(b) bacterium with genetic material in plasmid

genetic material in plasmid

genetic material

virus' genetic material passed into eukaryote and added to the eukaryote's own genome

replication

nucleus

bacterial genetic material passed into eukaryote and added to eukaryote's own genome

nucleus

Figure 1.30 Horizontal inheritance into a eukaryotic genome by **(a)** virus and **(b)** bacterium

Evolution by natural selection

Changes in genomic sequences in organisms result in changes to the organisms over time – this is called evolution. The changes depend on random alterations in the genome due to mutation. Mutations can be advantageous or detrimental to the survival of the organism.

Advantageous mutations help organisms to survive to reproduce, and so the mutation is passed on to offspring. Natural selection is the process by which selection pressure favours the genetic sequences that increase survival in a particular environment in a non-random way.

In sexual selection, the sequences that increase in a non-random way lead directly to successful reproduction. Figure 1.31 shows the link between mutation and survival.

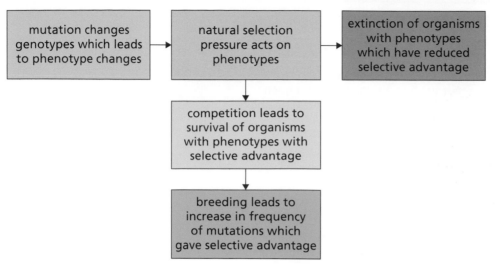

Figure 1.31 Summary of links between mutations and survival in evolution

Type of selection pressure

Stabilising selection

Stabilising selection tends to result in phenotypes in a range becoming more aligned with a mean value. An example of this is found in gall flies, which produce galls on plants that contain their offspring. Flies that produce small galls often have these parasitised by wasps, while those that produce large galls often have them predated by woodpeckers. There is selection pressure to produce galls of a medium size, as shown in the graph in Figure 1.32.

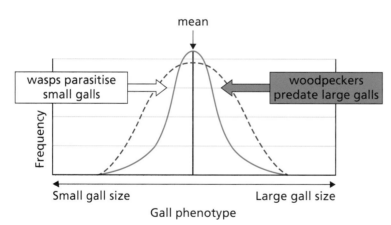

Figure 1.32 Stabilising selection pressure on gall fly gall sizes

Directional selection

Directional selection tends to move the average phenotype towards an extreme value in a range. In cliff swallows, for example, larger body size is a selective advantage, as shown in the chart in Figure 1.33.

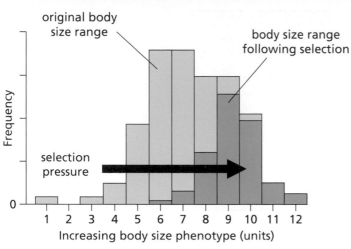

Figure 1.33 Directional selection for larger body size in cliff swallows

Disruptive selection

Disruptive selection tends to favour two extreme phenotypes, and results in two or more common phenotypes. In salmon, for example, larger male fish are better able to compete for territories, but smaller male fish without territories are able to sneak into those of larger fish and fertilise eggs without being detected, as shown in Figure 1.34.

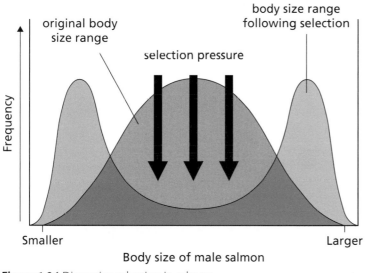

Figure 1.34 Disruptive selection in salmon

Genetic drift

Sometimes genetic frequencies increase or decrease randomly. This happens especially in small populations by chance events, neutral mutation or by colonisation and the founder effect, as shown in the following table. These random changes in frequency, especially in small populations, are called genetic drift.

Origin of genetic drift	Effect on gene frequency
Chance event	Eliminates individuals by chance, resulting in random changes to gene frequency among the survivors
Neutral mutation	Gene frequency changes by mutation but the effect on phenotypes is minor and gives no change to selective advantage
Colonisation	Founder effect – by chance the colonising population has different gene frequencies from the original population

Examples ⚑

Figures 1.35 and 1.36 show examples of genetic drift.

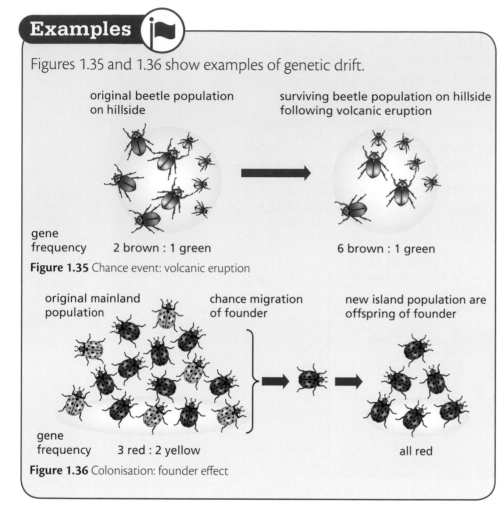

original beetle population on hillside

surviving beetle population on hillside following volcanic eruption

gene frequency   2 brown : 1 green   6 brown : 1 green

Figure 1.35 Chance event: volcanic eruption

original mainland population   chance migration of founder   new island population are offspring of founder

gene frequency   3 red : 2 yellow   all red

Figure 1.36 Colonisation: founder effect

Speciation

A species is a group of very similar interbreeding organisms that give rise to fertile offspring. The biological species is the basic unit of classification. Its members are reproductively isolated so do not normally attempt to interbreed with other species. Speciation is the evolution of two or more species from a common ancestor.

New biological species are produced by natural selection, usually acting over long periods of time in an evolutionary process called speciation.

Hints & tips ★

Remember that different species do not produce fertile young when they interbreed. They can only produce fertile young with members of the same species.

Hints & tips ★

Remember I'M A NEW SPECIES to represent the order of events in speciation – isolation, mutation then natural selection.

Allopatric speciation

In allopatric speciation, sub-populations of a species become isolated from each other by geographical barriers such as mountains or oceans. No gene flow occurs between the sub-populations and they build up separate genetic differences based on natural selection acting on different mutations in their different environments.

Example 🚩

Figure 1.37 shows an example of allopatric speciation involving Galapagos finches.

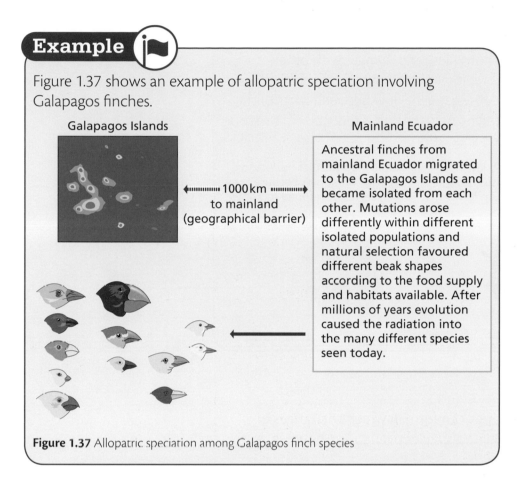

Galapagos Islands

Mainland Ecuador

◄·········· 1000 km ··········►
to mainland
(geographical barrier)

Ancestral finches from mainland Ecuador migrated to the Galapagos Islands and became isolated from each other. Mutations arose differently within different isolated populations and natural selection favoured different beak shapes according to the food supply and habitats available. After millions of years evolution caused the radiation into the many different species seen today.

Figure 1.37 Allopatric speciation among Galapagos finch species

Sympatric speciation

In sympatric speciation, isolation occurs when gene flow between populations is stopped by ecological or behavioural barriers to the exchange of genetic sequences. The sub-populations live side by side but do not interbreed and so natural selection is able to act separately on them.

Example 🚩

American maggot flies

The ancestors of American maggot flies laid their eggs only in native hawthorn berries. The species now lays eggs in hawthorn berries and in apples, which were introduced to America about 200 years ago.

Females generally choose to lay their eggs in the type of fruit in which they grew up. Males tend to look for mates on the type of fruit in which they grew up. So hawthorn flies tend to mate with other hawthorn flies and apple flies tend to mate with other apple flies, as shown in Figure 1.38. This means that gene flow between parts of the population that mate on different types of fruit is reduced. This may be the first step toward sympatric speciation.

Hawthorn maggot flies mate and lay eggs on hawthorn berries because they themselves developed in hawthorn berries.

Apple maggot flies mate and lay eggs on apples because they themselves developed in apples.

Figure 1.38 Sympatric isolation in American maggot flies

Hybrid zones

In a small number of cases, zones can form in which the ranges of two very similar and closely related species overlap, as shown in Figure 1.39.

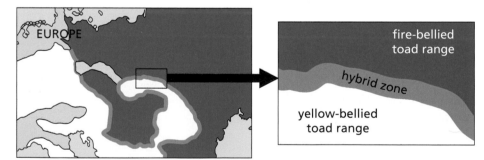

Figure 1.39 Hybrid zone for two species of European toad

In the zone of hybridisation, the fire-bellied toad lives alongside the yellow-bellied toad, and they interbreed under certain circumstances. Pure phenotypes of each species are found alongside hybrids between them. Hybrid offspring are usually either infertile or survive less well compared with non-hybrids. Hybrid zones persist because of repopulation with pure forms which then hybridise.

Hints & tips ⭐

Remember that hybrids formed between two species are infertile — fertile young are only produced when interbreeding is within one species.

Key words

Allopatric speciation – speciation in which gene flow is prevented by a geographical barrier
Behavioural barrier – barrier to gene flow caused by behavioural differences between individuals
Biological species – group of similar organisms interbreeding to produce fertile young
Deleterious sequence – DNA sequence that lowers survival rate
Directional selection – natural selection that tends to favour an extreme value of a varied characteristic
Disruptive selection – natural selection that favours two different values of a varied characteristic
Ecological barrier – barrier to gene flow caused by ecological preference differences between individuals
Evolution – changes to organisms over time that are mainly caused by natural selection
Genetic drift – random changes to DNA sequences
Geographical barrier – physical barrier to gene flow, such as a mountain or river
Horizontal inheritance – inheritance of genetic material within a generation
Hybrid zone – region in which frequent interbreeding between two species occurs
Natural selection – process that ensures survival of the fittest
Sexual selection – natural selection of characteristics that increase reproductive success
Speciation – evolutionary process by which new species are formed
Stabilising selection – natural selection that favours a middle value of a varied characteristic
Sympatric barrier – behavioural or ecological barrier to the flow of genes
Sympatric speciation – speciation in which gene flow is prevented by ecological or reproductive barriers
Vertical inheritance – inheritance of genetic material from parents by offspring
Virus – has genetic material enclosed in a protein coat

Questions ?

Restricted response (structured in 1- or 2-mark parts)

1 Gene sequences are inherited vertically from parent to offspring.
   Describe how genetic sequences are inherited horizontally. (2)
2 Give the meaning of the term sexual selection. (2)
3 Give the term that describes random changes in genetic frequencies, especially in small populations. (1)

Extended response (4–9 marks each)

4 One type of selection pressure is stabilising selection. Give an account of this type of selection
   pressure and the names and effects of **two** other types of selection pressure on populations. (5)
5 Give an account of the role of natural selection in evolution. (5)
6 Give an account of the formation and maintenance of zones of hybridisation. (4)

Answers are on page 41.

Key points !

1 The sequence of nucleotide bases can be determined for individual genes and entire genomes. ☐
2 Comparison of **sequence data** requires **bioinformatics**, which involves computer and statistical analyses. ☐
3 In **phylogenetics** sequence data can be used to study evolutionary relatedness among groups of organisms. ☐
4 Sequence divergence can be used as a **molecular clock** to estimate time since lineages diverged. ☐
5 Comparison of sequence data has provided evidence for three domains of life: the **bacteria**, the **archaea** and the eukaryotes. ☐
6 Sequence data and **fossil evidence** have been used to determine the main sequence of events in the evolution of life. ☐
7 Main events in the evolution of life include the last universal ancestor, the emergence of photosynthesis, appearance of eukaryotes and multicellular organisms. ☐
8 Comparison of genomes from different species shows that many genes are conserved across different organisms. ☐
9 Analysis of an individual's genome could lead to **personalised medicine**. ☐
10 Genetic components of disease and the likelihood of success of particular treatments could be revealed by genome analysis. ☐
11 Difficulties with personalised medicine arise in relating individual genome data to treatments and in the complex nature of many diseases. ☐

Summary notes
Genomics and phylogenetics

Sequences of nucleotide bases can be determined for individual genes and entire genomes. Amino acid sequences can be determined for individual proteins. The results are called sequence data. To compare sequence data, computer and statistical analyses are required. These techniques are known as bioinformatics.

Sequence data can be used to study evolutionary relatedness among groups of organisms. Sequence divergence can be used along with the fossil record in drawing molecular clock graphs, such as that for cytochrome C or haemoglobin. Molecular clock diagrams are based on the assumption that the mutation rate of genes leading to amino acid differences in proteins is constant through time.

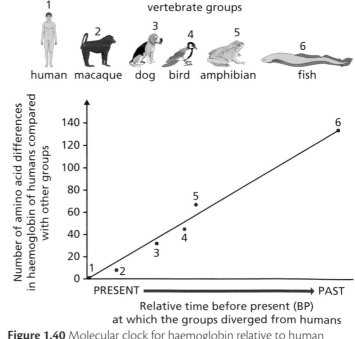

Figure 1.40 Molecular clock for haemoglobin relative to human haemoglobin

Figure 1.40 shows how differences in amino acid sequence in haemoglobin can confirm the evolutionary relatedness of vertebrate groups.

Phylogenetic trees

Sequence data results can be used in combination with fossil evidence to draw phylogenetic trees, as shown in Figure 1.41. In this figure, letter x shows the last common ancestor of A and B and letter y shows the last common ancestor of C, D and E.

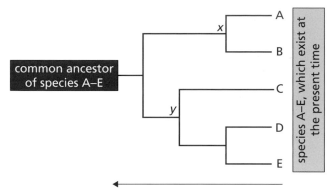

Figure 1.41 The basic features of a phylogenetic tree

The tree in Figure 1.42 shows the emergence of the three fundamental domains of life on Earth today – bacteria, archaea and eukaryotes.

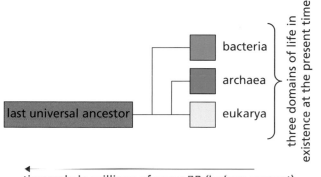

Figure 1.42 The three domains of life

Sequence data combined with fossil evidence is used to determine the main sequence of events in the evolution of life, as shown in the table below. Comparison of genomes from different species show that many genes are found in a conserved state across different organisms.

Event in evolution	Approximate time (million years BP)	Notes
appearance of prokaryotic cells	3600	first bacteria-like cells with no distinct nucleus
existence of the last universal ancestor (LUA)	3500	existence of the most recent organism from which all organisms now living on Earth have descended
photosynthesis	3400	first organisms which could use light energy in the synthesis of complex molecules
appearance of eukaryotic cells	2000	first organisms with cells containing a true nucleus
appearance of multicellular organisms	1000	first organisms whose bodies were composed of a group of interdependent cells
appearance of animals	600	first multicellular eukaryotic organisms which ingested other organisms as food
appearance of vertebrate animals	540	first animals which possessed backbones
appearance of land plants	475	first plants to live in terrestrial (land) habitats

Personal genomics and health

It is possible to sequence the genome of an individual human being. Many diseases have a genetic risk component and so analysis of an individual's genome could lead to personalised medicine through increased information on the likelihood of a treatment being successful in a specific individual. Pharmacogenetics refers to the study of how drugs might be designed to best suit individuals with particular genetic sequences.

There is significant difficulty in distinguishing between neutral mutations and potentially harmful mutations in genes and in regulatory genetic sequences, which makes relating genomic data to personalised medicine more problematic.

Figure 1.43 shows the effects of the genotype of a group of patients with liver disease on treatment with a new, potentially beneficial drug – this highlights the problem. If patient genotype could be related to the effects of the drug before treatment, this could maximise the benefits of the treatment by identification of the group for whom the drug would be most beneficial.

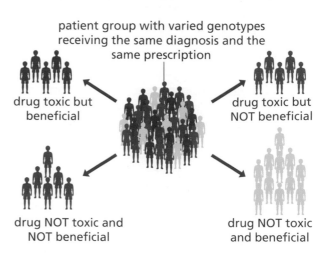

Figure 1.43 The effects of the genotype of a group of patients with liver disease

Key words

Archaea – a domain of life

Bacteria – a domain of life

Bioinformatics – use of computers and statistics in analysis of sequence data

Fossil evidence – information derived from the remains of extinct organisms

Molecular clock – graph that shows differences in sequence data for a protein against time

Personalised medicine – possible future development in which treatment is based on an individual's genome

Phylogenetics – study of evolutionary relatedness of species

Sequence data – information concerning amino acid or nucleotide base sequences

Questions ?

Restricted response (structured in 1- or 2-mark parts)

1 Give the **two** types of information needed to construct phylogenetic trees. (2)
2 Give the term applied to the statistical and mathematical treatment of sequence data. (1)
3 Name the **three** domains of life. (2)
4 Give an account of personalised genomics and medicine. (2)

Extended response (4–9 marks each)

5 Give an account of phylogenetics and molecular clocks. (6)

Answers are on page 42.

Answers

Key Area 1.1

Restricted response

1 a) double helix   [1]
   b) by hydrogen bonding; between
      complementary bases   [1 each = 2]
   c) a deoxyribose sugar molecule; a
      phosphate group; a nitrogenous base

                              [all 3 = 2; 2/1 = 1]

   d) (i) adenine pairs with thymine and
           guanine pairs with cytosine   [2]
      (ii) each strand runs in the opposite
           direction; to its complementary strand
                                      [1 each = 2]
2 a) packaged in circular chromosomes; and in
      plasmids   [1 each = 2]
   b) packaged in linear chromosomes; and in
      circular chromosomes in chloroplasts and
      mitochondria   [1 each = 2]

Extended response

3 Function: carries inherited information; in a
   chemical language; in its base sequence
                                        [any 2 = 2]
   Structure: double helix; chains/strands of
   nucleotides; nucleotide is deoxyribose, a
   phosphate and a base; sugar–phosphate
   backbone; complementary base pairing or A
   with T, G with C; antiparallel chains/strands
                                        [any 5 = 5]
                                        [total = 7]

Answers

Key Area 1.2

Restricted response

1 a) denatures/separates DNA strands   [1]
   b) allows primers to bind   [1]
   c) comes from bacteria adapted to live in
      hot springs   [1]
   d) 128 copies   [1]
   e) identification of individuals from blood/
      semen; showing place of extinct species
      in evolution; (there are many other
      acceptable answers)   [any 1 = 1]

Extended response

2 DNA uncoils and unzips; primers bind at end
   of lead template strand; DNA polymerase
   adds complementary DNA nucleotides
   to lead strand continuously; primers bind
   to lagging strand in many places; DNA
   polymerase adds complementary DNA
   nucleotides to lagging strand in fragments;
   fragments joined by ligase; replication occurs
   at several positions/at many replication
   forks on a DNA molecule at the same time;
   replication requires energy/ATP   [any 7 = 7]

Answers

Key Area 1.3

Restricted response

1 a) peptide bonds [1]
   b) by hydrogen bonds *and* other linkages [1]
   c) allows the protein to carry out its
      function [1]
2 alternative RNA splicing; post-translational
   modification [1 each = 2]
3 introns are non-coding regions *and* exons are
   coding regions [1]
4 cutting *and* combining chains; adding
   carbohydrates; adding phosphates
   [any 2 = 2]

Extended response

5 a) DNA unwinds and unzips; RNA polymerase
      adds complementary RNA nucleotides;
      (to make a) primary transcript; introns
      removed; exons spliced to make mature
      mRNA; occurs in nucleus [any 4 = 4]
   b) mRNA goes to ribosome; tRNA carries
      specific amino acids; anticodons on tRNA
      aligned with codons on mRNA; amino
      acids aligned in correct sequence; amino
      acids linked by peptide bonds
      [any 4 = 4]
      [total = 8]

Answers

Key Area 1.4

Restricted response

1 embryonic stem cells divide and then
   differentiate into any type of cell; adult stem
   cells also divide but then only differentiate
   into cells of the type found in the tissue from
   which they came [1 each = 2]
2 divide and differentiate to replace cells; which
   were/had become damaged/diseased cells
   [1 each = 2]

Extended response

3 in tissue cells some genes switched off and
   other genes switched on; producing proteins
   characteristic of that tissue; allow tissue to
   carry out its function [any 1 = 1]

   meristems contain unspecialised cells; found
   in root and shoot tips; lateral meristems in
   stems; meristem cells divide to produce cells
   which can differentiate; to produce mature
   plant tissues [any 3 = 3]
   [total = 4]

4 to obtain embryonic stem cells an embryo has
   to be sacrificed; but using embryonic stem
   cells can potentially relieve suffering and save
   life; stem cells could be used to treat healthy
   individuals; stem cells could be part of an
   illegal trade; other ethical issue explained
   [any 4 = 4]

Answers

Key Areas 1.5 and 1.6

Restricted response

1 a) 1 deletion; 2 insertion; 3 substitution
                                    [all 3 = 2; 2/1 = 1]
   b) 1/deletion gives frame-shift effect with
       major changes to amino acid sequence
       or all amino acids changed after the
       mutation   [1]

       3/substitution results in missense and gives
       minor changes to polypeptide *or* only one
       amino acid changed *or* results in nonsense
       if stop codon affected   [1]
2 single gene mutation provides the variation
   needed for evolution/natural selection;
   natural selection favours mutations that
   increase survival   [1 each = 2]
3 a) mutations that affect non-coding DNA
       sequences/introns   [1]
   b) mutation that can result in mRNA with
       the wrong introns or exons   [1]

Extended response

4 deletion; involves loss of section of
   chromosome; translocation; involves
   section of one chromosome joining to
   another; duplication; involves a section of
   one chromosome being copied within the
   chromosome; inversion; involves a set of
   genes rotating through 180°
           [any 2 names = 2 and matching effects = 2]
                                              [total = 4]
5 in duplication a second copy of a section
   of a chromosome is present; a single
   gene mutation in a duplicated region of a
   chromosome can produce an advantageous
   gene without the loss of an existing gene
                                            [1 each = 2]

   hybrid plants are often at a selective
   advantage/more vigorous; hybrid plants are
   usually sterile; polyploidy produces extra sets
   of chromosomes; this can give fertility to
   hybrids; polyploidy can make evolutionary
   change happen rapidly   [any 4 = 4]
                                              [total = 6]

Answers

Key Area 1.7

Restricted response

1 passed from one prokaryotic organism
   to another; passed into the genome of a
   eukaryote by a virus or prokaryote [1 each = 2]
2 selection that favours characteristics related
   to sex; and which then lead to better
   reproductive success   [1 each = 2]
3 genetic drift   [1]

Extended response

4 favours individuals with a central value in the
   range of variation; directional selection; favours
   individuals with characteristics at one extreme
   of the range; disruptive selection; favours
   individuals at two different points in the range
                       [1 each (effects must match) = 5]

5 individuals of a species vary; there is
   competition between individuals of the species;
   natural selection favours the survival of best-
   adapted individuals; they survive to reproduce
   and pass their beneficial genes to their offspring;
   this increases the frequency of the beneficial
   genes; after long periods of time new species
   may form   [any 5 = 5]
6 hybrid zones form where the ranges of two
   closely related species overlap; within hybrid
   zones members of the two species interbreed;
   the hybrid offspring are less fit/sterile; and are
   eliminated by natural selection; members of
   each species re-colonise the hybrid zone; and
   undergo further hybridisation to repopulate the
   zone
                                            [any 4 = 4]

Answers

Key Area 1.8

Restricted response

1 DNA/protein sequences; fossil record
[1 each = 2]

2 bioinformatics [1]

3 bacteria; archaea; eukaryotes
[all 3 = 2; any 2 = 1]

4 personalised genomics involves sequencing the genome of an individual; genomic differences are important in the effectiveness of treatments/drugs; so different treatments can be designed for an individual [any 2 = 2]

Extended response

5 genomics involves studying of gene sequences; gene sequences are used to show evolutionary relatedness; evolutionary relatedness is the basis of phylogenetic trees; to add timescales to phylogenetic trees fossils are needed [any 3 = 3]

molecular clocks are based on sequence differences of a particular protein; differences in sequences related to a protein in different species are graphed on one axis; the other axis shows the timescale of divergence based on relative sequence differences [all 3 = 3]

[total = 6]

Practice course assessment: Unit 1 (50 marks)

Section A (10 marks)

1 In the chloroplasts of plant cells, genetic material is organised into
   A linear chromosomes   B RNA molecules
   C circular chromosomes   D circular plasmids.

2 The graph below shows temperature changes involved in one cycle of the polymerase chain reaction (PCR).

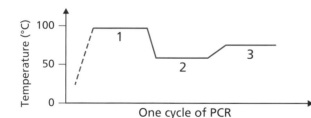

One cycle of PCR

Which row in the table below identifies the main events occurring in each region of the graph?

	Main event occurring during PCR cycle		
	1	2	3
A	Primers bind to target sequences on DNA	DNA polymerase replicates regions of DNA	DNA strands separate
B	DNA strands separate	DNA polymerase replicates regions of DNA	Primers bind to target sequences on DNA
C	DNA strands separate	Primers bind to target sequences on DNA	DNA polymerase replicates regions of DNA
D	Primers bind to target sequences on DNA	DNA strands separate	DNA polymerase replicates regions of DNA

⇨

3   The list shows steps in the synthesis of the protein mucin.
    1   Transcription of DNA
    2   Adding a carbohydrate group
    3   RNA splicing
    4   Translation of mRNA

    In which order would these steps occur?

    A   1 3 4 2
    B   1 4 2 3
    C   3 1 2 4
    D   3 4 2 1

4   Which of the following events in its habitat could give rise to changes in gene frequencies in a species by genetic drift?
    A   changes in the population of its predator
    B   a volcanic eruption
    C   increases in annual rainfall
    D   the appearance of a new disease

Questions 5 and 6 refer to the graph on the right, which shows changes in the number of human stem cells present in a culture over a period of 16 days. Also shown is the level of activity of an enzyme found in stem cell cytoplasm over the same period.

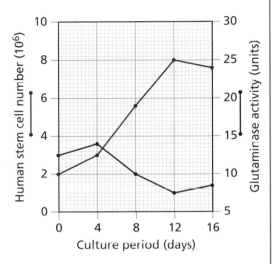

5   How many units of enzyme activity were recorded when the number of cells was at 25% of its maximum over the 16-day period?
    A   2
    B   3
    C   10
    D   12.5

6   What was the percentage decrease in enzyme activity between days 8 and 12 of the period?
    A   25
    B   50
    C   100
    D   200

7   What term is given to the random change in frequency of DNA sequences, particularly in small populations?
    A   genetic drift
    B   speciation
    C   natural selection
    D   the bottleneck effect

8   Bioinformatics is the
    A   production of phylogenetic tree diagrams
    B   development of personalised medicine
    C   use of mathematical and statistical techniques in genetic sequencing
    D   construction of molecular clocks in evolutionary studies.

⇨

9 The charts below show the effects of selection on the body mass of male birds in a population of barn swallows. Measurements were made before and after a period of extremely high temperatures during their breeding season.

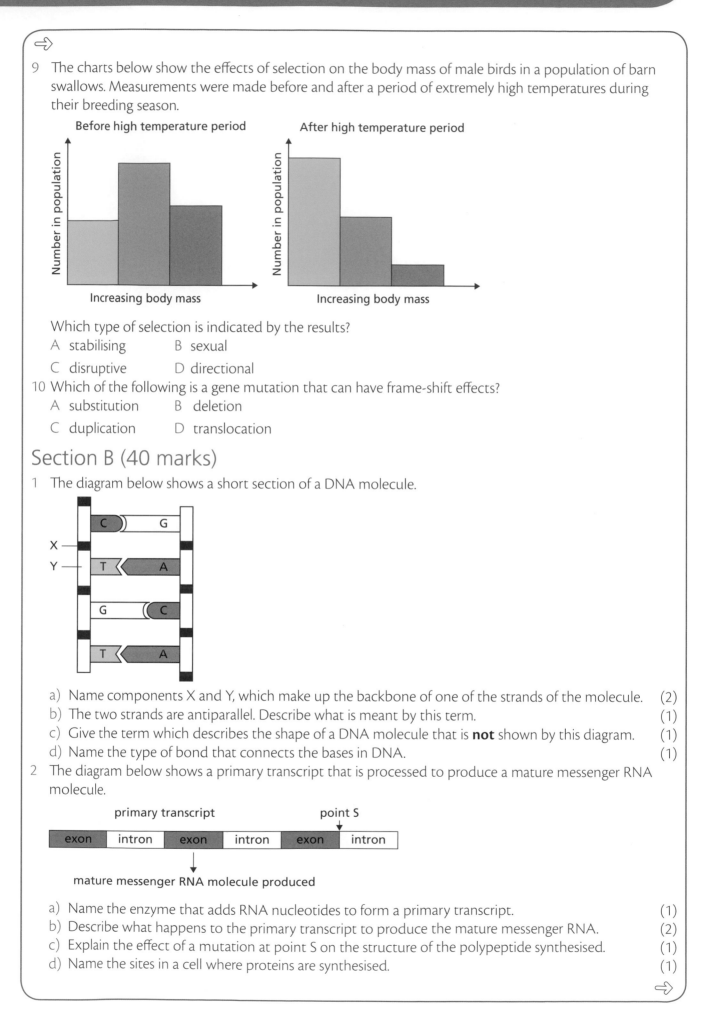

Which type of selection is indicated by the results?

A stabilising   B sexual

C disruptive   D directional

10 Which of the following is a gene mutation that can have frame-shift effects?

A substitution   B deletion

C duplication   D translocation

Section B (40 marks)

1 The diagram below shows a short section of a DNA molecule.

a) Name components X and Y, which make up the backbone of one of the strands of the molecule.   (2)
b) The two strands are antiparallel. Describe what is meant by this term.   (1)
c) Give the term which describes the shape of a DNA molecule that is **not** shown by this diagram.   (1)
d) Name the type of bond that connects the bases in DNA.   (1)

2 The diagram below shows a primary transcript that is processed to produce a mature messenger RNA molecule.

a) Name the enzyme that adds RNA nucleotides to form a primary transcript.   (1)
b) Describe what happens to the primary transcript to produce the mature messenger RNA.   (2)
c) Explain the effect of a mutation at point S on the structure of the polypeptide synthesised.   (1)
d) Name the sites in a cell where proteins are synthesised.   (1)

3 The diagram below shows the sequence of bases in some mRNA codons and the amino acids for which they code.

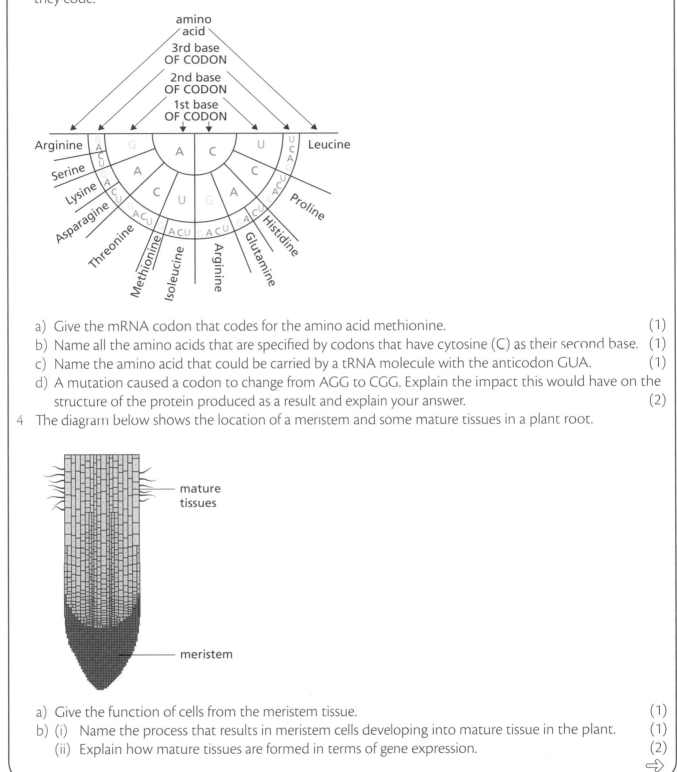

a) Give the mRNA codon that codes for the amino acid methionine. (1)
b) Name all the amino acids that are specified by codons that have cytosine (C) as their second base. (1)
c) Name the amino acid that could be carried by a tRNA molecule with the anticodon GUA. (1)
d) A mutation caused a codon to change from AGG to CGG. Explain the impact this would have on the structure of the protein produced as a result and explain your answer. (2)

4 The diagram below shows the location of a meristem and some mature tissues in a plant root.

a) Give the function of cells from the meristem tissue. (1)
b) (i) Name the process that results in meristem cells developing into mature tissue in the plant. (1)
   (ii) Explain how mature tissues are formed in terms of gene expression. (2)

5 a) Copy and complete the table below to show the differences between embryonic and adult stem cells.
(2)

	Embryonic stem cells	Adult stem cells
Location	In early embryo tissue	
Potential following cell division		Can differentiate into cells of one type of tissue

b) Describe **one** ethical issue that can arise when considering the use of embryonic stem cells in research or medicine.
(2)

6 The phylogenetic tree below shows how several species of carnivorous mammal are related.

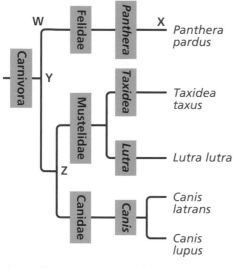

a) Identify the species with DNA sequences most different from *Taxidea taxus*. (1)
b) Identify the species with DNA sequences most similar to *Lutra lutra*. (1)
c) Identify the **two** species whose DNA sequences are **most** similar to each other. (1)
d) Give the letter on the phylogenetic tree that marks the point showing the position of the last common ancestor of the carnivorous mammals. (1)
e) Apart from DNA sequence data, give the other source of information that allows phylogenetic trees to be constructed. (1)

7 In Europe the ranges of the yellow-bellied toad and the fire-bellied toad overlap in a zone where the two species hybridise. The graph below shows the frequency of a certain allele in toad populations along a 70 km line running from north to south, passing from the range of one species through the hybrid zone and into the range of the other.

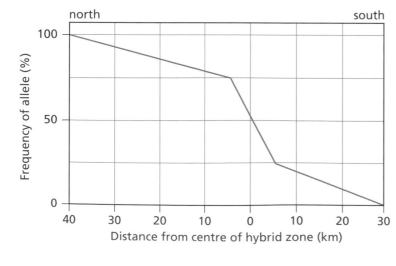

a) Estimate the average allele frequency in populations of toad at the centre of the hybrid zone. (1)

b) Use values from the graph to describe how the frequency of the allele changes along the line from north to south. (2)

c) The hybrid population at the centre of the hybrid zone has remained the same over many years. Suggest why the hybrid population numbers do not increase or decrease. (2)

Question 8 contains a choice.

8 *Either* A Give an account of the role of mutation and natural selection in the formation of new species. (7)

Or B Give an account of the replication of DNA in cells. (7)

Answers to practice course assessment: Unit 1

Section A

1 C, 2 C, 3 A, 4 B, 5 C, 6 A, 7 A, 8 C, 9 D, 10 B

Section B

1 a) X – phosphate; Y – deoxyribose [2]
  b) they run in/are aligned in opposite directions [1]
  c) double helix [1]
  d) hydrogen bond [1]
2 a) RNA polymerase [1]
  b) introns are removed; exons are spliced together [1 each = 2]
  c) intron may be left in mRNA *and* wrong amino acids included in polypeptide [1]
  d) ribosomes [1]
3 a) AUG [1]
  b) threonine *and* proline [1]
  c) histidine [1]
  d) there would be no difference in the protein produced; both codons code for arginine [1 each = 2]
4 a) can undergo cell division [1]
  b) (i) differentiation [1]
    (ii) some genes are switched on *and* others are switched off; so that the correct proteins are produced to form the mature tissue [1 each = 2]

5 a) Location: within brain/bone/heart/stomach/named tissue [1]
    Potential: can differentiate into any cell type [1]
  b) to access stem cells, embryo would be damaged; medical ethic is to preserve life *or* other possible answers [1 each = 2]
6 a) *Panthera pardus* [1]
  b) *Taxidea taxus* [1]
  c) *Canis latrans* and *Canis lupus* [1]
  d) Y [1]
  e) fossils [1]
7 a) 45% (+/−1%) [1]
  b) dropped from 100% at 40 km north to 75% at 5 km north; dropped from 75% at 5 km north to 25% at 5 km south; dropped from 25% at 5 km south to 0% at 30 km south
    [all 3 = 2; 2/1 = 1]
  c) hybrids removed by natural selection; replaced by further hybridisation [1 each = 2]
8A mutation produces variation within species; mutation can be deleterious or beneficial; there is a struggle for survival; those that are fittest/best suited/with beneficial mutations survive; the survivors breed;

⇒

survivors pass mutations/favourable or beneficial characteristics to offspring; mutations build up over long periods; new species cannot interbreed to produce fertile offspring [any 7 = 7]

B double helix (uncoils and) unzips; primers add onto template strands; primers allow DNA polymerase/enzyme to bind; DNA polymerase adds complementary DNA nucleotide to templates; lead/3′–5′ strand replicated continuously; lagging strand replicated in fragments; fragments joined by ligase; two new identical DNA molecules formed [any 7 = 7]

Metabolism and survival

Metabolic pathways

Key points ❗

1 **Metabolism** is the total of all integrated controlled enzyme-catalysed reactions that take place in cells. ☐
2 **Metabolic pathways** can involve the synthesis of molecules (**anabolic**) or the breakdown of molecules (**catabolic**) to provide energy and building blocks. ☐
3 Anabolic pathways require the input of energy and catabolic pathways release energy. ☐
4 Metabolic pathways can have reversible and irreversible steps and alternative routes may exist that can bypass steps in a pathway. ☐
5 Membranes form surfaces and **compartments** to localise metabolic activity and allow high concentrations of metabolites and high reaction rates. ☐
6 Proteins embedded in **phospholipid membranes** have functions such as forming **pores**, **pumps** or enzymes. ☐

Summary notes

Cell metabolism

Metabolism is the name given to the sum total of all the chemical reactions that take place within a living cell. It is the network of connected and integrated pathways involved in cell activities, and involves reversible and irreversible steps, sometimes with alternative routes, that are all controlled by enzymes.

Metabolic pathways

The control of metabolic pathways is essential to cell survival. A metabolic pathway is a series of stepwise chemical reactions controlled by enzymes, as shown in Figure 2.1.

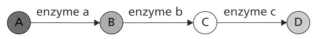

Figure 2.1 Metabolic pathway involving substances A–D and enzymes a–c

Anabolism

Anabolic pathways are biosynthetic processes that involve the building up of complex molecules from simpler substances. Anabolic pathways require the input of energy.

Protein synthesis is an example of an anabolic reaction, which requires ATP to provide the energy to build up amino acids to form a protein.

Catabolism

Catabolic pathways involve the breakdown of complex molecules into simpler substances. They usually release energy. Catabolism can also provide building blocks for use in other chemical reactions. Aerobic respiration is an example of a catabolic reaction, involving the breakdown of glucose and resulting in the release of energy in the form of ATP.

Figure 2.2 shows the two types of metabolic pathway.

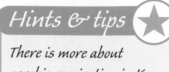

Hints & tips

More about protein structure can be found in Key Area 1.3 (page 11).

Hints & tips

There is more about aerobic respiration in Key Area 2.2 (page 61).

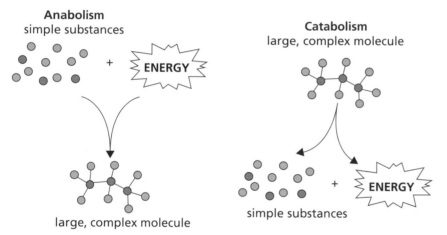

Figure 2.2 Summary of anabolism and catabolism

Metabolic pathways can have reversible and irreversible steps and alternative routes may exist that can bypass steps in a pathway. Figure 2.3 shows an example of a metabolic pathway, a reversible step, an irreversible step and an alternative bypass route.

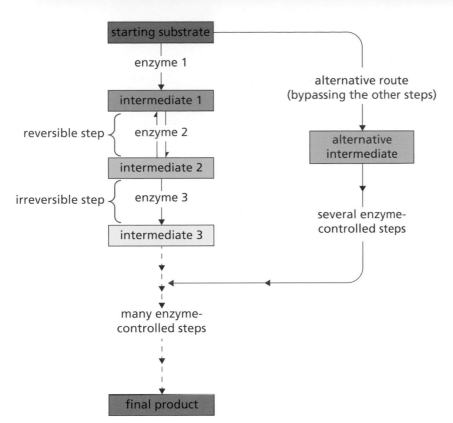

Figure 2.3 A metabolic pathway with characteristic features

Membrane structure

Membranes consist of protein and phospholipid. The phospholipid molecules form a double layer and are in constant motion, giving a fluid nature to membranes and making them flexible.

The proteins are scattered in a patchy mosaic pattern. Some proteins form pores, others are pumps that penetrate through the membrane and some are enzymes that catalyse chemical reactions, as shown in Figure 2.4.

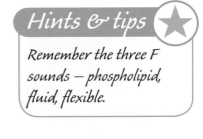

Hints & tips

Remember the three F sounds — phospholipid, fluid, flexible.

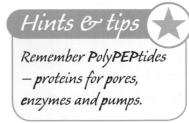

Hints & tips

Remember PolyPEPtides — proteins for pores, enzymes and pumps.

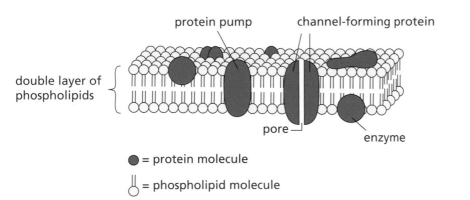

Figure 2.4 The fluid mosaic model of membrane structure

Pores, pumps and enzymes

Channel-forming proteins have pores that control the passive diffusion of certain molecules, depending on their size. These pores make cell membranes selectively permeable.

Active transport involves the movement of molecules from low to high concentration. This type of movement needs additional energy that is available from ATP. Cells must be respiring aerobically to produce enough ATP for active transport. It involves specialised protein pumps in the plasma membrane, which recognise specific molecules and transfer them across the membrane. The sodium–potassium pump is an example of a carrier protein involved in active transport. Figure 2.5 shows how it works in a nerve cell.

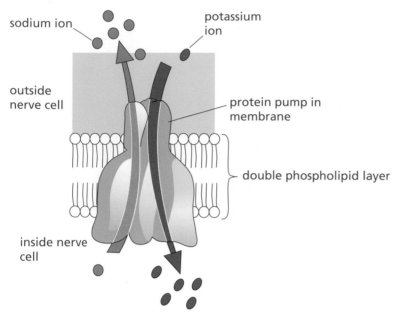

Figure 2.5 The sodium–potassium pump in a nerve cell

ATP synthase is an example of an enzyme embedded in the membranes of mitochondria and chloroplasts, where it catalyses the synthesis of ATP, as shown in Figure 2.6.

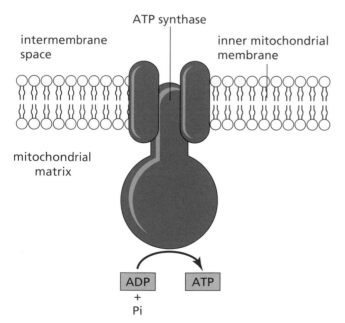

Figure 2.6 ATP synthase embedded in the inner membrane of a mitochondrion

Metabolic surfaces and compartments

The organelles in a cell are membrane-bound compartments in which metabolic pathways are localised. Some organelles, such as mitochondria and chloroplasts, have double membranes, with the inner membranes acting as highly metabolic membrane surfaces.

> **Hints & tips**
>
> There is more about ATP synthase in Key Areas 2.2 and 3.1b (pages 61 and 108, respectively).

> **Hints & tips**
>
> There is more about mitochondria in Key Area 2.2 (page 61) and chloroplasts in Key Area 3.1b (page 108).

The small compartments provide favourable conditions for reactions to take place by allowing high concentrations of reactants to occur, resulting in higher reaction rates. The large surface-to-volume ratio of numerous organelles allows the efficient exchange of materials between the organelles and their surroundings. Figure 2.7 shows the membranes of a mitochondrion and a chloroplast.

Hints & tips ⭐

There is more about the origin of chloroplasts and mitochondria in Key Areas 3.5 and 3.6 on page 126.

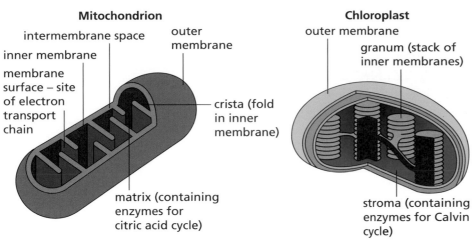

Figure 2.7 Membranes of a mitochondrion and a chloroplast

Key words

Anabolic – metabolic activity that requires energy input and builds up complex molecules
Catabolic – metabolic activity that releases energy in breakdown reactions
Compartment – small membrane-bound region of a cell
Metabolic pathway – enzyme-controlled sequence of chemical reactions in cells
Metabolism – total of all metabolic pathways in an organism
Phospholipid membrane – membrane of a cell made from fluid phospholipid molecules and proteins
Pore – small gap in a membrane created by a channel-forming protein
Pump – protein in a phospholipid membrane that carries substances across it by active transport

Questions ❓

Restricted response (structured in 1- or 2-mark parts)

1 a) Describe what is meant by a metabolic pathway. (1)
   b) State **two** differences between anabolic and catabolic pathways. (2)
2 a) Give **two** roles of proteins embedded in phospholipid membranes. (2)
   b) Give **two** examples of organelles bounded by double membranes. (2)
   c) Explain the advantage of membrane-bound compartments in cells. (2)

Extended response (4–9 marks each)

3 Write notes on each of the following:
   a) metabolic pathways (4)
   b) the functions of membranes (5)
   (total = 9)

Answers are on page 93.

Key Area 2.1b
Control of metabolic pathways

Summary notes
Control of metabolic pathways

Enzymes are coded for by genes. Each step in a metabolic pathway is controlled by a specific enzyme. A metabolic block can occur when a gene mutation results in the absence of a functional enzyme. Figure 2.8 shows the genetic control of a metabolic pathway, and the result of a block in the pathway.

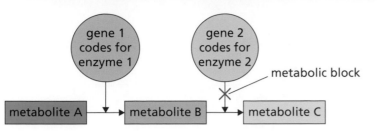

Figure 2.8 Genetic control of a metabolic pathway

If a mutation in gene 2 results in the absence of enzyme 2 then metabolite C will not be produced.

Enzyme action

Enzymes are biological catalysts that speed up the rates of chemical reactions by lowering the activation energy required for the reactions to proceed.

Activation energy

The energy required to initiate a reaction is called its activation energy. Before a substrate can change into a product, the substrate must overcome an energy barrier called the activation energy (E_A).

High temperatures often supply the activation energy in non-living situations, but in cells enzymes reduce the activation energy needed for a reaction to occur, as shown in Figure 2.9.

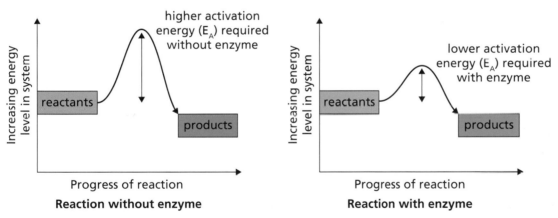

Figure 2.9 Activation energy

For example, in the breakdown of hydrogen peroxide:

E_A = 86 kJ mol⁻¹ without an enzyme
E_A = 1 kJ mol⁻¹ with the enzyme catalase

Induced fit

The active site of an enzyme is the location on its surface where substrate molecules bind and the chemical reaction takes place. Enzymes are specific and only act on one substrate because substrate molecules are complementary in shape to the enzyme's active site. Substrates are chemically attracted to the active site – they are said to have an affinity for it.

As the substrate starts to bind, the active site changes shape to fit the substrate more closely, increasing the rate of reaction, as shown in Figure 2.10.

Hints & tips

There is more about gene mutation in Key Area 1.6 on page 22.

Hints & tips

Induced fit is a bit like the fitting of a hand into a surgical glove – the glove change shape and then the fit is exact and very tight.

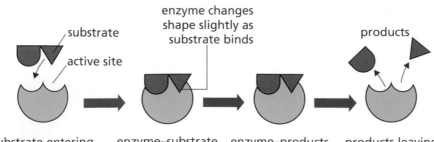

Figure 2.10 The induced-fit model of enzyme action

The active site orientates the substrate molecules and promotes the chemical reaction through the lowering of the activation energy required, as shown in Figure 2.11.

After the reaction takes place, the product, being a different shape from the substrate, moves away because it has low affinity for the active site. The active site returns to its original shape.

Rates of enzyme reaction

The maximum rate at which any enzyme-catalysed reaction can proceed depends on, among other things, the concentration of substrate molecules, as shown in Figure 2.12. An increase in substrate concentration drives the reaction in the direction of the end product and increases the rate of the reaction.

Multi-enzyme complexes

Some enzymes involved in a particular metabolic pathway occur grouped together in a membrane as a multi-enzyme complex. This helps ensure that the reactions proceed in the correct order. In respiration, the pyruvate dehydrogenase complex contains three enzymes, which act together to convert pyruvate into acetyl-CoA.

Hints & tips ⭐

There is more about the conversion of pyruvate to acetyl-CoA in Key Area 2.2 (page 61).

Many metabolic reactions are reversible and the concentration of the substrate and product affect the direction and rate of the reaction.

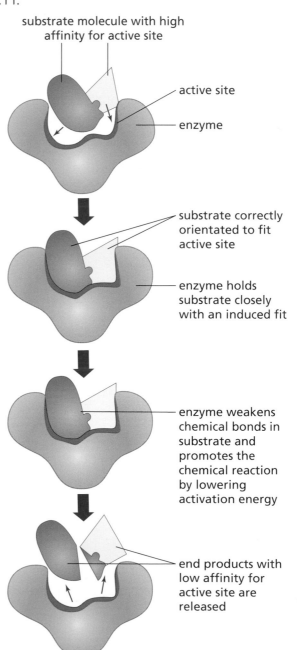

Figure 2.11 The role of the active site in orientating reactants

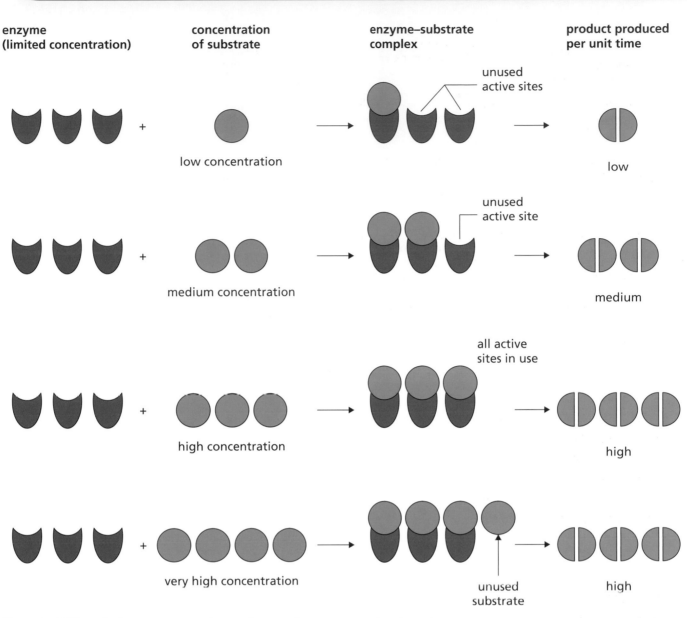

Figure 2.12 Effect of substrate concentration on the rate of an enzyme-catalysed reaction

Control of metabolic pathways through the regulation of enzyme action

Inhibitors

An inhibitor is a substance that reduces the rate of an enzyme reaction. Inhibitors occur naturally but are also produced artificially for uses such as drugs and pesticides. There are two main kinds of inhibitor.

Competitive inhibitors are molecules with a similar structural shape to the normal substrate of the enzyme and so can fit into its active site. They compete with substrate molecules for a position in the active site on the enzyme. Figure 2.13 shows the effect of a competitive inhibitor on the activity of an enzyme.

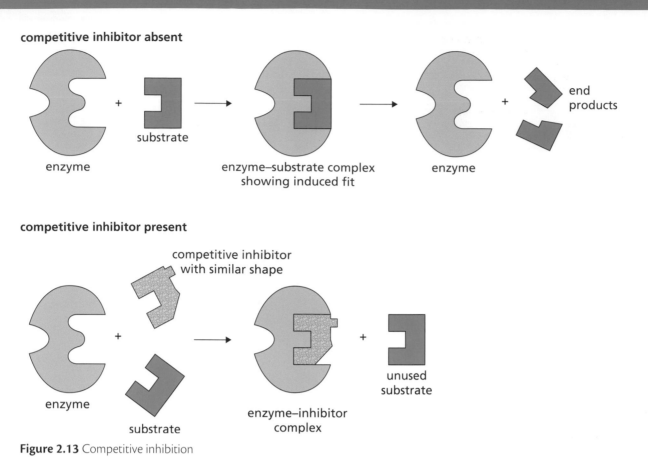

competitive inhibitor absent

substrate

enzyme

enzyme–substrate complex
showing induced fit

enzyme

end products

competitive inhibitor present

competitive inhibitor
with similar shape

enzyme

substrate

enzyme–inhibitor
complex

unused
substrate

Figure 2.13 Competitive inhibition

With some of the active sites occupied and blocked by the inhibitor, the rate of the reaction is reduced. However, if the substrate concentration is increased, the chance of the substrate binding to the enzyme is increased and the rate of the reaction can return to normal, as shown in Figure 2.14.

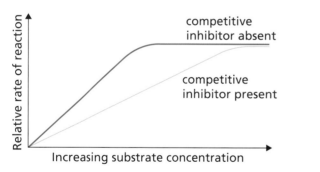

Relative rate of reaction

competitive
inhibitor absent

competitive
inhibitor present

Increasing substrate concentration

Figure 2.14 The effect of increasing substrate concentration on competitive inhibition

Non-competitive inhibitors are molecules with a quite different structure from the substrate molecule. They do not fit into the active site of the enzyme but bind to another part of the enzyme molecule. This changes the shape of the active site, so that it can no longer combine with the substrate molecule. Figure 2.15 shows the effect of a non-competitive inhibitor on the activity of an enzyme.

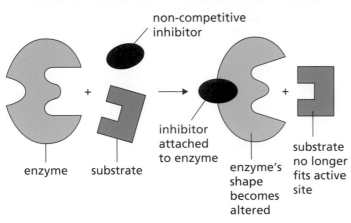

Figure 2.15 Non-competitive inhibition

The effect of non-competitive inhibitors is to reduce the amount of active enzyme and has a similar effect to decreasing the enzyme concentration. Cyanide, heavy metal ions and some insecticides are examples of non-competitive inhibitors. Increasing the substrate concentration does not increase the reaction rate in the presence of a non-competitive inhibitor and the effect of the inhibitor is permanent.

Feedback inhibition occurs when an end product inhibits the activity of an enzyme that catalysed a reaction earlier in the pathway that produced it, as shown in Figure 2.16.

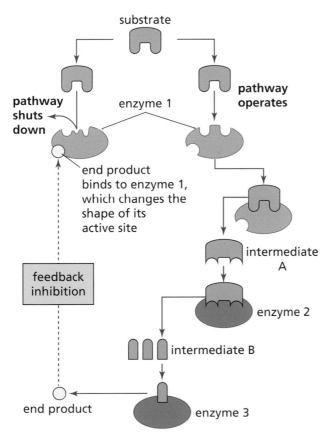

Figure 2.16 Feedback inhibition

Key words

Activation energy – input of energy required to start a chemical reaction
Active site – region on an enzyme molecule where the substrate binds
Competitive inhibition – the slowing of reaction rate due to the presence of a substance resembling the substrate
Feedback inhibition – enzyme inhibition caused by the presence of an end product of a metabolic pathway acting as an inhibitor of the pathway
Induced fit – change to an enzyme's active site brought about by its substrate
Non-competitive inhibition – enzyme inhibition by a substance that permanently alters the active site of an enzyme
Product – substance resulting from an enzyme-catalysed reaction
Substrate – substance on which an enzyme acts

Questions ?

Restricted response (structured in 1- or 2-mark parts)

1 Describe the role of genes in the control of metabolic pathways. (2)
2 **a)** Explain what is meant by the induced-fit model of enzyme action. (2)
   b) Describe the effect of an increase in substrate concentration on the direction and rate of an enzyme reaction. (2)
   c) Explain how enzymes speed up the rate of reactions in metabolic pathways. (2)

Extended response (4–9 marks each)

3 Give an account of enzyme action and of the effects of competitive and non-competitive inhibition. (9)

Answers are on page 94.

Key Area 2.2
Cellular respiration

Key points ❗

1. **Cellular respiration** pathways are present in cells from all three domains of life. ☐
2. The metabolic pathways of cellular respiration yield energy and are connected to many other pathways. ☐
3. In respiration, glucose is broken down in a series of enzyme-controlled steps. ☐
4. Hydrogen ions and high-energy electrons are removed by **dehydrogenase** enzymes and used to yield **ATP**. ☐
5. ATP is used to transfer the energy from cellular respiration to synthesis pathways and other cellular processes where energy is required. ☐
6. The breakdown of ATP to ADP and **phosphate (Pi)** releases energy. ☐
7. The regeneration of ATP from ADP and phosphate (Pi) uses the energy released from cellular respiration. ☐
8. **Phosphorylation** is the addition of a phosphate group to a molecule to alter its reactivity. ☐
9. **Glycolysis** is the first stage of respiration and involves the breakdown of glucose to **pyruvate**. ☐
10. In glycolysis, the phosphorylation of **intermediates** by ATP is an energy investment phase and the direct regeneration of ATP is an energy pay-off stage. ☐
11. Pyruvate progresses to the **citric acid cycle** if oxygen is available. ☐
12. In the absence of oxygen, pyruvate undergoes **fermentation** to **lactate** in mammal muscle cells or ethanol and CO_2 in plants and yeasts. ☐
13. Pyruvate is broken down to an **acetyl group**, which combines with **coenzyme A** to be transferred to the citric acid cycle as acetyl coenzyme A. ☐
14. Acetyl coenzyme A combines with **oxaloacetate** to form **citrate**, followed by the enzyme-mediated steps of the citric acid cycle, with some regeneration of ATP, the release of carbon dioxide and the regeneration of oxaloacetate. ☐
15. At certain steps in glycolysis and the citric acid cycle, dehydrogenase enzymes remove hydrogen ions from the substrate along with associated **high-energy electrons**. ☐
16. The hydrogen ions and high-energy electrons are passed to the coenzymes **NAD** or **FAD**, forming NADH or $FADH_2$. ☐
17. The **electron transport chain** is a collection of proteins attached to the inner membrane of the mitochondria. ☐
18. NADH and $FADH_2$ release the high-energy electrons to the electron transport chain where they cascade down the chain, releasing energy. ☐
19. Energy is used to pump H ions across the inner mitochondrial membrane. ☐
20. The return flow of H ions drives ATP synthase, which produces the bulk of the ATP generated by cellular respiration. ☐
21. The final electron acceptor is oxygen, which combines with hydrogen ions and electrons to form water. ☐
22. Glucose is the main substrate for respiration, but **alternative respiratory substrates** include other sugars, starch, glycogen, amino acids and fats. ☐

Summary notes

Cellular respiration

Cellular respiration pathways are present in the cells from all three domains of life.

The metabolic pathways of cellular respiration are of central importance to cells. They yield energy and are connected to many other pathways.

Transfer of energy via ATP

ATP is built up or regenerated from ADP and inorganic phosphate (Pi) using the energy released from cellular respiration. Respiration converts the chemical energy stored in glucose into chemical energy stored in ATP.

ATP is used to transfer the chemical energy from cellular respiration to synthetic pathways and other cellular processes where energy is required, for example the contraction of muscle fibres, active transport, DNA replication and protein synthesis. The energy held in the ATP is released when it is broken down into ADP + Pi. Figure 2.17 shows an example of the transfer of chemical energy by ATP to a synthetic pathway.

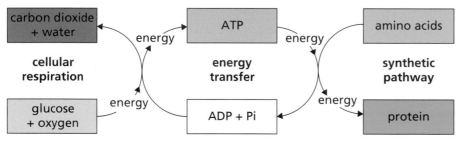

Figure 2.17 An example of the role of ATP in energy transfer

Synthesis of ATP in respiration

During respiration, glucose is broken down in a series of enzyme-catalysed steps. Hydrogen ions and high-energy electrons are removed by dehydrogenase enzymes and used in the synthesis of ATP.

Stages in aerobic respiration

The stages of respiration take place in different parts of the cell.

1 Glycolysis

Glycolysis is a series of enzyme-controlled reactions that take place in the cytoplasm of cells.

During glycolysis glucose is broken down to pyruvate in the absence of oxygen.

The phosphorylation of intermediates in glycolysis uses two molecules of ATP and is described as an energy investment phase. The later reactions in glycolysis result in the direct regeneration of four molecules of ATP for every glucose molecule and are referred to as the energy pay-off phase, giving a net gain of 2 ATP. During the energy pay-off phase, dehydrogenase enzymes remove hydrogen ions (H$^+$), which combine

Hints & tips

Glycolysis means the splitting of glucose.

with the hydrogen carrier NAD to form NADH. If oxygen is present, NADH transports hydrogen to the electron transport chain, which leads to the production of more ATP. Figure 2.18 shows the breakdown of glucose to pyruvate during glycolysis.

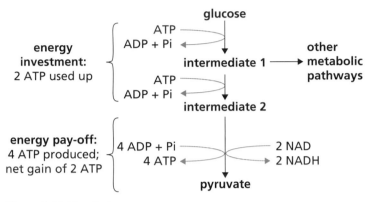

Figure 2.18 Glycolysis

2 Citric acid cycle

If oxygen is available, pyruvate progresses to the citric acid cycle. This stage takes place in the central matrix of the mitochondria. Pyruvate enters the mitochondria and is broken down by enzymes to an acetyl group and carbon dioxide (CO_2).

The acetyl group then combines with coenzyme A to be transferred to the citric acid cycle as acetyl coenzyme A. The acetyl group combines with oxaloacetate to form citrate (citric acid). The citrate then undergoes a series of enzyme-mediated steps resulting in the generation of one ATP molecule, the release of carbon dioxide and the regeneration of oxaloacetate in the matrix of the mitochondria. During the citric acid cycle, dehydrogenase enzymes remove hydrogen ions (H^+) and high-energy electrons, which combine with the coenzymes NAD and FAD to form NADH and $FADH_2$. Figure 2.19 shows the stages involved in the citric acid cycle.

In the absence of oxygen, the pyruvate undergoes fermentation to either lactate in mammal muscle cells or ethanol and CO_2 in plant cells and in yeast.

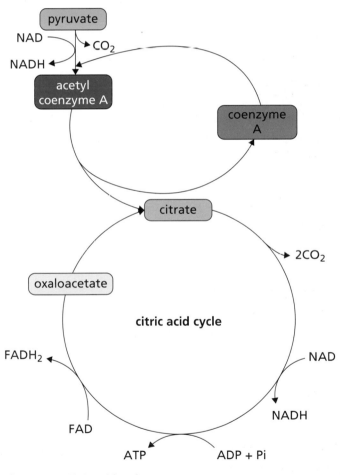

Figure 2.19 Citric acid cycle

3 Electron transport chain

NADH and FADH₂ transport and pass on the high-energy electrons to the electron transport chain. This final stage in aerobic respiration takes place on the inner membrane of the mitochondria. The electron transport chain is a collection of proteins attached to the membrane.

NADH and FADH$_2$ release the high-energy electrons to the electron transport chain where they pass down the chain of electron acceptors, releasing their energy. The energy is used to pump hydrogen ions (H^+) across the inner mitochondrial membrane from the matrix side of the mitochondria into the space between its membranes. The return flow of the hydrogen ions (H^+) back into the matrix drives the enzyme ATP synthase, which results in the synthesis of ATP from ADP + Pi. This stage produces most of the ATP generated by cellular respiration. Oxygen is the final acceptor of hydrogen ions and electrons, forming water.

Figure 2.20 shows the stages involved in the electron transport chain on the inner membranes of mitochondria.

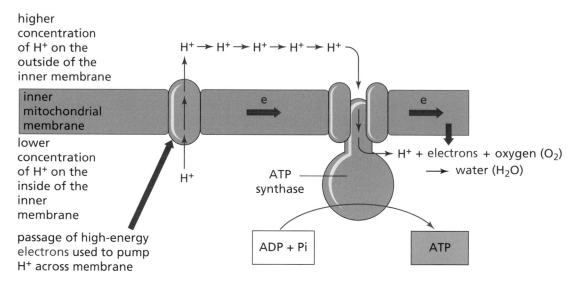

Figure 2.20 The electron transport chain of respiration on the inner membranes of mitochondria

Substrates for respiration

Starch and glycogen are broken down to glucose for use as a respiratory substrate.

Alternative respiratory substrates

Other sugar molecules can be converted to glucose or intermediates in glycolysis. Proteins can be broken down to amino acids, which are converted to intermediates of glycolysis or the citric acid cycle. Fats can also be broken down to fatty acids and glycerol, which are converted to intermediates of glycolysis and the citric acid cycle.

Key words

Acetyl group – produced by breakdown of pyruvate; joins with oxaloacetate in the citric acid cycle

Alternative respiratory substrate – substrate used for respiration other than carbohydrate

ATP – molecule used for energy transfer in cells

Cellular respiration – release of energy from respiratory substrates

Citrate – citric acid; first substance produced in the citric acid cycle

Citric acid cycle – second stage of aerobic respiration, occurring in the matrix of mitochondria

Coenzyme A – substance that carries an acetyl group into the citric acid cycle

Dehydrogenase – enzyme which removes hydrogen from its substrate; important in the citric acid cycle

Electron transport chain – group of proteins embedded in membranes of mitochondria and chloroplasts

FAD – hydrogen carrier important in the citric acid cycle

Fermentation – progression of pyruvate in the absence of oxygen

Glycolysis – first stage in cellular respiration

High-energy electron – electron that can yield energy as it passes through an electron transport chain

Intermediate – substance in a metabolic pathway between the original substrate and the end product

Lactate – produced by the anaerobic conversion of pyruvate in mammalian muscle cells

NAD – hydrogen carrier important in the citric acid cycle

Oxaloacetate – substance that combines with the acetyl group in the citric acid cycle to form citrate

Phosphate (Pi) – inorganic phosphate used to phosphorylate ADP

Phosphorylation – addition of phosphate to a substance

Pyruvate – end product of glycolysis

Questions ?

Restricted response (structured in 1- or 2-mark parts)

1 **a)** Explain why the phosphorylation of intermediates in glycolysis is described as an energy investment phase. (2)

   b) State the role of dehydrogenase enzymes in glycolysis and the citric acid cycle. (1)

   c) Describe the role of the coenzymes NAD and FAD. (2)

2 **a)** Name the enzyme embedded in the inner membrane of a mitochondrion responsible for the regeneration of ATP. (1)

   b) Describe the role of the high-energy electrons transported to the electron transport chain. (2)

   c) State the role of oxygen in the electron transport chain. (1)

   d) Name **two** alternative respiratory substrates. (2)

Extended response (4–9 marks each)

3 Give an account of glycolysis and the citric acid cycle in respiration. (9)

4 Give an account of the electron transport chain and the transfer of energy by ATP. (9)

Answers are on pages 94–95.

Key Area 2.3
Metabolic rate

Key points !

1. The **metabolic rate** of an organism is the amount of energy used in a given period of time. ☐
2. The metabolic rates of different organisms at rest can be compared through the measurement of oxygen consumption, carbon dioxide production and heat production. ☐
3. High metabolic rates require efficient delivery of oxygen to cells. ☐
4. Fish have a **single circulatory system**, which has a heart with two chambers – an **atrium** and a **ventricle**. ☐
5. Amphibians and reptiles have an **incomplete double circulatory system**, with a three-chambered heart made up of a right and left atrium and one ventricle in which oxygenated and deoxygenated blood mix. ☐
6. Birds and mammals have a **complete double circulatory system**, with a four-chambered heart made up of two atria and two ventricles in which oxygenated and deoxygenated blood do not mix. ☐
7. Amphibians exchange gases through their skin, and their lungs have a relatively small surface area for gas exchange. ☐
8. Reptile and mammal lungs have a highly branched system of tubes, with many thin-walled, moist **alveoli** providing a large surface area for the efficient exchange of gases. ☐
9. Birds are very active and have a very efficient system of gas exchange that allows them to obtain the large quantities of oxygen needed for their very high metabolic rates. ☐
10. Some organisms show physiological adaptations that enable them to survive in, and to exploit, **low-oxygen niches**, for example at high altitudes or in deep oceans. ☐
11. The maximum volume of oxygen that an organism can take up and use during intense exercise is called the maximum oxygen uptake, or **VO$_2$ max**. ☐
12. VO$_2$ max (or maximum oxygen uptake) is used as a measure of fitness in humans. ☐

Summary notes

Metabolic rate

The metabolic rate of an organism is the amount of energy used in a given period of time and can be measured in terms of the oxygen consumed, the carbon dioxide produced or the heat produced in the time period.

Oxygen delivery

Oxygen is consumed during aerobic respiration, and organisms that have high metabolic rates require the efficient delivery of oxygen to their cells. In vertebrates, oxygen is delivered in blood pumped by the heart.

Vertebrate hearts and circulatory systems have evolved to increase efficiency of the delivery of oxygen to tissues.

Circulatory systems in vertebrates

1 Single circulatory system

Fish have a single circulatory system, which has a heart with two chambers – an atrium and a ventricle. It is called a single circulatory system because the blood only passes through the heart once in each complete circuit, as shown in Figure 2.21.

When blood passes through a capillary bed a drop in pressure occurs. In fish, this means that blood is delivered to the capillary bed in the body tissues at low pressure.

2 Incomplete double circulatory system

Amphibians and most reptiles have incomplete double circulatory systems. Their hearts have three chambers – right and left atria and a ventricle. The right atrium receives deoxygenated blood returning from the capillary bed in the body tissues. The left atrium receives oxygenated blood returning from the lungs. The blood from both atria is then passed into the one ventricle, which means that the oxygenated and deoxygenated blood mix before being pumped out of the ventricle to supply the body tissues with the oxygen they require, as shown in Figure 2.22.

3 Complete double circulatory system

Birds and mammals have a complete double circulatory system. The heart has four chambers – two atria and two ventricles – allowing complete separation of oxygenated and deoxygenated blood. Blood passes through the heart twice during each complete circuit of the body with no mixing of the oxygenated and deoxygenated blood, as shown in Figure 2.23.

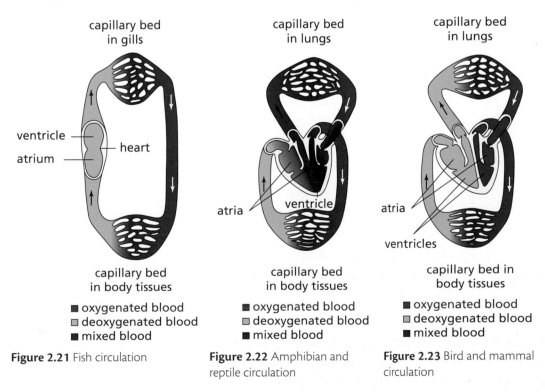

Figure 2.21 Fish circulation

Figure 2.22 Amphibian and reptile circulation

Figure 2.23 Bird and mammal circulation

The various circulatory systems are compared in the following table.

Vertebrate group(s)	Type of circulation	Heart	Features
Fish	Single	Two chambers – an atrium and a ventricle	Loss of pressure a problem
Amphibians and reptiles	Incomplete double	Three chambers – a right and left atrium and a ventricle	Pressure maintained, but tissue blood is incompletely oxygenated
Birds and mammals	Complete double	Four chambers – two atria and two ventricles	Pressure maintained and tissue blood completely oxygenated

Complexity of lungs

Amphibians can exchange gases through their skin. They use their lungs for gas exchange during very active periods. Their lungs are small, thin-walled sacs without alveoli. In comparison with mammals, their lungs have a relatively smaller surface area for gas exchange.

Reptiles and mammals have lungs with a highly branched system of tubes called bronchioles ending in many thin-walled, moist alveoli, providing a large surface area for the efficient exchange of gases. This provides them with the large quantities of oxygen that their metabolism requires. Figure 2.24 shows an alveolus and capillary network.

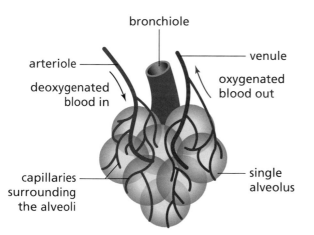

Figure 2.24 Alveolus and capillary network in reptiles and mammals

Birds are the most active vertebrates and have a very efficient system of gas exchange that allows them to obtain the large quantities of oxygen needed for their very high metabolic rates. They have a system of large air sacs associated with their lungs, designed to keep air flowing through the lungs in one direction rather than having to go in and out by the same route, as shown in Figure 2.25.

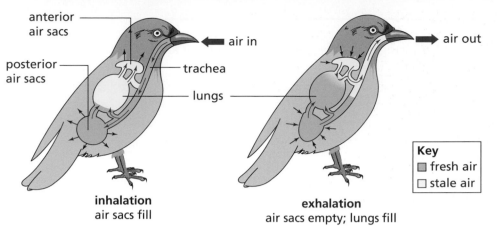

Figure 2.25 Respiratory system of birds

When the bird breathes in, fresh air fills its posterior air sacs. Stale air moves into the anterior air sacs from the lungs. When the bird breathes out, the fresh air passes from the posterior sacs to the lungs and the stale air passes from the anterior sacs to the outside.

Physiological adaptations of animals for low oxygen niches

Some organisms show physiological adaptations that enable them to survive in and exploit low oxygen niches, for example at high altitude, deep in the ocean or in deoxygenated muds.

Humans respond to high altitude by increasing the number of red blood cells by up to 20% when moving from sea level to 4000 metres. It takes several weeks for this adaptation to take effect.

Diving mammals, such as seals, whales and dolphins, can make deep-water dives for long periods of time. They have physiological adaptations that enable them to do this. One adaptation is to slow their heart rate down to conserve oxygen. Another adaptation is to collapse their lungs. This reduces their buoyancy and allows them to sink quickly, saving energy to hunt for food.

Bloodworms (*Tubifex*) live in low-oxygen bottom sediments of fresh water. Their bodies contain haemoglobin, which allows them to absorb oxygen from the limited amount present.

The use of maximum oxygen uptake as a measure of fitness in humans

The maximum volume of oxygen that the body can take up and use during intense exercise is called the maximum oxygen uptake or VO_2 max. This is used as a measure of fitness in humans. It is measured using a procedure involving exercising on an ergometer – a treadmill or exercise bike. VO_2 max is reached when the oxygen uptake stays steady even when the workload continues to be increased. It improves with training.

Key words

Alveoli – microscopic parts of the gas exchange system in vertebrate lungs (*sing.* alveolus)

Atrium – chamber receiving blood entering a vertebrate heart

Complete double circulation – double circulation with complete separation of oxygenated and deoxygenated blood (e.g. in birds and mammals)

Double circulation – blood flows through the heart twice during a full circulation of the body

Incomplete double circulation – double circulation with some mixing of oxygenated and deoxygenated blood (e.g. in amphibians and some reptiles)

Low-oxygen niche – way of life in a habitat with little oxygen present, such as at high altitude or in a deep ocean

Metabolic rate – rate of consumption of energy by an organism

Single circulatory system – blood flows through the heart once during a full circulation of the body (e.g. in fish)

Ventricle – chamber of a vertebrate heart that distributes blood

VO$_2$ max – maximum volume of oxygen that can be absorbed by an organism in a period of time

Questions ?

Restricted response (structured in 1- or 2-mark parts)

1 a) State what is meant by an organism's metabolic rate. (1)
   b) Describe **two** methods of measuring the metabolic rate of an organism. (2)
   c) Describe how the gas exchange system of birds is adapted to enable them to maintain their very high metabolic rates. (2)
2 a) Give **two** examples of low-oxygen niches. (1)
   b) Describe **one** physiological adaptation for low-oxygen niches. (1)
   c) Explain the term VO$_2$ max and why it can be used as a measure of fitness in humans. (2)

Extended response (4–9 marks each)

3 Compare and contrast the heart structure and circulation of fish, amphibians and mammals. (9)

Answers are on page 95.

Key Area 2.4
Metabolism in conformers and regulators

Key points !

1. The ability of an organism to maintain its metabolic rate is affected by external abiotic factors such as temperature, salinity and pH. ☐
2. The internal environment of a **conformer** is dependent upon its external environment. ☐
3. Conformers cannot alter their metabolic rate using physiological means, but as a result their metabolic costs can be low. ☐
4. Conformers can have a narrow **ecological niche** unless they can tolerate or resist variation in their external environment. ☐
5. Behavioural responses can help to maintain a conformer's optimum metabolic rate. ☐
6. **Regulators** adjust their metabolic rate using physiological mechanisms to maintain a steady state. ☐
7. Regulators use metabolism to control their internal environment, which increases the range of possible ecological niches. ☐
8. **Homeostasis** is the maintenance of steady conditions within an organism. ☐
9. Regulators require energy to achieve homeostasis and as a result have high metabolic costs. ☐
10. **Negative feedback** is the control mechanism by which homeostasis is achieved. ☐
11. Negative feedback systems have monitoring centres with receptor cells, a system for sending messages and effectors, which carry out a response. ☐
12. **Thermoregulation** is important for optimal enzyme-controlled reaction rates and diffusion rates for maintenance of metabolism. ☐
13. The **hypothalamus** is the temperature-monitoring centre of the mammalian brain and contains **thermoreceptors**, which detect changes in blood temperature. ☐
14. The hypothalamus sends out nerve impulses to effectors in skin and body muscles. ☐

Summary notes
Metabolism in conformers and regulators

External abiotic factors such as temperature, salinity and pH can affect the ability of an organism to maintain its metabolic rate.

Conformers

Organisms that cannot maintain their metabolic rate by physiological mechanisms are called conformers. A conformer's internal environment is directly dependent upon its external environment. Their ecological niches are narrow and they lack the ability to tolerate change should it occur.

They do not use physiological mechanisms that require energy to alter their metabolic rate and so they have low metabolic energy costs. Conformers live in stable environments such as the ocean depths. Many conformers manage to maintain their optimum metabolic rate by employing behavioural responses, such as reptiles basking on rocks to increase body temperature.

Regulators

Regulators are organisms that can control their internal environment and maintain a steady state known as homeostasis by using physiological mechanisms. This ability widens the range of possible ecological niches that they can occupy. Regulation requires energy to maintain homeostasis. The control mechanism by which homeostasis is achieved is called negative feedback.

Negative feedback control

Negative feedback systems have monitoring centres with receptor cells, a system for sending messages and effectors. The receptors are special cells that constantly monitor the internal environment and detect changes. If a change from the optimum is detected, a corrective mechanism is switched on and messages are sent to the effectors. The messages can either be hormones in the blood or nerve impulses. The effectors are the parts of the body, such as muscles or glands, that respond to the messages. The effectors respond to correct the change and return conditions to their optimum. Figure 2.26 shows the general mechanism of negative feedback control.

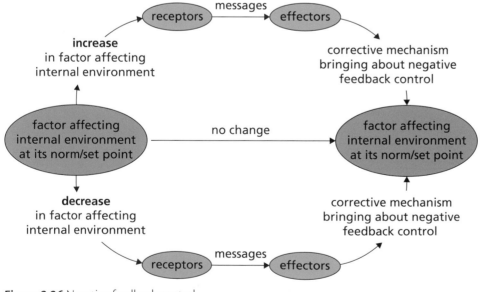

Figure 2.26 Negative feedback control

Thermoregulation in mammals

Mammals are thermoregulators and have a homeostatic mechanism to regulate their body temperature. Figure 2.27 shows the effect of external temperature on the body temperature of a mammal regulator compared with a reptile conformer.

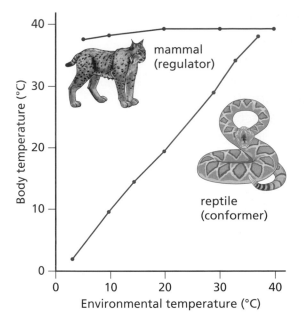

Figure 2.27 Temperature in a regulator and a conformer

The hypothalamus is the temperature-monitoring centre and contains thermoreceptors, which detect changes in blood temperature. The hypothalamus sends out nerve impulses to the effectors, skin and body muscles, as shown in Figure 2.28.

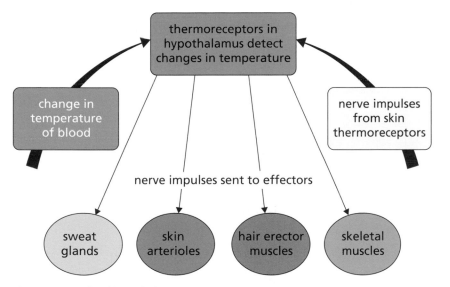

Figure 2.28 Role of hypothalamus

Hot conditions, exercise or illness can increase the body temperature above normal. The thermoreceptors in the hypothalamus detect this increase and send nerve impulses to the effectors. Sweat glands increase sweat production and heat from the body evaporates the water, lowering the body temperature by convection. Vasodilation occurs – the skin arterioles become dilated (wider) – allowing a larger volume of blood to flow through the capillaries on the skin surface, increasing heat loss by radiation. These corrective mechanisms lower the body temperature back to normal.

If the body temperature falls below normal, the thermoreceptors in the hypothalamus detect the decrease and send nerve impulses to the effectors. The sweat glands decrease sweat production. Vasoconstriction occurs – the skin arterioles become constricted (narrower) – reducing the volume of blood that flows through the capillaries on the skin surface, so less heat is lost by radiation. Hair erector muscles contract to raise hairs, which trap air, providing insulation and reducing heat loss. Shivering of the skeletal muscles generates heat. There is also an increase in the metabolic rate, which increases heat production. These corrective mechanisms raise the body temperature back to normal. Figure 2.29 shows the homeostatic control of body temperature in humans.

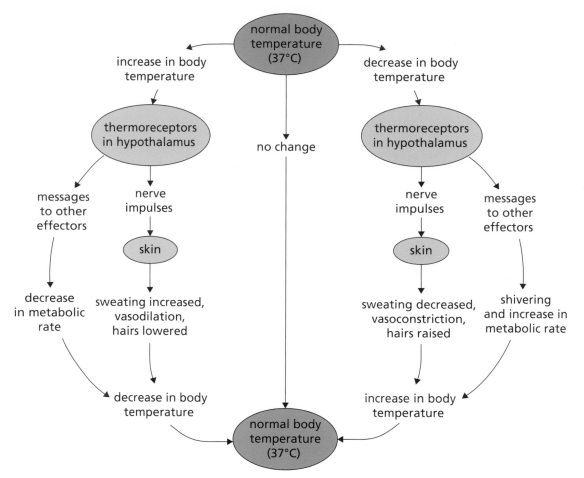

Figure 2.29 Control of body temperature in humans

Advantages of maintaining a constant body temperature

Enzymes have an optimum temperature at which they work best. Animals that can maintain the optimum temperature for enzyme activity can maintain a high metabolic rate.

Temperature also affects diffusion rates. Rates of diffusion of substances such as oxygen and carbon dioxide are faster at warmer temperatures and maintaining these contributes towards the ability to maintain high metabolic activity.

Key words

Conformer – animal whose internal environment is dependent on its environment

Ecological niche – the way of life and the role of an organism in its community

Homeostasis – maintenance of a steady state in the cells of a living organism

Hypothalamus – region of the mammalian brain in which blood temperature is monitored

Negative feedback – system of maintaining homeostasis in regulator organisms

Regulator – animal that can adjust its metabolic rate to maintain a steady internal state

Thermoreceptor – heat-sensitive cell in the hypothalamus of mammals

Thermoregulation – use of negative feedback in regulation of body temperature in mammals

Questions ?

Restricted response (structured in 1- or 2-mark parts)

1 Mammals maintain their body temperature by homeostatic control.
  a) Name the temperature-monitoring centre in the brain that detects temperature changes. (1)
  b) In the following sentence, identify which of the alternatives in each pair makes the sentence correct.
  The corrective mechanism in response to a decrease in body temperature includes (vasoconstriction/vasodilation), which (increases/decreases) blood flow in the skin. (1)
  c) Describe how the messages from the temperature-monitoring centre are relayed to the effectors in the skin. (1)
  d) State **two** reasons why body temperature in humans is important to metabolic processes. (2)
2 a) Give **two** abiotic factors that affect the ability of an organism to maintain its metabolic rate. (2)
  b) Give the meaning of the term homeostasis. (1)
  c) Explain why conformers usually have a narrow ecological niche. (2)
  d) Give the name of the control system used by regulators to maintain a relatively stable internal environment. (1)

Extended response (4–9 marks each)

3 Give an account of the mechanisms of thermoregulation in mammals. (9)
4 Give an account of metabolism in conformers in relation to their ecological niches. (7)

Answers are on page 96.

Metabolism and adverse conditions

Key points !

1 Many environments vary beyond the tolerable limits for the normal metabolic activity of an organism. ☐

2 To cope with these cyclic or unpredictable fluctuations, organisms must have adaptations to survive or to avoid adverse conditions. ☐

3 To allow survival during a period when the costs of continued normal metabolic activity would be too high, the metabolic rate can be reduced. ☐

4 **Dormancy** is part of an organism's life cycle and is the stage associated with resisting or tolerating periods of environmental adversity. ☐

5 Dormancy can be **predictive** or **consequential**. ☐

6 Examples of dormancy include **hibernation** and **aestivation**. ☐

7 Hibernation is often defined in terms of mammals and is a common survival strategy in response to a metabolic energy crisis brought about by low temperatures and lack of food. ☐

8 Aestivation allows survival in periods of high temperature or drought. ☐

9 Daily **torpor** is a period of reduced activity in organisms with high metabolic rates. ☐

10 **Migration** avoids metabolic adversity by expending energy to relocate to a more suitable environment. ☐

11 Specialised techniques are used in studies of long-distance migration. For example, individual marking and types of tracking have been developed to overcome the difficulties involved in the study of migratory vertebrates and invertebrates. ☐

12 Experiments have been designed to investigate the **innate** and **learned** influences on migratory behaviour. ☐

13 **Extremophiles** are organisms that live under extreme conditions that most life forms are unable to tolerate. ☐

14 Some species have enzymes that are extremely tolerant and allow them to thrive in environments that would be lethal to almost all other species. ☐

15 Examples of extremophiles include **thermophilic bacteria**, which live in hot springs or seabed vents. ☐

Summary notes

Maintaining metabolism during environmental change

Many environments vary beyond the tolerable limits for normal metabolic activity of an organism. In some environments, extremes of temperature can result in lack of food and drought. To cope with these fluctuations, which can be cyclic or unpredictable, organisms have adaptations to survive them or avoid them.

1 Surviving adverse conditions

Dormancy

To allow survival during a period when the energy costs required for normal metabolic activity would be too high, the metabolic rate can be reduced. This can be achieved by a period of dormancy. Dormancy is part of an organism's life cycle and can be predictive or consequential.

Predictive dormancy occurs when an organism becomes dormant before the onset of the adverse conditions. It occurs in advance of the adverse conditions and is usually genetically programmed. It is typical in predictable seasonal environments where the temperature and photoperiod can be used as environmental cues.

Consequential dormancy is when an organism becomes dormant after the onset of the adverse conditions. It is a typical response of organisms living in unpredictable environments.

Examples of dormancy in animals include hibernation, aestivation and torpor.

Hibernation is often defined in terms of mammals. It is a widespread and common survival strategy in response to the threat of a metabolic energy crisis brought about by low temperatures and lack of food. Before hibernating, a mammal eats extra food and stores it as fat. During hibernation, metabolic rate is reduced, resulting in a decrease in body temperature, heart rate and breathing rate. This reduces energy expenditure and allows a mammal to survive the winter period.

Aestivation is a form of dormancy that allows some animals to survive in periods of high temperature or drought in the summer. It occurs not just because of food supply issues, but also because the conditions become too hot and dry for the animal to survive. The process typically involves burrowing into the ground, where the temperature stays cool, and reducing metabolic activity in a similar manner to hibernation.

Examples 🚩

In Australia, the water-holding frog has an aestivation cycle to conserve energy. It buries itself in sandy ground in a secreted, water-tight, mucus cocoon during periods of hot, dry weather and remains in this state of dormancy until the arrival of the rain when conditions improve.

Lungfish are capable of a form of aestivation that allows them to live without water for as long as 3 years. Lungfish are fish that have lungs as well as gills, allowing them to breathe air. When its lake dries up, the fish burrows into the mud, secreting mucus until its entire body is covered. The mucus dries into a sack that holds moisture in. Even when the mud dries completely, the lungfish stays moist and breathes through a mucus tube.

Daily torpor is a period of reduced activity in organisms with high metabolic rates such as small birds and mammals. Daily torpor is similar to short-term hibernation.

Torpor results in a decrease in body temperature, heart rate and breathing rate and increases an organism's chances of survival by reducing the energy required to maintain a high metabolic rate. Small mammals and birds can reduce their rate of energy consumption during daily torpor by up to 90%.

Example

Hummingbirds have an extremely high metabolic rate, with a heart rate that can exceed 1200 beats per minute. Their energy consumption is so great that hummingbirds use daily torpor to conserve energy, even in the tropics.

2 Avoiding adverse conditions

Migration is a relatively long-distance movement of individuals, which usually takes place on a seasonal basis. Migration enables animals to avoid metabolic adversity brought about by lack of food and low temperatures by expending energy to relocate to a more suitable environment.

Hints & tips

Make sure you know the difference between surviving adverse conditions and **avoiding** them.

Innate and learned influences on migratory behaviour

Migration is found in all major animal groups, including birds, mammals, reptiles, amphibians, fish and insects. An organism's migratory behaviour is thought to be inherited or innate. Migratory behaviour is also influenced by learning, which is gained by experience.

Migration occurs in response to an external trigger stimulus such as the day length, local climate, the availability of food, the season of the year or for mating reasons. To be counted as a true migration, the movement of the animals should be an annual or seasonal occurrence, such as birds migrating for the winter or the annual migration of wildebeest for grazing. It can also involve a major habitat change as part of the life cycle, as in the case of the Atlantic salmon, which migrate from fresh water to seawater in an annual cycle.

Tracking migration

Scientists have developed specialised techniques to overcome the difficulties involved in the study of the long-distance migration of vertebrates and invertebrates. These include the individual marking of animals, such as the ringing of a bird's leg with an identification tag, and attempting recaptures. Transmitters, attached to animals' bodies, which send out a signal that can be picked up by a receiver have also been developed. One advantage of these is that the animals being tracked do not need to be recaptured.

Extremophiles

Extremophiles are organisms that live under extreme conditions that most life forms are unable to tolerate. These conditions might be extremes of heat (over 42°C), cold (below 4°C), salinity, pH and pressure. The majority of extremophiles are microorganisms belonging to the taxonomic domain of life archaea, but some bacteria also live under extreme conditions.

Extremophiles have been found in the ice of the Arctic and Antarctic, in deserts, in deep-sea vents, in volcanic fissures and in areas of high salinity. Examples of extremophiles include thermophilic bacteria that live in hot springs or seabed vents and that thrive at temperatures of 50–80°C.

Biotechnologists have found ways to make use of many of these microorganisms, or their enzymes, in industrial processes. For example, enzymes from cryophiles or psychrophiles (cold-loving organisms) are used to enhance the cleaning power of washing detergents in cold water. Heat-loving or thermophilic organisms and their enzymes are probably the most highly studied extremophiles and have many uses in industrial processes and in enzyme products in the home. 'Taq polymerase' is a DNA polymerase from the bacterium *Thermus aquaticus*. *T. aquaticus* lives in the hot springs of Yellowstone National Park, Wyoming, and its discovery led to the development of a highly useful technique called the polymerase chain reaction (PCR). This is used for a wide variety of purposes, including forensic genetic fingerprinting, medical diagnosis and screening for genetic and other diseases.

Hints & tips

There is more about PCR in Key Area 1.2 (page 6).

Some species living in hot springs or seabed vents are able to generate their ATP by removing high-energy electrons from inorganic molecules such as hydrogen sulfide. For example, snottites are colonies of single-celled bacteria that hang from the walls and ceilings of caves. They generate ATP from hydrogen sulfide and produce sulfuric acid.

Methanogens generate ATP from hydrogen and produce methane. They are found in low-oxygen niches, for example the digestive systems of humans and ruminants. Other species of methanogens are found in hot springs, hydrothermal vents and under layers of ice.

Key words

Aestivation – reaction of an organism to tolerate extreme drought

Consequential dormancy – dormancy that occurs in response to the onset of adverse conditions

Dormancy – response by an organism to tolerate adverse conditions (e.g. hibernation, aestivation)

Extremophile – organism that lives in an environment with extreme abiotic conditions

Hibernation – response by an animal to avoid adverse conditions by reduction of metabolic rate

Innate behaviour – unlearned instinctive behaviour

Learned behaviour – behaviour of an individual organism not common to all members of its species and which is acquired by experience

Migration – response by an organism to avoid adverse conditions by relocating

Predictive dormancy – dormancy that occurs before the onset of adverse conditions

Thermophilic bacteria – bacteria that live in hot springs or seabed vents

Torpor – state of reduced metabolic activity in response to adverse conditions

Questions ?

Restricted response (structured in 1- or 2-mark parts)

1   **a)**   Give the meaning of the term dormancy.   (1)
    b)   Give **two** examples of dormancy.   (2)
    c)   Describe the difference between consequential and predictive dormancy.   (2)
    d)   Explain the benefit to some animals of being able to undergo daily torpor.   (1)

2   **a)**   Give the meanings of innate and learned behaviour in bird migration.   (2)
    b)   Give **two** methods of tracking migratory animals.   (2)

3   **a)**   Give the term for organisms that live under extreme conditions in environments that most species are unable to tolerate.   (1)
    b)   Give **one** example of these organisms and the conditions that it is able to tolerate.   (2)
    c)   Describe **one** application of an enzyme extracted from a thermophilic bacterium.   (2)

Extended response (4–9 marks each)

4   Give an account of the adaptations of organisms to surviving and avoiding adverse environmental conditions.   (8)
5   Give an account of extremophiles.   (4)

Answers are on pages 96–97.

Key Area 2.6
Environmental control of metabolism in microorganisms

Key points !

1 Microorganisms include archaea, bacteria and some species of eukaryote such as yeasts and protozoans. □

2 Microorganisms include species that use a wide range of substrates for metabolism and produce a wide range of products from their metabolic pathways. □

3 As a result of their adaptability, microorganisms are found in a wide range of ecological niches. □

4 Microorganisms can be used for a variety of research and industrial uses because of ease of cultivation and their speed of growth. □

5 The growth of microorganisms is influenced by the composition of their **growth medium** and by environmental conditions. □

6 Microorganisms require an energy source and raw materials for biosynthesis. □

7 Energy is derived from either chemical substrates or from light in photosynthetic microorganisms. □

8 Many microorganisms can produce all the complex molecules required for biosynthesis, including all the amino acids required for protein synthesis, from simple chemical compounds in growth media. □

9 Some microorganisms require complex compounds such as vitamins or fatty acids in their growth medium. □

10 Growth media can be composed of simple substances or can contain complex ingredients such as **beef extract**. □

11 Culture conditions include **sterility** to eliminate any effects of contaminating microorganisms, control of temperature, control of oxygen levels by aeration and control of pH by buffers or the addition of acid or alkali. □

12 The growth of unicellular organisms such as bacteria and yeast is recorded by measuring the increase in cell number in a given period of time. □

13 The time it takes for a unicellular organism to divide into two is called the doubling or **generation time**. □

14 Populations of microorganisms can be estimated by making **total cell counts** which consist of **viable** (live) and dead cells. □

15 **Exponential growth** can be illustrated on logarithmic and semi-logarithmic graph paper. □

16 The **lag phase** of growth is when microorganisms adjust to the conditions of the culture by inducing enzymes that metabolise the available substrates. □

17 The **log** (exponential) **phase** of growth is when the population doubles with each round of cell division. □

18 The **stationary phase** of growth is when the culture medium becomes depleted, some metabolites accumulate and **secondary metabolites** are produced. □

⇒

⇒

19 Secondary metabolism can confer an ecological advantage to microorganisms by producing substances not associated with growth, such as antibiotics. ☐

20 The **death phase** is when lack of substrate and the accumulation of toxic metabolites cause the death of cells. ☐

21 Some industrial fermentations involving microorganisms may require addition of metabolic **precursors**, **inducers** or inhibitors to control metabolism and give required products. ☐

Summary notes

Metabolism in microorganisms

Microorganisms include archaea, bacteria and some species of eukaryote such as yeasts and protozoans. Microorganisms include species that use a wide range of substrates for metabolism and produce a wide range of products from their metabolic pathways.

As a result of their adaptability, microorganisms are found in a wide range of ecological niches and can be used for a variety of research and industrial applications because they reproduce and grow quickly. They are easy to culture and they produce many different useful products.

Environmental control of metabolism

Culture media

The growth of microorganisms is influenced by the composition of their growth medium and the environmental conditions in which they are being cultured. Microorganisms require an energy source and a supply of raw materials in their growth medium. They use the raw materials for the biosynthesis of more complex substances such as proteins and nucleic acids.

Many microorganisms can produce all the molecules required for biosynthesis, including the amino acids required for protein synthesis, from simple chemical compounds in growth media. Others require specific complex compounds such as vitamins or fatty acids. Growth media can be composed of simple substances suitable for specific microorganisms. Others contain complex ingredients such as beef extract.

Energy is derived either from chemical substrates such as carbohydrates or from light in the case of photosynthetic microorganisms.

Culture conditions

Culture conditions include sterility to eliminate any effects of contaminating microorganisms, and the control of temperature, oxygen levels by aeration and pH by buffers or the addition of acid or alkali.

Hints & tips ⭐

Remember STOP –
Sterility
Temperature
Oxygen
pH.

Industrial fermenters or bioreactors, which are used to culture microorganisms on a huge scale, are controlled automatically by computers. Sensors monitor the culture conditions and maintain the factors affecting growth at their optimum level, as shown in Figure 2.30.

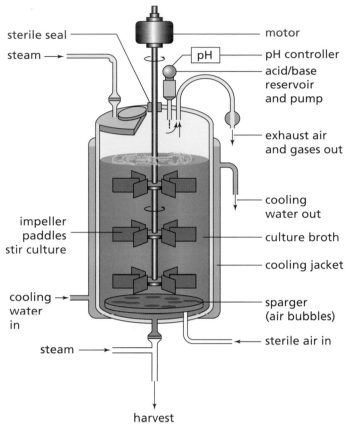

Figure 2.30 Industrial fermenter

Growth

Growth can be defined as the irreversible increase in dry biomass of an organism.

Growth of unicellular organisms such as bacteria and yeast is recorded by measuring the increase in cell number in a given period of time.

Phases of microorganism growth

The time it takes for a unicellular organism to divide into two is called the doubling or generation time. When microorganisms are cultured in a liquid medium, they use up the substrate and nutrients available and release metabolites back into the medium. These changes result in the four characteristic phases of growth: the lag, log (exponential), stationary and death phases, as shown in Figure 2.31. To estimate microbial populations, cell counts are made. Viable cells are those which are alive and capable of further cell division. Dead cells contribute to the total cell count.

Hints & tips

The dry mass is a more reliable measurement of growth than the fresh mass because fresh mass includes the water content in the cells of the organisms, which can vary independently of growth.

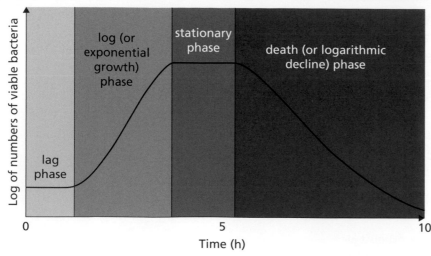

Figure 2.31 Phases of growth in microorganisms

In the lag phase of growth the microorganisms adjust to the conditions of the culture by inducing the production of enzymes that metabolise the available substrates. No cell division occurs at this stage.

In the log or exponential phase of growth the population doubles with each round of cell division. The rate depends on the culture medium used and the temperature.

In the stationary phase the culture medium becomes depleted and nutrients or oxygen start to run out. Metabolites released by the microorganisms begin to accumulate and these may be toxic to the microorganism. Secondary metabolites are also produced, which may give the microorganism a selective advantage in a natural setting.

The stationary phase is reached when the rate of production of new cells is equal to the death rate of the older cells and there is therefore no increase in cell number in the culture.

In the death phase the lack of substrate and the toxic accumulation of metabolites causes the death rate of the cells to be greater than the production of any new cells. More cells die than are being produced. By the end of this phase a bacterial population might be completely eliminated or resistant spores might remain.

Figure 2.32 shows the exponential growth phase of a unicellular culture using semi-log graph paper, which gives a straight-line graph. Note that on the cell number scale the division between 1 and 10 is the same size as that between 10 and 100.

Hints & tips

There is more about selective advantage in Key Area 1.7 (page 28).

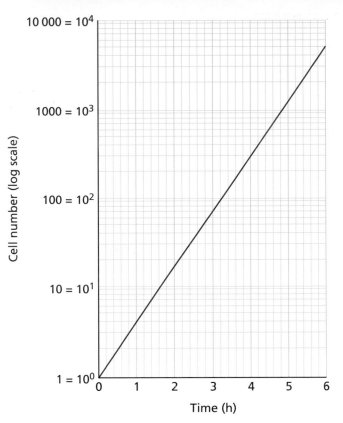

Figure 2.32 Exponential growth plotted on semi-log graph paper

Controlling metabolism

Microorganisms are able to control their metabolic pathways naturally by processes such as the induction or inhibition of enzymes and end-product inhibition. Some industrial fermentations involving microorganisms might require the addition of metabolic precursors, inducers or inhibitors to control metabolism and ensure that the required substance is produced. The required product might be an intermediate metabolite and not the final product.

Precursors

A precursor is a substance that is acted upon by an enzyme to ensure the production of a desired metabolite later on in the same pathway.

Inducers

An inducer is a substance that triggers the production of a specific enzyme, which then produces a desired metabolite.

Inhibitors

Inhibitors can be used to avoid the breakdown of a required product. They affect the enzyme catalysing the breakdown of the required metabolite by acting competitively or non-competitively.

Figure 2.33 shows a metabolic pathway and how the addition of metabolic precursors, inducers or inhibitors can be used to control the metabolism of microorganisms in order to give the required product.

Hints & tips

There is more about inhibitors in Key Area 2.1b (page 54).

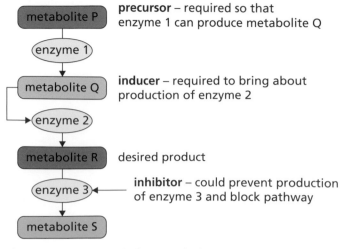

Figure 2.33 Precursors, inducers and inhibitors in a metabolic pathway

Primary and secondary metabolism

Primary metabolism refers to the metabolism of a microorganism that occurs during the lag and log phases of its growth. This is when it breaks down the available substrate to obtain energy and produces primary metabolites that can be used for the biosynthesis of substances such as proteins and nucleic acids.

Secondary metabolism occurs at the end of the log phase and during the stationary phase of growth. Secondary metabolism produces substances that are not associated with growth but which may confer an ecological advantage. Examples of these secondary metabolites include antibiotics, which inhibit the growth of other species of bacteria and so reduce competition for the available resources.

Key words

Beef extract – complex growth medium for microorganisms

Death phase – phase of microorganism growth in which death rate of cells exceeds rate of cell division

Exponential growth – growth phase of microorganisms involving a rapid geometric increase in numbers

Generation time – time taken for a microorganism cell to divide

Growth medium – substance in which microorganisms are encouraged to grow

Inducer – substance that causes a gene to be expressed, often leading to production of an enzyme

Lag phase – earliest growth stage in microorganisms

Log phase – exponential phase of microorganism growth

Precursor – substance needed to start a metabolic pathway

Secondary metabolite – substance produced during the stationary phase of growth of a culture of microorganisms

Stationary phase – phase of microorganism growth during which secondary substances can be made

Sterile – not containing contaminating microorganisms

Total cell count – total number of cells in a culture including viable (live) cells and dead cells

Viable cell count – number of live cells from a total cell count

Questions ?

Restricted response (structured in 1- or 2-mark parts)

1 **a)** Describe **two** features of microorganisms that make them useful for a variety of research and industrial uses. (2)
  b) Give **two** complex compounds that are sometimes added to culture media to enable certain microorganisms to grow. (2)
  c) Explain why sterile conditions must be maintained in the culture of a microorganism. (1)
  d) Explain why temperature, pH and oxygen levels must be monitored and controlled during the culture of microorganisms. (2)
2 **a)** Name **two** types of substance that may need to be added to some fermentations to control the metabolism of microorganisms so that the desired product is obtained. (2)
  b) Describe what happens during the primary metabolism of a microorganism in culture. (2)
  c) Explain why substances produced during secondary metabolism might give an ecological advantage to a microorganism. (2)

Extended response (4–9 marks each)

3 Give an account of the different culture conditions required for the growth of microorganisms. (9)
4 Give an account of the phases of growth of microorganisms cultured in a fermenter. (7)

Answers are on pages 97–98.

Genetic control of metabolism in microorganisms

Key points !

1 Wild strains of microorganisms can be improved by **mutagenesis**, selective breeding and culture, or **recombinant DNA technology**. ☐
2 Mutagenesis is the process of inducing mutations. ☐
3 Exposure to ultraviolet (UV) light, other forms of radiation or mutagenic chemicals results in random mutations, some of which might produce an improved strain with desirable qualities. ☐
4 Some bacteria can transfer plasmids or pieces of chromosomal DNA to each other or take up DNA from their environment to produce new strains. ☐
5 In fungi and yeast, new genotypes can be brought about by sexual reproduction between existing strains. ☐
6 Recombinant DNA technology involves the joining together of DNA molecules from two different species. ☐
7 Plant or animal gene sequences can be transferred to microorganisms to produce plant or animal proteins. ☐
8 Genes that remove inhibitory controls or amplify specific steps in a metabolic pathway can be introduced to increase the yield of a desired protein. ☐
9 As a safety mechanism, genes are often introduced that prevent the survival of a modified microorganism in an external environment. ☐
10 Extra-chromosomal DNA molecules can be transferred to microorganisms by recombinant plasmids or artificial chromosomes. ☐
11 Recombinant plasmids or artificial chromosomes act as **genetic vectors**. ☐
12 A vector carries the DNA from the donor organism into the host cell. ☐
13 The vectors must contain restriction sites and marker genes in addition to genes for self-replication and regulatory sequences to allow control of gene expression. ☐
14 **Restriction endonucleases** cut target sequences of DNA from chromosomes, leaving sticky ends. ☐
15 Treatment of vectors with the same restriction endonuclease forms complementary sticky ends that are then combined using DNA ligase to form recombinant DNA. ☐
16 Plant or animal recombinant DNA in bacteria can result in polypeptides that are folded incorrectly or lack post-translational modifications. ☐
17 These polypeptides can be produced more successfully in a recombinant yeast cell. ☐
18 The development of biotechnology products raises **ethical issues** and the consideration of **hazards** and the control of **risks**. ☐

Summary notes

Genetic control of metabolism

Wild strains of microorganisms, with the potential to be used in industry in the production of a desirable product, can be improved by processes such as mutagenesis, selective breeding and culture, or recombinant DNA technology.

Mutagenesis

Mutagenesis is the process of inducing mutations. Exposure to ultraviolet (UV) light, other forms of radiation or mutagenic chemicals results in random mutations, some of which might produce an improved strain of microorganism with desirable qualities, which can then be selected and cultured for use. Improved microorganisms for an industrial application could refer to their ability to be cultured in a low-cost medium or to the fact that the production of the required product is increased.

Selective breeding

Bacteria reproduce asexually and so variation does not arise due to reproduction.

However, new strains of bacteria can arise by the transfer of plasmids or pieces of chromosomal DNA between bacteria. This is called **horizontal transfer** of genetic material. They can also take up DNA from their environment to produce new strains. These processes produce new strains of microorganism with different genotypes. Figure 2.34 shows how new strains of bacterial species can arise as a result of the horizontal transfer of DNA.

> ⭐ *Hints & tips*
>
> *There is more about horizontal inheritance in Key Area 1.7 (page 28).*

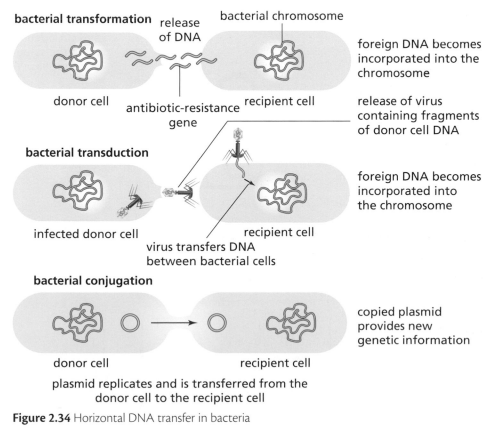

Figure 2.34 Horizontal DNA transfer in bacteria

Sexual reproduction in fungi

In fungi and yeast, new genotypes can be brought about by sexual reproduction between existing strains.

Recombinant DNA technology

Microorganisms can be transformed by transferring plant or animal gene sequences to them. Recombinant DNA technology involves the joining together of DNA molecules from two different species. The DNA sequences used in the construction of recombinant DNA molecules can originate from any species. It can then be inserted into a host organism to produce new genetic combinations that are of value to science, medicine, agriculture and industry.

Plant or animal gene sequences can be transferred to microorganisms to produce plant or animal proteins. Genes that remove inhibitory controls or amplify specific metabolic steps in a pathway can be introduced to increase the yield of a desired protein.

As a safety mechanism, genes are often introduced that prevent the survival of the microorganism in an external environment.

Control of gene expression in recombinant plasmids and artificial chromosomes

Extra-chromosomal DNA molecules can be transferred to microorganisms.

Genetic engineers can identify, locate and extract a gene coding for a desirable characteristic and then insert and seal it into the DNA of a vector, such as a bacterial plasmid, before inserting it into the host cell such as a bacterium. Figure 2.35 shows some of the stages involved in recombinant DNA technology.

The recombinant plasmid is called a vector because it carries the DNA from the donor organism into the host cell.

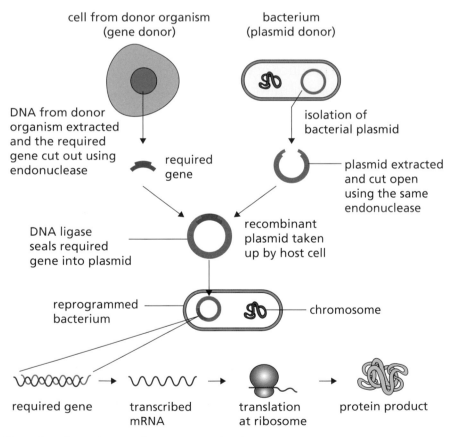

Figure 2.35 Stages in recombinant DNA technology

To be an effective vector, the plasmid must contain restriction sites and marker genes, in addition to genes for self-replication and regulatory sequences, to allow the control of gene expression.

Figure 2.36 shows the features of an effective plasmid vector.

The plasmid must have a restriction site, which is a location on the plasmid that can be cut open by the same restriction endonuclease used to extract the gene from the donor's DNA. Restriction endonucleases cut target sequences of DNA, leaving sticky ends. Treatment of vectors with the same restriction endonuclease forms complementary sticky ends that are then combined with the target sequences using DNA ligase to form recombinant DNA.

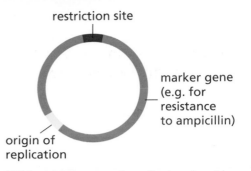

Figure 2.36 Features of an effective plasmid vector

The plasmid acting as a vector also requires a marker gene. A marker gene is a gene which is deliberately transferred along with the required gene during the process of genetic engineering. It is easily recognised and used to identify those cells to which the gene has been successfully transferred. Thus, a marker gene is a gene used to determine if a DNA sequence has been successfully inserted into the host organism's DNA.

There are two types of marker genes.

A selectable marker gene is a gene that protects the organism from a selective agent that would normally kill it. Only one in several million cells may take up donor DNA and, rather than checking every single cell, the genetic engineers use a selective agent to kill all cells that do not contain the new DNA, which means that only the modified ones survive. Antibiotics are the most common selective agents.

A marker gene for screening is a gene that makes the cell containing the gene look different, for example, a marker gene that produces a green fluorescent protein which makes the modified cells glow green under UV light.

The plasmid also requires an origin of replication. This contains genes for the self-replication of the plasmid, which is essential for the future copying of the plasmid.

Plant or animal recombinant DNA in bacteria can result in the production of polypeptides that are folded incorrectly or lack post-translational modifications. These proteins can be produced more successfully in recombinant yeast cells, which are eukaryotic and so have the enzymes needed for post-translational modifications.

Ethical issues

Ethics is about the application of moral frameworks concerning the principles of conduct governing individuals and groups. In the context of gene technology, it is to do with issues of whether it is right or wrong to conduct research into and develop these technologies.

The following table shows some of the ethical arguments that can be linked to genetic modification technology.

Arguments in favour of the technology	Arguments against the technology
It might improve nutrition and food security by increasing quantity and quality of food	The potential impact of the technology is unknown and many aspects of it such as the safety of foods or drugs remain to be understood
It might improve the environment by allowing reduction of the use of pesticides or fertilisers	The risks of the organisms or the genes they contain escaping are too great and could not be reversed
It might improve health by the production of drugs that are otherwise difficult to produce	Genes are self-perpetuating, and the risks that they might bring in the future are unknown

Hints & tips ★

It is probably better to answer questions about ethical issues using examples such as those in this table rather than to talk about humans 'playing God'.

Hazards and risks

A hazard is a danger that could arise when carrying out a microbiological procedure.

A risk is the likelihood of the hazard actually arising. Microbiological procedures should be assessed for risk before they are undertaken and the assessment used to control the risk.

Key words

Ethical issue – issue affecting human attitudes and decisions regarding various choices

Genetic vector – used to carry genetic material from one cell to another

Hazard – a danger derived from an activity

Mutagenesis – stimulation of mutations in a species

Recombinant DNA technology – activities in which DNA is moved from one species to another

Restriction endonuclease – enzyme that cuts genetic material from a chromosome or is used to open a plasmid

Risk – calculated chance of a potential hazard arising

Questions ?

Restricted response (structured in 1- or 2-mark parts)

1 a) State **two** methods by which wild strains of microorganisms could be improved. (2)
   b) Explain what is meant by the term mutagenesis. (1)
   c) Give **one** example of a mutagenic agent that can increase the rate of mutation in an organism. (1)

2 Bacterial plasmids can be modified by inserting a gene from another organism.
   a) Two enzymes are required to produce the modified plasmid.
      (i) Name the enzyme that cuts the plasmid at specific restriction sites. (1)
      (ii) Name the enzyme that seals the gene from the donor organism into the plasmid. (1)
   b) Give **two** reasons for the transfer of gene sequences to microorganisms **other than** for the production of plant or animal proteins. (2)
   c) (i) Explain why animal DNA that has been transferred to bacteria might produce proteins that are not functional. (1)
      (ii) Suggest how this problem might be overcome. (1)

⇨

3 Give **two** reasons for the transfer of gene sequences to microorganisms other than for the production of a desired protein. (2)

Extended response (4–9 marks each)

4 Give an account of the production of protein by recombinant DNA technology. (9)

Answers are on page 98.

Answers

Key Area 2.1a

Restricted response

1 a) sequence of chemical reactions controlled by enzymes [1]
   b) anabolic pathways are biosynthetic processes/involve the building up of complex molecules from simpler substances *and* catabolic pathways involve the breakdown of complex molecules into simpler substances [1]

   anabolic pathways require the input of energy *and* catabolic pathways usually release energy [1]
2 a) pores; pumps; enzymes [any 2 = 2]
   b) mitochondria; chloroplasts; nucleus [any 2 = 2]
   c) localise the metabolic activity of the cell; provide more favourable conditions for reactions to take place; membrane folds in organelles provide a large surface area for metabolic reactions to take place; the large surface-to-volume ratio of small compartments allow high concentrations of reactants to occur; higher reaction rates possible [any 2 = 2]

Extended response

3 a) a metabolic pathway is a sequence of chemical reactions controlled by enzymes; chemical reactions are anabolic and catabolic; anabolic pathways are biosynthetic processes/involve the building up of complex molecules from simpler molecules; anabolic pathways require the input of energy; catabolic pathways involve the breakdown of complex molecules into simpler molecules; catabolic pathways usually release energy [any 4 = 4]
   b) membrane separates the internal contents of the cell from its surrounding environment; membranes can form compartments to localise the metabolic activity of the cell; compartments provide more favourable conditions for reactions to take place; membrane folds in organelles provide a large surface area for metabolic reactions to take place; large surface-to-volume ratio of small compartments in organelles allow high concentrations of reactants to occur/higher reaction rates; channel-forming proteins/pores allow diffusion of small molecules; carrier proteins/pumps involved in active transport; some proteins act as enzymes [any 5 = 5]
   [total = 9]

Answers

Key Area 2.1b

Restricted response

1 each step in a metabolic pathway is controlled by a specific enzyme; each enzyme is coded for by a gene; order of bases in the gene determines the order of amino acids, which determines structure, shape and function of the protein/enzyme   [any 2 = 2]

2 a) enzyme is flexible and so the active site can change shape; substrate induces the active site to change shape; active site can alter the position or orientate the substrate molecules so that they fit more closely
    [any 2 = 2]

   b) increase in substrate concentration drives the chemical reaction in the direction of the end product; increases the rate of reaction   [1 each = 2]

   c) active site can alter the position of/ orientate the substrate molecules so that they fit more closely; activation energy is lowered when an enzyme is involved
    [1 each = 2]

Extended response

3 enzyme activity depends on the flexible/ dynamic shape of enzyme molecules; substrate has an affinity for the active site; induced fit; active site orientates the reactants; enzymes lower the activation energy; products have a low affinity for the active site; substrate and product concentration affects the direction and rate of reactions *or* increasing the substrate concentration increases/speeds up/drives forward the rate of the reaction; enzymes act in groups/ multi-enzyme complex   [any 6 = 6]
in competitive inhibition the inhibitor resembles the substrate molecule; inhibition is reduced by increase in substrate concentration; in non-competitive inhibition the shape of the active site is changed; product inhibition/feedback inhibition
    [any 3 = 3]
    [total = 9]

Answers

Key Area 2.2

Restricted response

1 a) phosphorylation of intermediates in glycolysis uses 2 ATP; later reactions in glycolysis result in the direct regeneration of 4 ATP for every glucose molecule and so this gives a net gain of 2 ATP   [1 each = 2]

   b) dehydrogenase enzymes remove hydrogen ions from a substrate along with high-energy electrons   [1]

   c) NAD and FAD transport H^+ and high-energy electrons; to the electron transport chain   [1 each = 2]

2 a) ATP synthase   [1]

   b) high-energy electrons pass down the chain of electron acceptors; releasing their energy, which is then used to pump hydrogen ions (H^+) across the inner mitochondrial membrane   [1 each = 2]

   c) oxygen acts as the final electron acceptor and combines with hydrogen ions and electrons to form water   [1]

   d) other sugars; glycogen; starch; fats; amino acids; fatty acids; glycerol   [any 2 = 2]

Extended response

3 glycolysis is the breakdown of glucose to pyruvate; 2 ATP molecules are used to phosphorylate intermediates in glycolysis; an energy investment phase; 4 ATP molecules are produced/generated/made in a pay-off stage; H carried away by NAD   [any 3 = 3]
if oxygen is available/in aerobic conditions pyruvate progresses to the citric acid cycle; pyruvate is converted/broken down to an acetyl group; acetyl group combines with coenzyme A; acetyl (coenzyme A) combines with oxaloacetate to form citrate; citric acid
    ⇒

⇨ cycle is enzyme controlled/involves dehydrogenases; ATP generated/synthesised/produced/released at substrate level in the citric acid cycle; carbon dioxide is released from the citric acid cycle; oxaloacetate is regenerated; NAD/NADH/NADH$_2$/FAD/FADH/FADH$_2$ transports electrons/transports hydrogen ions to the electron transport chain

[any 6 = 6]

[total = 9]

4 electron transport chain on the inner membrane of the mitochondria; electron transport chain is a collection of proteins attached to a membrane; NADH and FADH$_2$ release the high-energy electrons to the electron transport chain on the inner mitochondrial membrane; electrons pass down the chain of electron acceptors, releasing their energy; energy is used to pump hydrogen ions (H$^+$) across the inner mitochondrial membrane; return flow of the hydrogen ions (H$^+$) back into the matrix drives the enzyme ATP synthase; synthesis of ATP from ADP + Pi; this stage produces most of the ATP generated by cellular respiration; final electron acceptor is oxygen; oxygen combines with hydrogen ions and electrons to form water

[any 7 = 7]

regeneration of ATP from ADP and phosphate uses the energy released from cellular respiration; ATP is used to transfer the energy from cellular respiration to synthetic pathways/cellular processes where energy is required; breakdown of ATP to ADP and phosphate/Pi releases energy

[any 2 = 2]

[total = 9]

Answers

Key Area 2.3

Restricted response

1 a) metabolic rate of an organism is the amount of energy consumed in a given period of time [1]

   b) can be measured in terms of the oxygen consumed in a given period of time; carbon dioxide produced in a given period of time; the energy released as heat in a given period of time

[any 2 = 2]

   c) have a system of large air sacs associated with their lungs; air flows through the lungs in one direction/does not go in and out by the same route [1 each = 2]

2 a) high altitude; deep in the ocean; deoxygenated water; water-logged soil (other answers possible) [any 2 = 1]

   b) humans respond to high altitude by increasing their number of red blood cells; diving mammals for example slow their heart rate down to conserve oxygen *or* collapse their lungs to reduce buoyancy, allowing them to sink quickly and save energy (either) [any 1 = 1]

   c) VO$_2$ max is the maximum volume of oxygen that the body can take up and use; the oxygen can be used in respiration to release energy for exercise [1 each = 2]

Extended response

3 Fish circulation and heart structure: single circulatory system/heart to gills to body to heart; heart with only two chambers/atrium and a ventricle; loss of pressure a problem
Amphibian circulation and heart structure: incomplete double circulatory system; heart with three chambers/right and left atrium and one ventricle; pressure maintained; tissue blood is incompletely oxygenated
Mammal circulation and heart structure: complete double circulatory system; heart has four chambers/two atria and two ventricles; pressure maintained; tissue blood completely oxygenated [any 9 = 9]

Answers

Key Area 2.4

Restricted response

1 a) hypothalamus [1]
   b) vasoconstriction and decreases [1]
   c) nerve impulses [1]
   d) enzymes controlling the metabolism are maintained at their optimum temperature; affects rates of diffusion [1 each = 2]

2 a) temperature; salinity; pH [any 2 = 2]
   b) homeostasis is the maintenance of a steady state/a constant internal environment within an organism [1]
   c) conformers' internal environments are directly dependent upon their external environment; conformers lack the ability to tolerate change should it occur [1 each = 2]
   d) negative feedback control [1]

Extended response

3 temperature monitoring centre/thermoreceptors are located in the hypothalamus *or* information about temperature detected/received by hypothalamus; endotherms/mammals derive most of their body heat from respiration/metabolism/chemical reactions; nerve message/communication/impulse sent to skin/effectors; vasodilation/widening of blood vessels to skin in response to increased temperature; more/increased blood to skin/extremities; increased/more heat radiated from skin/extremities *or* vasoconstriction/narrowing of blood vessels to skin in response to decreased temperature; less blood to skin/extremities; decreased/less heat radiated from skin/extremities; increased temperature/body too hot leads to increase in sweat production *or* converse; increase in heat loss due to evaporation of water in sweat *or* converse; decrease in temperature causes hair erector muscles to raise/erect hair; traps warm air *or* forms insulating layer; decrease in temperature causes muscle contraction/shivering, which generates heat/raises body temperature; temperature regulation involves/is an example of negative feedback [any 9 = 9]

4 ability of an organism to maintain its metabolic rate is affected by external abiotic factors such as temperature/salinity/pH; conformer's internal environment is dependent upon its external environment; conformers cannot alter their metabolic rate using physiological means; conformers usually have a narrow ecological niche/limited range; conformers lack the ability to tolerate change should it occur; conformers live in stable environments; conformers do not use energy-requiring physiological mechanisms to alter their metabolic rate; conformers have low metabolic energy costs; many conformers manage to maintain their optimum metabolic rate by employing certain behavioural responses [any 7 = 7]

Answers

Key Area 2.5

Restricted response

1 a) dormancy is part of an organism's life cycle and is the stage associated with resisting/tolerating periods of environmental adversity [1]
   b) hibernation; aestivation; torpor [any 2 = 2]
   c) predictive dormancy is when an organism becomes dormant before onset of the adverse conditions; consequential dormancy is when an organism becomes dormant after the onset of adverse conditions [1 each = 2]
   d) torpor increases an organism's chances of survival by reducing the energy required to maintain a high metabolic rate [1]

⇨

⇨

2 a) innate means that it is inherited; migratory behaviour is also influenced by learning, which is gained by experience [1 each = 2]

 b) ringing; tagging; transmitters [any 2 = 2]

3 a) extremophiles [1]

 b) thermophilic bacteria/*Thermus aquaticus* or other named example; high temperatures/hot springs/seabed vents (other answers possible) [1 each = 2]

 c) DNA polymerase/Taq polymerase; polymerase chain reaction (other answers possible) [1 each = 2]

Extended response

4 Surviving adverse conditions: some environments vary beyond tolerable limits; the extremes of conditions do not allow the normal metabolism of the organisms present; variation in conditions can be cyclical or unpredictable; metabolic rate can be reduced when conditions would make the cost of metabolic activity too high; dormancy may be predictive or consequential; example from hibernation *or* aestivation; daily torpor is a period of reduced activity; example of an organism and the adverse conditions that it survives [any 6 = 6]

Avoiding adverse conditions: migration avoids metabolic adversity by relocation; methods used to study migration – marking example *or* tracking example; example of a vertebrate animal and the adverse conditions that it avoids [any 2 = 2]

[total = 8]

5 thrive in environment that would be lethal to almost all other species; named example (e.g. thermophilic bacteria); named habitat (e.g. hot springs, seabed vents, saline lakes); have tolerant enzymes *or* have heat-tolerant DNA polymerase [all 4 = 4]

Answers

Key Area 2.6

Restricted response

1 a) use a wide range of substrates for metabolism; produce a wide range of products from their metabolic pathways; ease of cultivation; speed of growth [any 2 = 2]

 b) vitamins; fatty acids; beef extract [any 2 = 2]

 c) to eliminate any contaminating microorganisms [1]

 d) optimum temperature and pH for microorganism enzymes; oxygen for aerobic respiration of microorganisms [1 each = 2]

2 a) precursors; inducers; inhibitors [any 2 = 2]

 b) substrate is broken down to obtain energy; produces primary metabolites used for the biosynthesis of substances such as proteins/nucleic acids [1 each = 2]

 c) results in the production of secondary metabolites such as antibiotics; inhibit the growth of bacteria and so reduce competition for the available resources [1 each = 2]

Extended response

3 require an energy source; energy is derived from substrates such as carbohydrates/ light in the case of photosynthetic microorganisms; supply of raw materials for the biosynthesis of proteins/nucleic acids; many microorganisms only require simple chemical compounds in growth media; other

⇨

⇨ microorganisms require specific complex compounds; example of complex compound e.g. vitamins/fatty acids; growth media can contain complex ingredients such as beef extract; sterility to eliminate any effects of contaminating microorganisms; control of temperature/pH/oxygen; control of oxygen levels by aeration; control of pH by buffers or the addition of acid or alkali   [any 9 = 9]

4 growth is recorded by measuring the increase in cell number in a given period of time; the time it takes for a unicellular organism to divide into two is called the doubling or generation time; the lag phase of growth

is where the microorganisms induce the production of enzymes that metabolise the substrates; no cell division occurs at this stage; log or exponential phase of growth is where the population doubles with each cell division; stationary phase is where the culture medium becomes depleted/nutrients or oxygen start to run out; stationary phase is reached when the rate of production of new cells is equal to the death rate of the older cells; death phase occurs due to lack of substrate/toxic accumulation of metabolites; more cells die than are being produced

   [any 7 = 7]

Answers

Key Area 2.7

Restricted response

1 a) mutagenesis; selective breeding and culture; recombinant DNA technology
      [any 2 = 2]
   b) the process of inducing mutations   [1]
   c) exposure to ultraviolet (UV) light; other forms of radiation; mutagenic chemicals
      [any 1 = 1]

2 a) (i) restriction endonuclease   [1]
      (ii) DNA ligase   [1]
   b) genes that remove inhibitory controls to increase the yield of a desired protein; genes that amplify specific metabolic steps to increase the yield of a desired protein; genes preverting the survival of the microorganism in an external enivironment   [any 2 = 2]
   c) (i) production of polypeptides that are folded incorrectly; production of polypeptides that lack post-translational modifications   [any 1 = 1]
      (ii) use yeast instead of bacteria   [1]

3 marker genes; genes which prevent survival in an external environment   [1 each = 2]

Extended response

4 recombinant DNA technology involves the joining together of DNA molecules from two different species; plant or animal gene sequences can be transferred to microorganisms to produce plant or animal proteins; genes that remove inhibitory controls/amplify specific metabolic steps in a pathway can be introduced to increase the yield of a desired protein; genes to prevent the survival of the microorganism in an external environment can be introduced as a safety mechanism; recombinant plasmids or artificial chromosomes act as vectors; vector carries the DNA from the donor organism into the host cell; vectors must contain restriction sites/marker genes/genes for self-replication and regulatory sequences; restriction endonucleases cut target sequences of DNA, leaving sticky ends; treatment of vectors with the same restriction endonuclease; complementary sticky ends are then combined using DNA ligase to form recombinant DNA   [any 9 = 9]

Practice course assessment: Unit 2 (50 marks)

Section A (10 marks)

1 The diagram below shows how a molecule might be biosynthesised from building blocks in a metabolic pathway.

building blocks   biosynthesised molecule

Which row in the table below correctly describes the metabolic process shown in the diagram and energy relationship involved in the reaction?

	Metabolic process	Energy relationship
A	Anabolic	Energy used
B	Anabolic	Energy released
C	Catabolic	Energy used
D	Catabolic	Energy released

2 The diagram on the right shows a metabolic pathway that is controlled by end product inhibition. For substance S to bring about end product inhibition, with which of the following must it interact?
   A substance P
   B substance Q
   C enzyme 1
   D enzyme 4

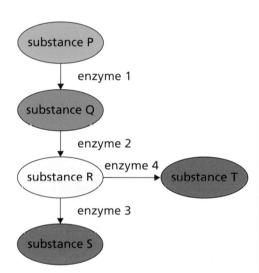

3 Membranes can form small compartments within cells that provide
   A high surface-to-volume ratios and allow low concentrations of substrates inside
   B high surface-to-volume ratios and allow high concentrations of substrates inside
   C low surface-to-volume ratios and allow low concentrations of substrates inside
   D low surface-to-volume ratios and allow high concentrations of substrates inside.

4 During fermentation in muscle fibres, pyruvate is
   A converted to citrate
   B broken down by the mitochondria
   C broken down to carbon dioxide and water
   D converted to lactate.

5 Four athletes were weighed and then given a treadmill test during which their maximum oxygen uptake (VO$_2$) was measured. Oxygen uptake is measured in litres per minute. Which row in the table below shows results for the athlete considered the **fittest**?

	Mass (kg)	Oxygen uptake (litres per minute)
A	60	3.6
B	55	3.6
C	60	3.7
D	55	3.7

$\Rightarrow$

6   Which of the following abiotic factors does **not** affect an animal's ability to maintain its metabolic rate?
    A   light intensity
    B   temperature
    C   salinity
    D   pH

7   The South African giant bullfrog lives in a habitat in which drought conditions can occur at any time of the year. To survive, the bullfrog responds by becoming dormant. The name given to this type of dormancy is
    A   predictive aestivation
    B   predictive hibernation
    C   consequential aestivation
    D   consequential hibernation

8   A viable count of bacteria grown in batch culture is shown in the graph below.

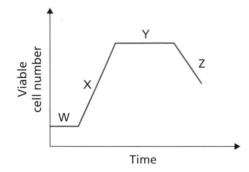

Four stages of growth are labelled W, X, Y and Z. Which row in the table below correctly identifies each stage of the bacterial growth curve?

	W	X	Y	Z
A	Lag	Log	Stationary	Death
B	Stationary	Log	Lag	Death
C	Lag	Log	Death	Stationary
D	Log	Lag	Stationary	Death

9   A bacterial culture contains 10 000 cells. If the doubling time for this bacterium is 30 minutes at 20°C, how many cells will be present after 3 hours at 20°C?
    A   60 000
    B   80 000
    C   320 000
    D   640 000

10 Yeast is often used as an alternative to bacteria as a recipient for foreign DNA because of yeast's ability to
    A   grow rapidly in culture
    B   carry out post-translational modification
    C   undergo sexual reproduction
    D   produce complex proteins.

Section B (40 marks)

1   The following graph shows how the rate of an enzyme-catalysed reaction varies with the substrate concentration and how the reaction is affected by a competitive and a non-competitive inhibitor.

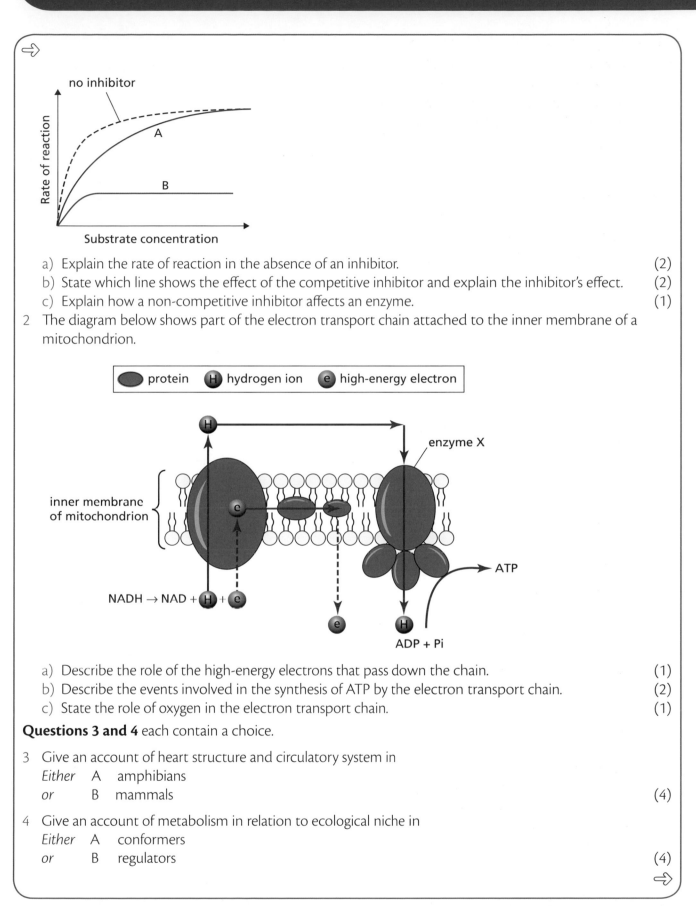

a) Explain the rate of reaction in the absence of an inhibitor. (2)
b) State which line shows the effect of the competitive inhibitor and explain the inhibitor's effect. (2)
c) Explain how a non-competitive inhibitor affects an enzyme. (1)

2 The diagram below shows part of the electron transport chain attached to the inner membrane of a mitochondrion.

a) Describe the role of the high-energy electrons that pass down the chain. (1)
b) Describe the events involved in the synthesis of ATP by the electron transport chain. (2)
c) State the role of oxygen in the electron transport chain. (1)

Questions 3 and 4 each contain a choice.

3 Give an account of heart structure and circulatory system in
   Either A amphibians
   or   B mammals (4)

4 Give an account of metabolism in relation to ecological niche in
   Either A conformers
   or   B regulators (4)

5　The following diagram shows some stages in the control of body temperature in a mammal.

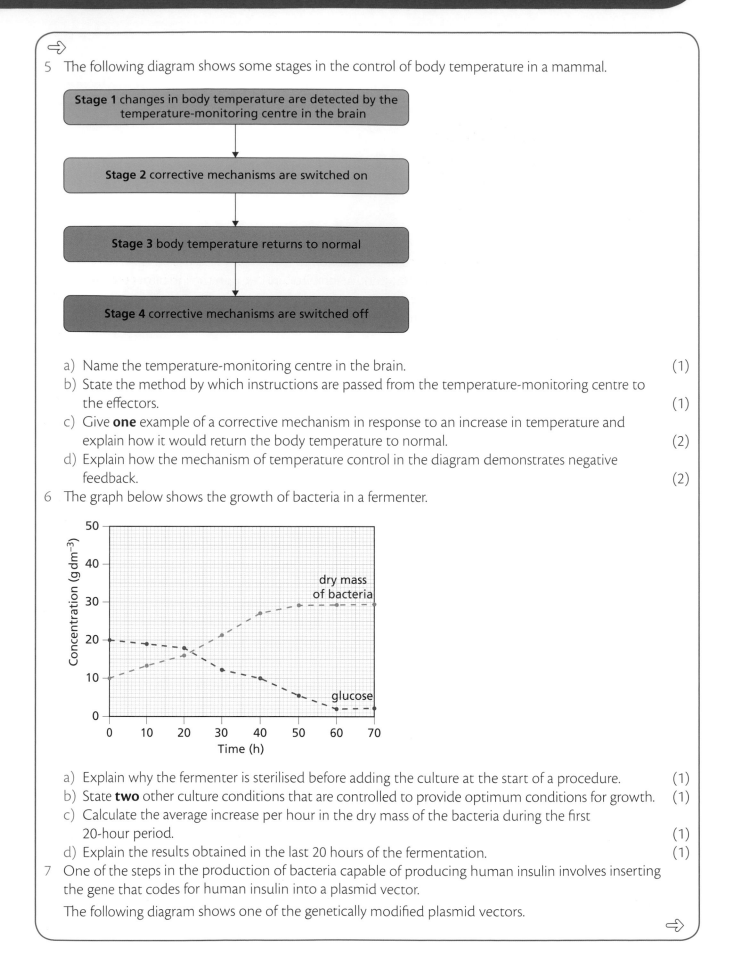

Stage 1 changes in body temperature are detected by the temperature-monitoring centre in the brain

Stage 2 corrective mechanisms are switched on

Stage 3 body temperature returns to normal

Stage 4 corrective mechanisms are switched off

   a)　Name the temperature-monitoring centre in the brain.　(1)

   b)　State the method by which instructions are passed from the temperature-monitoring centre to the effectors.　(1)

   c)　Give **one** example of a corrective mechanism in response to an increase in temperature and explain how it would return the body temperature to normal.　(2)

   d)　Explain how the mechanism of temperature control in the diagram demonstrates negative feedback.　(2)

6　The graph below shows the growth of bacteria in a fermenter.

   a)　Explain why the fermenter is sterilised before adding the culture at the start of a procedure.　(1)

   b)　State **two** other culture conditions that are controlled to provide optimum conditions for growth.　(1)

   c)　Calculate the average increase per hour in the dry mass of the bacteria during the first 20-hour period.　(1)

   d)　Explain the results obtained in the last 20 hours of the fermentation.　(1)

7　One of the steps in the production of bacteria capable of producing human insulin involves inserting the gene that codes for human insulin into a plasmid vector.

The following diagram shows one of the genetically modified plasmid vectors.

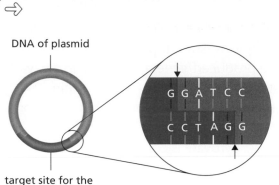

DNA of plasmid

target site for the
restriction enzyme

a) With reference to the diagram, explain the importance of using the same restriction enzyme to remove the insulin gene from a human chromosome and also to cut open the bacterial plasmid. (2)
b) Name the enzyme used to seal the insulin gene into the plasmid vector. (1)
c) Other than to make a desired protein, give **two** functions of gene sequences that are transferred to microorganisms by genetic engineering. (2)

Question 8 contains a choice.

8 *Either* A Give an account of aerobic respiration under the following headings:
a) glycolysis (2)
b) the citric acid cycle (6)
[total = 8]

or B Write notes on
a) adaptations shown by organisms to survive adverse conditions (5)
b) extremophiles (3)
[total = 8]

Answers to practice course assessment: Unit 2

Section A

1 A, 2 C, 3 B, 4 D, 5 D, 6 A, 7 C, 8 A, 9 D, 10 B

Section B

1 a) rate of reaction increases as substrate concentration increases because more substrate becomes available for available enzyme to work on/substrate concentration had been the limiting factor; rate of reaction then remains constant as all the enzyme molecules are being used/all available active sites are occupied/enzymes are now the limiting factor [1 each = 2]
b) A; as substrate concentration increases effect of inhibitor decreases [1 each = 2]
c) binds to the enzyme and changes the shape of the active site [1]

2 a) release/provide energy to pump H ions across the inner mitochondrial membrane [1]
b) return flow of H ions drives ATP synthase; ADP + Pi combine to form ATP [1 each = 2]
c) combines with hydrogen ions and electrons to form water [1]
3A Amphibians: incomplete double; heart with three chambers; made up of a right and left atrium and one lower ventricle; pressure maintained; but tissue blood is incompletely oxygenated [any 4 = 4]
B Mammals: complete double; heart has four chambers; made up of two atria and two ventricles; pressure maintained; and tissue blood completely oxygenated [any 4 = 4]

⇨

4A Conformers: internal environment is dependent upon their external environment; their metabolic costs may be low; conformers cannot alter their metabolic rate using physiological means; conformers may have a narrow ecological niche; behavioural responses may help to maintain optimum metabolic rate [any 4 = 4]

B Regulators: can control their internal environment and maintain a steady state; regulators adjust their metabolic rate using physiology; regulation requires energy to maintain a constant internal environment; increases the range of possible ecological niches that can be occupied; negative feedback is the control mechanism by which homeostasis is achieved [any 4 = 4]

5 a) hypothalamus [1]
  b) nerve impulses [1]
  c) vasodilation; increased heat loss by radiation [1 each = 2]
     increased sweating; increased
     or heat loss by evaporation [1 each = 2]
  d) any change away from the norm is detected by receptor cells which switches on a corrective mechanism; once the conditions are returned to normal the corrective mechanism is switched off [1 each = 2]

6 a) to eliminate contaminating microorganisms [1]
  b) temperature; pH; oxygen [any 2 = 1]
  c) 0.3 g dm^{-3} [1]
  d) growth/dry mass of bacteria levels off/stops as glucose/substrate decreases/runs out/is used up · [1]

7 a) cuts DNA/chromosome *and* plasmid at certain base/target sequences; produces complementary base pairs or sticky ends that can then be combined [1 each = 2]
  b) ligase [1]
  c) sequences that increase yield of desired protein; sequences that prevent survival in external environment; sequences which are marker genes [any 2 = 2]

8A a) glycolysis is the breakdown of glucose to pyruvate; 2 ATP molecules are used to phosphorylate intermediates in glycolysis; energy investment phase; 4 ATP molecules are produced/generated/made in a pay-off stage [any 2 = 2]
  b) if oxygen is available/in aerobic conditions pyruvate progresses to the citric acid cycle; pyruvate is converted/broken down to an acetyl group; acetyl group combines with coenzyme A; acetyl group combines with oxaloacetate to form citrate; citric acid cycle is enzyme-controlled/involves dehydrogenases; ATP generated/synthesised/produced/released at substrate level in the citric acid cycle; carbon dioxide is released from the citric acid cycle; oxaloacetate is regenerated; NAD/NADH/FAD/FADH$_2$ transports electrons/transports hydrogen ions to the electron transport chain [any 6 = 6]
  [total = 8]

8B a) some environments vary beyond tolerable limits; the extremes of conditions do not allow the normal metabolism of the organisms present; variation in conditions can be cyclical or unpredictable; metabolic rate can be reduced when conditions would make the cost of metabolic activity too high; dormancy may be predictive or consequential; example from hibernation/aestivation/leaf fall; daily torpor is a period of reduced activity; example of an organism and the adverse conditions that it survives [any 5 = 5]
  b) organisms that live under extreme conditions that most life forms are unable to tolerate *or* example; conditions might be extreme heat (over 42°C), cold (below 4°C), salinity, pH or pressure [any 1 = 1]
     some species have enzymes that are extremely tolerant; thermophilic bacteria or other example [2]
  [total = 8]

Sustainability and interdependence

Food supply

Key points !

1 **Food security** involves the ability to access sufficient quality and quantity of food. ☐
2 Human population growth has increased the demand for food and the concern for food security. ☐
3 Food production must be sustainable. ☐
4 Food production must not degrade the natural resources needed for **agriculture**. ☐
5 All food production depends on **photosynthesis**. ☐
6 Crop production is limited by the growing area and factors that affect plant growth. ☐
7 Crop production can be increased by breeding and growing higher-yielding **cultivars**, the use of **fertilisers** and by protecting crops from **pests**, disease and **competition**. ☐
8 **Livestock** animals produce less food per unit area than crop plants due to the loss of energy between **trophic levels**. ☐

Summary notes

Food security and agricultural production

Food security is a measure of the extent to which human populations can access and use food over a sustained period to avoid starvation or malnutrition. The following table shows some aspects that underpin food security.

Aspect of food security	Notes
Availability	Existence of food in sufficient quantities and of appropriate quality
Accessibility	Sufficient economic and infrastructure resources to access available food resources
Usage	Level of nutritional knowledge needed to use food resources properly
Sustainability	Degree to which food security can be guaranteed over extended time periods

An increase in the global human population has raised the overall requirement for food and increased the difficulty in ensuring food security for all. Figure 3.1 shows the increase in the human population over the last 2000 years. It is estimated that possibly 30% of the current population of 7 billion humans lack sufficient food security and so are liable to starvation or malnutrition.

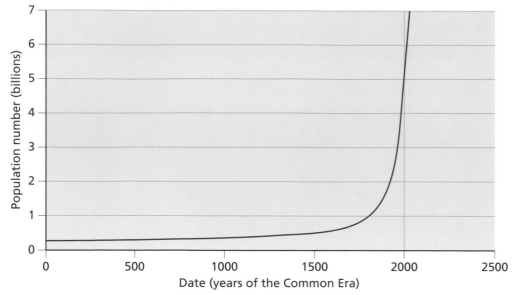

Figure 3.1 Human population growth

Energy from the Sun drives all of the Earth's food chains. Green plants trap light energy in photosynthesis. Some of this is passed to animal consumers. Humans can occupy different trophic levels, as shown in the energy pyramids in Figure 3.2. Due to the loss of energy between trophic levels, it is more energy-efficient for humans to act as primary consumers and eat crops rather than eating livestock as secondary consumers.

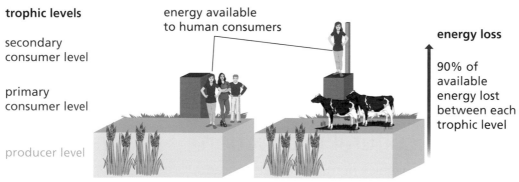

Figure 3.2 Humans and the pyramid of energy

Agriculture

In agriculture, certain green plants and animals are grown and harvested for food.

Crop plants

A small number of green plant species, such as sugar cane, cereals, potatoes and legumes, are the main producers of human food, as shown in the following table.

Crop	Average world production (millions of tonnes per annum)
Sugar cane	1800
Maize	885
Rice	723
Wheat	701
Potato	373
Soya bean (legume)	262

Production depends on a large number of factors, as shown in the following table. The environmental factors are mainly those that affect photosynthesis. Production can be increased by controlling these factors.

Soil factors	Environmental factors	Crop factors
Area of soil under crop	Temperature	Cultivar of crop
Fertiliser levels in soil	Rainfall	Pests
Soil type	Atmospheric carbon dioxide levels	Disease
Drainage	Light availability	Competition

Livestock animals

Since energy is lost between trophic levels, keeping animal livestock can result in less food production per unit area of land in agriculture. Land planted with a cereal crop such as wheat can be more productive in terms of overall food than the same area of pasture land kept for cattle.

Key words

Agriculture – human practice of growing crops and keeping livestock to maintain food security
Competition – struggle for existence between two organisms
Cultivar – variety of cultivated crop
Fertiliser – chemical addition to soil to increase plant growth
Food security – measure of the human ability to produce and use food
Livestock – agricultural animals
Pest – organism that damages agricultural produce and reduces food security
Photosynthesis – production of carbohydrate by a plant using the energy of light
Trophic level – feeding level in a food chain

Questions ?

Restricted response (structured in 1- or 2-mark parts)

1 Explain why there has been a major increase in concern about food security in recent years. (1)
2 State what is meant by the following terms:
   a) photosynthesis
   b) trophic level (2)
3 Give **three** examples of methods of increasing yield of food from a crop plant such as wheat. (2)
4 Explain why the yield of food from cultivated crops would be greater than the yield of meat from livestock kept in an equivalent area of land. (2)

Extended response (4–9 marks each)

5 Give an account of food security under the following headings:
   a) availability and accessibility (3)
   b) usage and sustainability (2)
   (total = 5)

Answers are on page 139.

Key Area 3.1b
Plant growth and productivity

Key points !

1 Photosynthesis captures **light energy** to produce carbohydrates. ☐
2 Photosynthetic **pigments** absorb light of specific wavelengths. ☐
3 Light that is not absorbed by pigments undergoes **transmission** and **reflection**. ☐
4 The **absorption spectrum** shows the range and extent to which light wavelengths are absorbed by a pigment. ☐
5 The **action spectrum** shows the rate of photosynthesis of a plant across a range of light wavelengths. ☐
6 **Chlorophyll** is the main photosynthetic pigment in green plants. ☐
7 **Carotenoids** such as carotene and xanthophyll extend the range of wavelengths absorbed by photosynthesis. ☐
8 Carotenoids pass energy to chlorophyll. ☐
9 Absorbed energy creates high-energy electrons by exciting electrons in pigment molecules. ☐
10 High-energy electrons release their energy as they pass through electron transport chains. ☐
11 Energy released by high-energy electrons generates ATP production by **ATP synthase**. ☐
12 Absorbed energy is also used in **photolysis**, in which water molecules are split into hydrogen and oxygen. ☐
13 Hydrogen is transferred by the **coenzyme NADP** to the **Calvin cycle** and oxygen is evolved. ☐
14 In the Calvin cycle the enzyme **RuBisCo** fixes carbon dioxide by attaching it to **ribulose bisphosphate (RuBP)** to produce an intermediate compound called **3-phosphoglycerate**. ☐
15 3-phosphoglycerate is phosphorylated by ATP and combined with hydrogen from NADPH to produce **glyceraldehyde-3-phosphate (G3P)**. ☐
16 G3P is used for the synthesis of glucose and to regenerate RuBP. ☐
17 Glucose produced by the Calvin cycle can be converted to **starch** or **cellulose** or passed to other biosynthetic pathways to form a variety of metabolites. ☐
18 **Net assimilation** is the increase in dry mass of a plant due to photosynthesis minus the loss due to respiration. ☐
19 Net assimilation can be measured by the increase in dry mass of a plant per unit area of leaf. ☐
20 **Productivity** is the rate of generation of new biomass per unit area of leaf per unit of time. ☐
21 **Biological yield** of a crop is the total plant biomass produced. ☐
22 **Economic yield** is the mass of the desired product. ☐
23 The **harvest index** is calculated by dividing the dry mass of the economic yield by the dry mass of the biological yield. ☐

Summary notes

Photosynthesis

Photosynthesis is a process in which green plants trap light energy and use it in the production of food. Carbon dioxide from the atmosphere is combined with water from the soil to make glucose. Oxygen is produced and released as a by-product. Photosynthesis is summarised in Figure 3.3.

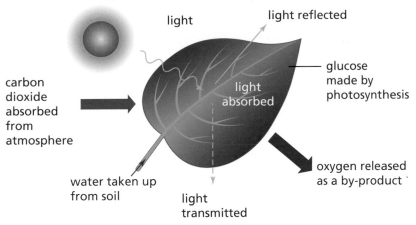

Figure 3.3 Summary of photosynthesis

Light energy and pigments

Light energy travels in waves. Green plants have several pigments that are able to absorb light energy. Chlorophyll a and b and carotenoids are the commonly occurring pigments. Light that strikes pigment molecules is absorbed, transmitted or reflected, as shown in Figure 3.3 above.

Hints & tips

*Remember **ART** – absorbed, reflected and transmitted.*

The absorption spectrum is a graph that shows the extent to which each wavelength of light is absorbed by a pigment. Figure 3.4 shows the absorption spectrum for chlorophyll a. The action spectrum shows the extent to which wavelengths of light can be used for photosynthesis in a green plant, as shown in Figure 3.5.

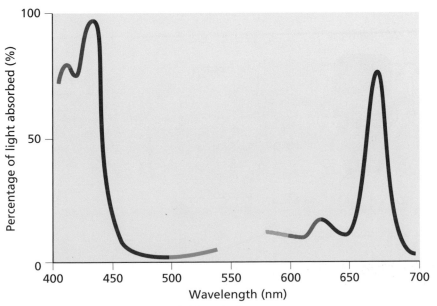

Figure 3.4 Absorption spectrum of chlorophyll a

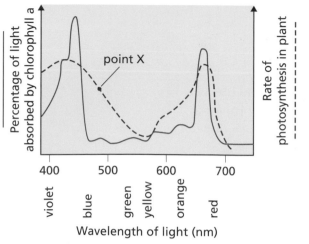

Figure 3.5 Absorption spectrum for chlorophyll a compared with the action spectrum for a green plant

Notice how the absorption spectrum and the action spectrum are broadly similar, though not identical. Comparison of the two spectra helps to confirm that pigments other than chlorophyll a are used in photosynthesis. At point X on the graph, the rate of photosynthesis remains high although the absorption by chlorophyll a is low.

Energy capture

When pigments absorb light, the energy excites electrons in the pigment molecules. These high-energy electrons move through a series of electron carrier molecules attached to the membranes of chloroplasts, releasing their energy, which is then used by ATP synthase to generate ATP from ADP + Pi. Some energy is also used to split water into oxygen, which is released, and hydrogen, which becomes bound to the coenzyme NADP, as shown in Figure 3.6. The ATP and NADPH are passed to the next stage, the Calvin cycle.

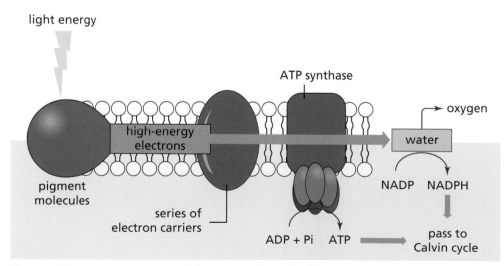

Figure 3.6 Light-dependent stage of photosynthesis on the chloroplast membrane

Calvin cycle (carbon fixation stage)

Carbohydrate is produced by a metabolic pathway called the Calvin cycle. The enzyme RuBisCo fixes carbon dioxide (CO_2) from the air by attaching it to ribulose bisphosphate (RuBP) to form 3-phosphoglycerate (3PG). The 3-phosphoglycerate accepts hydrogen from NADPH and is phosphorylated by ATP to form glyceraldehyde-3-phosphate (G3P). The G3P is then converted into glucose or can be used to regenerate RuBP, as shown in Figure 3.7.

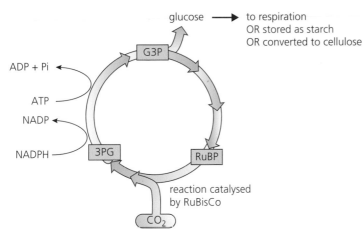

Figure 3.7 Calvin cycle

The glucose produced can be used in respiration to drive the plant's life processes or can be converted to cellulose or starch. Other carbohydrate formed in photosynthesis can be used in the synthesis of a variety of different metabolites, including proteins and lipids.

Figure 3.8 shows a summary of the stages of photosynthesis.

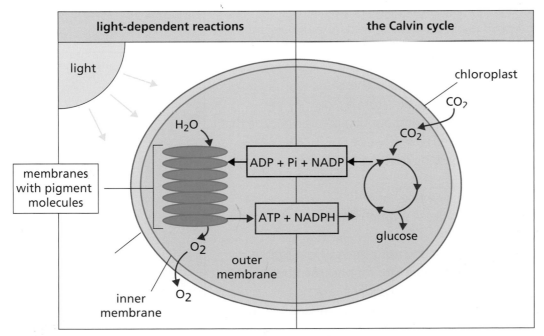

Figure 3.8 The two stages of photosynthesis summarised

Plant productivity

Net assimilation is the increase in mass of a plant produced in photosynthesis minus the mass used in respiration. This can be measured as the increase in dry mass per unit area of leaf.

The biological yield is the total biomass produced and the economic yield is the mass of desired product produced, as shown in Figure 3.9.

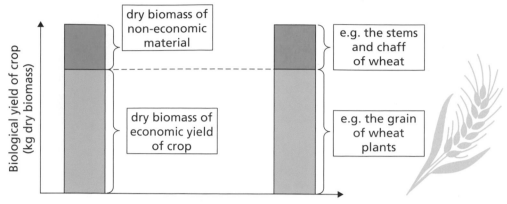

Figure 3.9 Various measurements of yield of wheat

The harvest index of a crop can be found by dividing the dry mass of the economic yield by the dry mass of the biological yield.

Key words

3-phosphoglycerate (3PG) – produced when CO_2 is fixed to RuBP by RuBisCo

Absorption spectrum – graph showing wavelengths of light absorbed by a pigment

Action spectrum – graph showing the wavelengths of light involved in photosynthesis

ATP synthase – membrane-bound enzyme that synthesises ATP

Biological yield – total dry mass increase

Calvin cycle – carbon fixation stage of photosynthesis

Carotenoids – orange and yellow accessory pigments in plants

Cellulose – structural carbohydrate in cell walls derived from photosynthesis

Chlorophyll – green pigment molecule in plants that absorbs red and blue light for photosynthesis

Coenzyme NADP – hydrogen carrier in photosynthesis

Economic yield – dry mass of desired product from a crop

Glyceraldehyde-3-phosphate (G3P) – compound in the Calvin cycle that can be converted to glucose or used to regenerate RuBP

Harvest index – value obtained by dividing dry mass of economic yield by dry mass of biological yield

Light energy – radiant energy used in photosynthesis

Net assimilation – total dry mass increase through photosynthesis minus the loss from respiration

Photolysis – breakdown of water molecules using energy from light

Pigment – coloured substance that absorbs light for photosynthesis

Productivity – measure of the performance of a plant

Reflection – light that strikes a leaf passes away from its surface back to the atmosphere

Ribulose bisphosphate (RuBP) – acceptor of carbon dioxide in the Calvin cycle

RuBisCo – ribulose bisphosphate carboxylase; fixes carbon dioxide in the Calvin cycle

Starch – storage carbohydrate in plants

Transmission – physical process of passing light energy through a surface

Questions ?

Restricted response (structured in 1- or 2-mark parts)

1 State what can happen to light that strikes a green leaf. (2)
2 Explain the difference between the absorption spectrum of a pigment and the action spectrum of a green plant. (2)
3 Describe the part played by carotenoid pigments in photosynthesis. (2)
4 Describe **three** fates of the glucose produced by photosynthesis. (2)
5 **a)** State what is meant by the following terms:
    (i) biological yield (1)
    (ii) economic yield (1)
  b) State how harvest index can be calculated. (1)

Extended response (4–9 marks each)

6 State what is meant by the term net assimilation and describe how it can be measured. (4)
7 Give an account of photosynthesis under the following headings:
  a) the capture of light energy (5)
  b) the Calvin cycle (4)
                                 (total = 9)

Answers are on page 140.

Key Area 3.2
Plant and animal breeding

Key points ❗

1 **Plant and animal breeding** involves manipulating heredity to improve new crops and animal stock to support sustainable food production. ☐

2 Desirable qualities in improved organisms include higher food yields, higher nutritional values, increased resistance to pests and diseases, resistance to harsh growing conditions and characteristics that assist rearing and harvesting. ☐

3 Plant **field trials** are carried out in a range of environments to compare different cultivars or treatments they receive, or to evaluate **GM crops**. ☐

4 In field trials, selection of treatments must ensure fair comparisons between cultivars. ☐

5 In field trials, the number of **replicates** involved must take account of the variability within the sample. ☐

6 In field trials, the treatments must be **randomised** to eliminate bias when measuring their effects. ☐

7 Animals and cross-pollinating plants are naturally **outbreeding**. ☐

8 Certain plants and animals can be inbred for several generations until the population is **true breeding** for the desired type due to elimination of heterozygotes. ☐

9 **Test crosses** can be used to identify unwanted **heterozygous** individuals with recessive alleles, which can then be eliminated from the stock. ☐

10 **Inbreeding** can produce individuals **homozygous** for unwanted **recessive** alleles. ☐

11 **Inbreeding depression** is the accumulation in individuals of homozygous recessive alleles that are deleterious (harmful). ☐

12 **Self-pollinating** plants are less susceptible to inbreeding depression because natural selection removes individuals homozygous for deleterious recessive alleles. ☐

13 In outbreeding species, inbreeding depression is avoided by selecting for desired characteristics but maintaining an otherwise genetically-diverse population. ☐

14 In animals, **cross-breeding** individuals from different breeds can produce a new F_1 cross-breed population with improved characteristics. ☐

15 A cross-bred F_2 **generation** can contain a wide variety of genotypes and so be of little use for further production, but might provide a source of new varieties. ☐

16 A process of selection and **back-crossing** is required to maintain the F_1 cross-breed population. ☐

17 Parent breeds can be maintained and cross-bred to produce the desired individuals when needed. ☐

⇒

18 Cross-breeding of different inbred plant lines can produce a relatively uniform heterozygous crop in the **F₁ generation**. ☐
19 F₁ hybrids often have increased vigour and yield. ☐
20 As a result of genome sequencing, organisms with desirable genes can be identified and used in breeding programmes. ☐
21 Single genes can be inserted into genomes using **genetic transformation techniques**. The transformed organism can then be used in breeding programmes. ☐

Summary notes

Breeding programmes

One method of increasing food security is to develop new varieties of crops and livestock breeds using breeding programmes. These programmes allow desirable features to be bred into particular plants or animals. Desirable features include higher yields, higher nutritional values, pest and disease resistance, the ability to thrive in particular environmental conditions, and characteristics that assist rearing and harvesting. The following table shows some of the desirable characteristics that have been bred into plant crops and animal breeds.

Plant crop or animal breed	Desirable characteristic that increases food security
Wheat	High grain yield
Potato	Resistance to fungal disease
Soya bean	High protein content of seeds
Strawberry	Resistance to frost
Dairy cattle	High milk yield
Beef cattle	High meat yield

Dwarf varieties

Fifty years ago, plant breeders discovered dwarf varieties of some cereal crops with much shorter stems than normal. These plants put more of their energy into creating seed and were easier to harvest, thus increasing the yield of these crops and improving food security.

Selecting and breeding

Plant and animal breeders work to cross individuals with desired characteristics such as high milk yielding cattle or dwarf crop plants.

Inbreeding and its results

Inbreeding involves crossing close relatives and is at its most intensive in naturally self-pollinating plants such as peas or wheat. Inbreeding ensures that offspring receive the alleles desired and eventually form a homozygous stock that will continue to breed true for the desired characteristic over many generations.

A disadvantage of inbreeding is that deleterious recessive alleles also become homozygous. In nature this is avoided because natural selection eliminates individuals with harmful alleles. It can be a problem in agriculture where natural selection is largely prevented or natural cross-breeders are forced to inbreed, and is known as inbreeding depression. The following table shows how repeated inbreeding increases the percentage of homozygous offspring.

Generation	P	F_1 ratio	F_2 ratio	F_3 ratio
Genotypes	Aa (self-pollinated)	1**AA**:2**Aa**:1**aa** (all allowed to self-pollinate)	6**AA**:4**Aa**:6**aa** (all allowed to self-pollinate freely)	28**AA**:8**Aa**:28**aa**
Percentage of generation that are homozygous	0%	2 out of 4 = 50%	12 out of 16 = 75%	56 out of 64 = 87.5%

Outbreeding and its results

Outbreeding involves crossing unrelated individuals, and occurs in animals and cross-pollinating plants such as tomato and maize. Outbreeding maintains heterozygosity and generally prevents the effects of inbreeding depression. However, offspring are varied and so not guaranteed to show the desired characteristics of their parents.

Cross-breeding and its results

Breeders often deliberately maintain stock by cross-breeding regularly. The F_1 individuals produced often show hybrid vigour because they combine the qualities of their parents. Figure 3.10 shows how hybrid vigour is obtained by cross-breeding pig varieties A and B.

The F_1 performs well in the quality sought, but in most cases it is used for food because further breeding of hybrids results in varied offspring, some of which would be totally unsuitable. Sometimes F_2 generations are produced with the hope of producing new desirable variants.

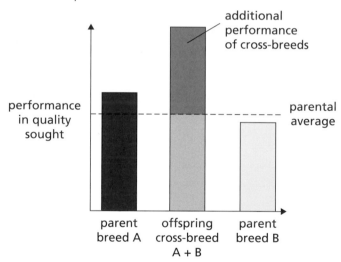

Figure 3.10 Results of cross-breeding two pig varieties

Back-crossing

In some cases, F_1 hybrids are back-crossed with parental individuals or individuals genetically similar to the parent. This increases the chances of their offspring showing the improved characteristics which had originally been sought in the hybrid.

Test crosses

These crosses can be used to identify animals carrying unwanted recessive alleles. **H** is an allele that gives a hornless or polled phenotype in cattle whereas **h** produces a horned phenotype. An animal with the genotype **Hh** might look the same as another with the genotype **HH** but a breeder might want to use only **HH** individuals to breed because hornless individuals might be more desirable in a farm situation. Crossing the animal with unknown genotype with a double recessive individual allows the unknown genotype to be confirmed when the offspring are examined, as shown in Figure 3.11.

polled bull of unknown genotype (either **HH** or **Hh**) × horned cow of genotype **hh**

HH × hh

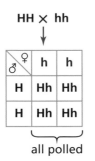

all polled

Hh × hh

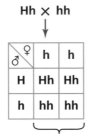

one polled : one horned

Figure 3.11 Diagram to show outcomes of a test cross on a polled bull

If the offspring are all polled then the genotype of the unknown bull must be **HH**. Presence of any horned calves shows that the unknown bull was **Hh**.

Genomic sequencing and genetic transformation

Organisms can have their genome sequenced and those with desirable alleles can be identified and used in breeding programmes to improve stock.

Genetic transformation techniques allow genetic material from one species to be inserted into the genome of another. The transformed organisms can then be used in breeding programmes. The potential benefits are huge because the genetic material of the transformed organism is undisturbed apart from the insertion of a gene.

In many cases the transformation involves adding genetic material to a crop plant genome by infecting the plant with bacteria which have plasmids modified to contain a desired gene. The desired gene is passed horizontally into the crop plant genome directly from the bacterial cell plasmids (see Figure 1.30(b) on page 29).

The following table shows examples of how genetic transformation techniques have been used very successfully in recent years.

> **Hints & tips ★**
>
> *There is more about gene sequencing in Key Area 1.8 (page 36).*

> **Hints & tips ★**
>
> *There is more about transformation in Key Area 2.7 (page 88).*

Crop plant transformed	Genetic material added	Food security benefit
Rice	Genes for vitamin A	Rice plants providing better nutrition for human consumers
Maize	Gene for Bt toxin, which kills insects	Maize plants resistant to insect pests, so increasing yield
Soya bean	Gene for herbicide resistance	Soya fields can be sprayed with herbicide, killing weeds without damaging the crop and so increasing crop yield

Field trials

Field trials are controlled experiments to compare the performance of plots of different varieties of crop plant (cultivars) or how plots of one cultivar perform with a range of treatments, such as different fertiliser application levels. Figure 3.12 shows how field trials on different fertiliser treatments and different cultivars could be set up.

TRIAL X	
1 kg of cultivar A seed and 1 kg fertiliser per hectare	1 kg of cultivar A seed and 2 kg fertiliser per hectare
1 kg of cultivar A seed and 3 kg fertiliser per hectare	1 kg of cultivar A seed and 4 kg fertiliser per hectare

TRIAL Y	
1 kg of cultivar A seed and 1 kg fertiliser per hectare	1 kg of cultivar B seed and 1 kg fertiliser per hectare
1 kg of cultivar C seed and 1 kg fertiliser per hectare	1 kg of cultivar D seed and 1 kg fertiliser per hectare

Figure 3.12 Diagram of field trials X and Y

Trial X shows four field plots with the *same* cultivar at *different* fertiliser treatments but all other factors held constant.

Trial Y shows four field plots with *different* cultivars at the *same* fertiliser treatment but all other factors held constant.

The plots can be harvested after a set time and yields compared. There are some flaws in these procedures. In order to ensure that the trials are fair, replication and randomisation of treatments should be carried out. Figure 3.13 shows an improved version of trial X.

1 kg of cultivar A seed and 2 kg fertiliser per hectare	1 kg of cultivar A seed and 4 kg fertiliser per hectare	1 kg of cultivar A seed and 4 kg fertiliser per hectare	1 kg of cultivar A seed and 3 kg fertiliser per hectare
1 kg of cultivar A seed and 1 kg fertiliser per hectare	1 kg of cultivar A seed and 2 kg fertiliser per hectare	1 kg of cultivar A seed and 3 kg fertiliser per hectare	1 kg of cultivar A seed and 1 kg fertiliser per hectare

Figure 3.13 Diagram of an improved field trial X with plots replicated and randomised

Notice that each plot is of the same size and planted with the same mass and cultivar of seed, so that a fair comparison is ensured. The fertiliser treatments have been replicated so that variation in the individual seed samples can be eliminated. The positioning of the plots is randomised to eliminate bias created by the environment when measuring the effects of the treatments. This version could be carried out again with each of the four cultivars in trial Y.

Key words

Back-cross – cross between an F_1 hybrid organism with a parental type to maintain characteristics of a new breed

Cross-breeding – breeding organisms of different genotype together

F_1 generation – first generation of offspring from a genetic cross

F_2 generation – offspring of an F_1 generation

Field trial – non-laboratory test on the performance of a crop in various environmental conditions

Genetic transformation – changes made to the genetic material of a cell by the addition of DNA from another cell

Genome sequencing – procedure to produce the nucleotide sequence of an entire genome

GM crop – genetically modified crop that contains a gene from other species

Heterozygous – having two different alleles of the same gene and so not breeding true

Homozygous – having two identical alleles of the same gene and so breeding true

Inbreeding – crossing organisms of the same or similar genotype

Inbreeding depression – accumulation of homozygous recessive alleles that lower biological fitness

Outbreeding – breeding of organisms of different genotypes

Plant and animal breeding – methods of crossing domestic animals and plants

Randomised – applies to values that have been arrived at by chance

Recessive – allele that only shows in the phenotype when homozygous

Replicate – repeat experiment in an investigation

Self-pollinating – passing pollen within the flowers of a single individual

Test cross – cross between an organism of unknown genotype and a homozygous recessive organism

True breeding – homozygous

Questions ?

Restricted response (structured in 1- or 2-mark parts)

1 Give **two** desirable qualities that might be selected by breeders seeking to improve a crop plant species. (2)

2 In some varieties of cattle, the allele for hornless **H** is dominant to the allele **h**, which produces horned animals. Homozygous hornless animals are more desirable for breeding purposes.
   Describe how a breeder could perform a test cross to identify the genotype of a hornless bull. (2)

3 In plant breeding, F_1 hybrids of different varieties of a species are often produced because they combine desired features of their parent varieties.
   a) Explain why F_2 plants produced from the hybrid are considered of little use for further production. (2)
   b) Give **one** potential benefit of allowing F_1 plants to breed to give an F_2 generation. (1)

4 Give the reasons for the following features of a plant breeding field trial:
   a) replication (1)
   b) randomisation of treatments. (1)

Extended response (4–9 marks each)

5 Give an account of inbreeding and outbreeding and outline the likely effects of carrying out these breeding approaches. (6)

Answers are on page 140.

Crop protection and animal welfare

Key points ❗

1 In agricultural **ecosystems**, weeds compete with crops while pests and disease organisms damage them, reducing their productivity. ☐

2 **Annual plant weeds** have rapid growth, a short life cycle, high seed output and long-term seed viability. ☐

3 **Perennial weeds** have competitive adaptations such as storage organs and vegetative reproduction. ☐

4 Most **crop pests** are invertebrate animals such as insects, nematode worms and molluscs. ☐

5 Crop plant diseases can be caused by fungi, bacteria and viruses, which are often carried by invertebrate animals. ☐

6 Weeds, pests and diseases can be controlled by **cultural** means. ☐

7 **Selective** plant protection chemicals can target broad-leaved species. ☐

8 **Systemic** plant protection chemicals enter the plant's transport system and are effective against weeds with underground storage organs by preventing regeneration. ☐

9 **Fungicides** can often be more effective when applied protectively, based on disease forecasts, than when treating a diseased crop. ☐

10 Plant protection chemicals can be toxic to animal species or be **persistent** and so **accumulate** or become magnified in **food chains**. ☐

11 Crop plants can become resistant to **pesticides** through natural selection. ☐

12 **Biological control** of pests involves the use of their natural predators, parasites or diseases. ☐

13 Risks with the use of biological control occur when the control agent escapes into the wider environment and affects natural ecosystems. ☐

14 **Integrated pest management (IPM)** combines cultural, chemical and biological controls. ☐

15 Provision of animal welfare in livestock production raises issues of costs, benefits and ethics. ☐

16 Poor **welfare of livestock** can be indicated by **stereotypic** and **misdirected behaviour** or failure of sexual or parental behaviour and altered levels of activity. ☐

17 **Ethology** is the observation of animal behaviour. ☐

18 The observed behaviour of domesticated animals in natural or semi-natural settings can provide information that can be used to improve the environment and welfare of domesticated animals. ☐

19 **Preference tests** and measurement of motivation can be used in animal welfare studies. ☐

Summary notes

Agricultural ecosystems

Agricultural ecosystems are often very uniform, with only one species, the crop, making up the bulk of the community. This type of situation provides opportunities for weed plants, pests and diseases, which are liable to affect the crop plants and reduce yield. A variety of methods of control are used to protect crops and reduce impact on food security.

Crop weeds

Crop weeds grow among crop plants where they reduce yields by competing for resources needed by crops. Weeds can be annual plants or perennial plants. The following table defines and lists the main adaptations of the types of weed.

Type of weed	Definition	Adaptations
Annual	Grow from seed and complete their life cycle in 1 year	Grow quickly following germination Have a short life cycle Produce many seeds Seeds are viable for long periods
Perennial	Persist from year to year	Have competitive advantage through being established prior to crop growth Have storage organs Reproduce vegetatively using special structures such as runners and bulbs

Invertebrate pests

These animals come from three main invertebrate groups. The following table shows the main groups with notes on their adaptations.

Invertebrate group	Example(s)	Adaptations
Nematodes (tiny worms)	Eel worms	Bore into host plant and live parasitically within the plant tissues
Molluscs	Slugs, snails	Have rasping mouthparts, which can deal with tough plant material
Insects	Greenfly, caterpillars	Have piercing or biting mouthparts, which penetrate or chew plant tissues

Diseases of crop plants

Many crop plant diseases are caused by microorganisms such as fungi, bacteria and viruses, as shown in the following table. Some of these microorganisms can be carried by invertebrates acting as vectors.

Hints & tips

There is more about vectors in Key Area 3.5 (page 126).

Microorganism	Example	Affected crop plant
Fungus	Blight fungus	Potato
Bacterium	Soft rot	Parsley
Virus	Stunt virus	Tomato

Fungal diseases of crop plants often spread quickly and do huge damage rapidly. Protective applications of fungicide based on disease forecasts are often more effective than trying to treat an already diseased crop.

Control methods

Cultural methods

Cultural methods of pest control are often traditional and preventative and have been embedded in farming practices over many generations. The following table shows some examples and their effects.

Cultural practice	Effect
Ploughing	Perennial weeds damaged or buried
Weeding	Early hoeing removes annual weeds
Crop rotation	Specific pests die out between plantings of the same crop

Chemical methods

Herbicides are weed-killers. Selective herbicides work by over-stimulating plant metabolism and killing the leafy part of the plant. The substances are absorbed through green leaves and so kill broadleaved plants quickly but not narrow-leaved ones such as cereals whose leaves absorb very little of the substance. Systemic herbicides are absorbed and transported through the vascular system of the weed and totally destroy all parts of it, so preventing regeneration.

Fungicides kill fungal parasites of crops and are often sprayed onto crops. Fungicides can be used as a protective measure when environmental conditions and disease forecasts suggest fungal infections are likely.

Insecticides kill insect pests. One of the most effective early insecticides was DDT. Unfortunately this substance is persistent, which means that, after spraying, it remains in the ecosystem and can be passed along food chains, gradually accumulating in the bodies of predatory animals at the end of the chain.

Figure 3.14 shows how DDT can accumulate along a food chain. Loss of the predators sets the chain out of balance and ultimately the system collapses. This effect is especially damaging when the pesticide leaches in an uncontrolled way into water near to farming areas.

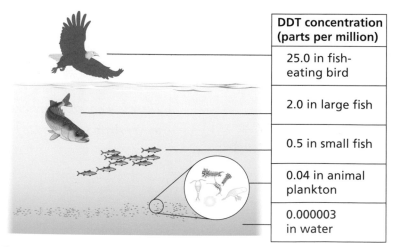

DDT concentration (parts per million)
25.0 in fish-eating bird
2.0 in large fish
0.5 in small fish
0.04 in animal plankton
0.000003 in water

Figure 3.14 Accumulation of DDT along a food chain

Biological control

In biological control, a natural enemy of the pest, such as a predator, parasite or disease-causing pathogen, is used to control the pest numbers. The following table shows examples of the various categories of biological control organisms.

Category	Example of pest controlled
Predator	Ladybirds act as predators of adult greenfly
Parasite	*Encarsia* wasp larvae are parasitic on whiteflies
Pathogen	*Bacillus thuringiensis* causes disease in caterpillars

Biological control has the advantage of not requiring chemicals that could persist in the ecosystem and cause unintended damage. Biological control works especially well in closed systems such as greenhouses, where the control agent cannot escape into the wider environment and cause unintended problems.

There are risks linked to the escape of biological control agents into natural ecosystems. If the agents are introduced from a different part of the world, they may be free from predators, parasites and disease. Their numbers could increase rapidly and they may threaten indigenous species.

Hints & tips

There is more about introduced and invasive species in Key Area 3.8 (page 136).

Integrated pest management (IPM)

Integrated pest management uses a combination of methods to control pest numbers. It combines cultural, chemical and biological control methods and allows reduction in the application of chemical pesticides.

Animal welfare

Domesticated animals should behave in natural ways, live free from disease and grow vigorously. Methods of livestock production should ensure the well-being of the animals involved. This raises issues of costs and benefits and also ethical questions.

Improving conditions for animals is expensive and results in food that is more costly for human consumers. However, contented animals grow and reproduce better and produce better quality meat, milk and eggs.

Ethical questions involve evaluating human moral conduct. Poor welfare of domesticated animals could be seen as unethical. Is the need to provide better food security a higher priority than the need to behave ethically? In the UK, the Farm Animal Welfare Council (FAWC) advises the government on the changes to legal regulations needed to ensure animal welfare.

Indicators of poor animal welfare

Poor welfare is often indicated by changes to behaviour, leading to reproductive failure. Some examples are shown in the following table.

Behaviour indicating poor welfare	Example
Stereotypy	Repetitive actions such as aimless chewing movements in pigs
Misdirected behaviour	Inappropriate use of normal behaviour, such as over-grooming of feathers by chickens, leading to feather damage
Abnormal activity levels	Hyper-aggressive stamping and head lowering in bulls
Failure of reproductive behaviour	Rejection or abandoning of offspring by female sheep

Ethology

Ethology is the study of animal behaviour. Observation of animals in their natural environment can give information about treatment of domestic animals to avoid the problems listed in the table above. Ethograms are lists or diagrams that describe animal behaviour.

Ethograms from animal behaviour studies in wild populations can be used to infer the welfare needs of animals in domestication. Figure 3.15 shows an ethogram for a wild mammal, which could be compared with one from a domesticated member of the same species.

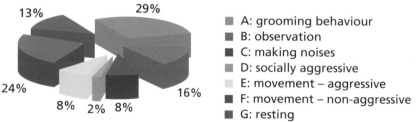

- A: grooming behaviour
- B: observation
- C: making noises
- D: socially aggressive
- E: movement – aggressive
- F: movement – non-aggressive
- G: resting

Figure 3.15 Ethogram for a wild mammal, showing the percentage of time spent on different activities

Preference testing

Preference tests are set up to check the conditions that animals prefer by providing them with controlled choices. Figure 3.16 shows a radial arm maze designed to investigate the grain preferred by domesticated chickens. Conditions in each of the arms are kept the same and many individual chickens are used in a number of trials. Preferences could be inferred from the masses of grain left in the hoppers after a set period of time.

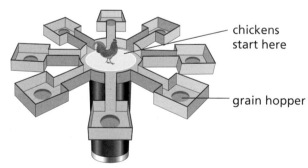

chickens start here

grain hopper

Figure 3.16 Radial arm maze

Motivation

Motivation is a measure of the extent to which an animal is driven to seek out a basic need such as food or water. Degree of motivation can affect the results of a preference test. Chickens prefer to walk on thin rather than thicker wire mesh. Hungry chickens might prefer to be in an area with an unsuitable mesh floor if that area provides the food they need at the time, compared with a suitable mesh floor in an area with no food available.

Key words

Accumulate – build up or magnify
Annual weed – weed plant that completes its life cycle in 1 year
Biological control – method of controlling pests using natural predators, parasites or diseases
Crop pest – organism that reduces the yield of crops
Cultural – based on human behaviours and activities
Ecosystem – interaction between communities and their habitats
Ethology – the observation and study of animal behaviour
Food chain – diagram to show the flow of energy in an ecosystem
Fungicide – chemical substance that kills fungal pest species
Integrated pest management – IPM; use of chemical, biological and cultural means to control pests
Misdirected behaviour – normal behaviour that has been directed inappropriately, such as over-grooming
Perennial weed – weed that persists in the community by continuing to grow year after year
Persistent – unable to be broken down by enzymes
Pesticide – chemical that kills pests
Preference test – experiment in which animals are given choices to guide the planning of their welfare
Selective – applies to pesticides whose action is targeted
Stereotypic behaviour – repetitive movements, such as apparently aimless pacing
Systemic – affecting all tissues of an organism's body
Welfare of animals – relating to activities designed to be humane to livestock while maximising their yield

Questions ?

Restricted response (structured in 1- or 2-mark parts)

1 Give **two** issues that arise when deciding on the level of animal welfare provision on a farm. (2)
2 Describe how the following experimental procedures are used in the study of behaviour in domesticated animals.
   a) ethograms (2)
   b) preference tests (2)

Extended response (4–9 marks each)

3 Give an account of chemical methods used to protect plants from named pests and of the environmental damage that can result from their use. (9)
4 Describe the properties of plants that allow them to be successful weeds of crop plants, under the following headings:
   a) adaptations of annual plants (3)
   b) adaptations of perennial plants (2)
   (total = 5)
5 Give an account of biological control and outline a risk linked with using this method of crop protection. (4)

Answers are on page 141.

Symbiosis, social insects and social behaviour

Key points !

1 **Symbiosis** is an intimate relationship that has coevolved between members of two different species. ☐

2 **Parasites** benefit in terms of energy or nutrients and their **hosts** are harmed by the loss of these resources. ☐

3 Parasites often have limited metabolism and cannot survive out of contact with their hosts. ☐

4 Parasites can be transmitted to new hosts using direct contact, **resistant stages** and **vectors**. ☐

5 Some parasitic life cycles have evolved to include **secondary hosts**. ☐

6 In **mutualism**, both partner species benefit in the interdependent relationship. ☐

7 Examples of mutualism include cellulose-digesting microbes in the guts of herbivores and photosynthetic algae in the polyps of coral. ☐

8 There is evidence for the symbiotic origins of chloroplasts and mitochondria in eukaryotic cells. ☐

9 Many animals live in social groups and have behaviours such as **social hierarchies**, cooperative hunting and cooperative defence, which are adaptations to group living. ☐

10 **Cooperative hunting** can benefit **subordinate** animals as well as **dominant animals**. ☐

11 By cooperative hunting, subordinate animals might gain more food than by hunting alone. ☐

12 In cooperative hunting, food sharing will occur as long as the reward for sharing exceeds that for foraging alone. ☐

13 **Altruistic behaviour** harms the donor individual but benefits the recipient.☐

14 In social animals, **reciprocal altruism** often occurs. ☐

15 In reciprocal altruism, altruistic behavioural roles are later reversed. ☐

16 Behavioural altruism occurs between related individuals (kin). ☐

17 In **kin selection**, the donor benefits in terms of increased chances of survival of genes they share with the recipient's offspring. ☐

18 In **social insects**, such as bees, wasps, ants and termites, only certain individuals contribute to reproduction. ☐

19 Most members of a colony of social insects are workers, who cooperate with close relatives to raise offspring related to them. ☐

20 Many social insects are **keystone species** and have a central and important stabilising role in their ecosystems. ☐

21 Some social insects are of economic importance to humans as pollinators or controllers of pests. ☐

22 In **primates** there is a long period of **parental care** during which offspring can learn complex social behaviours. ☐

23 To reduce unnecessary conflict, social primates use ritualistic display and appeasement behaviours. ☐

24 In monkeys and apes, **alliances** form between individuals, which are often used to increase social status within the group. ☐

25 The complexity of social structure in primates is related to ecological niche, the distribution of resources and **taxonomic group**. ☐

Summary notes

Symbiosis

Symbiosis is an intimate ecological relationship between members of two different species that have coevolved alongside each other over millions of years.

Parasitism

A parasite has an intimate ecological relationship with its host. The parasite species is dependent on its host species for energy or nutrients, whereas the host is harmed by the loss of these resources. Parasites often have limited metabolism, which prevents their survival out of contact with their host.

Parasites are transmitted to their hosts by direct contact, through resistant stages or by vectors. Some parasites have life cycles that involve a secondary host. The following table shows some examples of parasite species.

Parasite species	Host	Secondary host	Transmission
Human head lice	Human	None	Direct physical contact between humans
Cat fleas	Domestic cat	None	Direct physical contact between cats when adult fleas passed, or by resistant-stage larvae or pupae of the flea being picked up from the environment
Malaria parasite (*Plasmodium*)	Human	None	Mosquito acts as a vector, which carries the parasite stages from human to human through biting
Pork tapeworm	Human	Pig (also damaged by stages of the tapeworm)	Consumption of undercooked pork from an infected pig by a human

Figure 3.17 shows the life cycle of the cat flea.

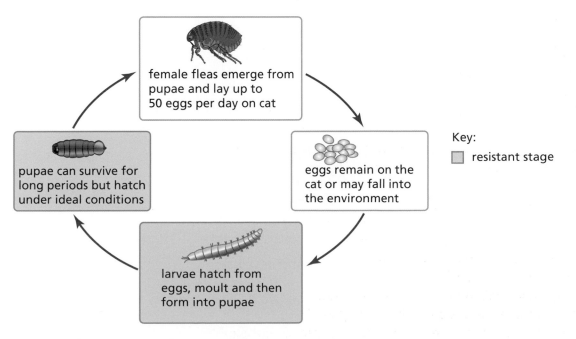

Figure 3.17 Life cycle of the cat flea

Figure 3.18 shows how a secondary host is involved in the life cycle of the pork tapeworm.

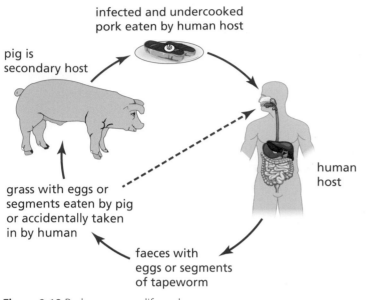

Figure 3.18 Pork tapeworm life cycle

Mutualism

In mutualism, both partner species benefit from the interdependent relationship. The following table shows some examples of mutualistic relationships between species.

Partner species	Notes on interdependence
Herbivorous grazers (e.g. cattle) with cellulose-digesting bacteria	Their gut provides a safe, warm, moist habitat with a continuous supply of food for the cellulose-digesting bacteria that live there. The bacteria digest cellulose to produce simple sugars used by the herbivores as an energy source because many do not have the required digestive enzymes themselves.
Polyp stages of coral with photosynthetic *Zooxanthella* algae	The soft-bodied part of sessile corals provides a safe, nitrogen-rich habitat for *Zooxanthella* algae, which live there and produce photosynthetic sugars that supply carbohydrate to the coral polyp, which it would otherwise lack.

The symbiotic origin of chloroplasts and mitochondria

Chloroplasts and mitochondria are organelles that occur within the cells of eukaryotic organisms. Mitochondria are found in all eukaryote cells while chloroplasts are found only in those of green plants.

There is a theory that proposes that these organelles started as free-living prokaryotic cells that were engulfed into larger cells and developed a mutualistic relationship with them, as shown in Figure 3.19. The relationship was favoured by natural selection. The body of evidence that supports this theory is summarised in the following table.

Sources of evidence from chloroplasts and mitochondria	How the evidence from organelles supports a symbiotic origin
Nucleic acid	They have DNA that is circular, like that of some prokaryotic cells
Ribosomes	Their ribosomes are similar to those of prokaryotic cells
Size	They are similar in size to prokaryotic bacteria
Membranes	Their inner membranes have electron transport systems and bound enzymes similar to those of prokaryotic bacteria
Method of replication	Their replication method is similar to cell division in prokaryotic bacteria

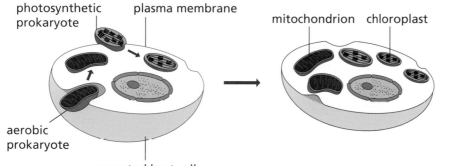
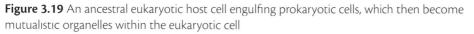

Figure 3.19 An ancestral eukaryotic host cell engulfing prokaryotic cells, which then become mutualistic organelles within the eukaryotic cell

Social behaviour

Many animal species live in social groups of various sizes. The groups are kept together by behaviours that have evolved by natural selection. Some behavioural adaptations are summarised in the following table.

Behavioural adaptation	Species as an example	Survival value
Social hierarchy	Grey wolf	Lowers aggression and saves energy Experienced leadership guaranteed Most favourable genes passed on
Cooperative hunting	African wild dogs	Larger prey can be killed Subordinate animals benefit Energy usage per individual reduced
Cooperative defence	Baboons	Early warning can be given Younger individuals defended Predators intimidated or confused

Altruistic behaviour

Altruistic behaviour involves a donor harming itself to the benefit of the recipient. Explanations for different types of altruism are shown in the following table.

Altruism	Example	Explanation
Reciprocal	Vampire bats who have hunted successfully might share food at the roost with those who have not	The successful hunter on one occasion might be unsuccessful later and need to obtain food from a previous recipient
Kin selection	Donor long-tailed tits with no offspring might feed the recipient offspring of other parents in times of food shortage	Long-tailed tits live in loose colonies with related individuals, so that recipient offspring of one parent might share some of the donor's genes

Social insects

Some insects live in social colonies, for example bees, wasps, ants and termites. Only a few individuals carry out reproduction while other, sterile individuals called workers carry out most of the food collection. This is known as a division of labour and is an adaptation that increases the survival of the species. The feeding of offspring of the fertile by the sterile is an example of kin selection since the breeding system ensures that the offspring are close relatives of all of the colony members.

Keystone species

In some ecosystems, stability can be brought about by one species called a keystone species. Many social insects are keystone species because their absence could lead to instability and the collapse of the system. Honey bees, for example, are often keystone species because their pollinating activities are needed by the flowering plants that form the base of the food pyramids in their ecosystem.

Figure 3.20 shows some general benefits of different keystone species to ecosystems.

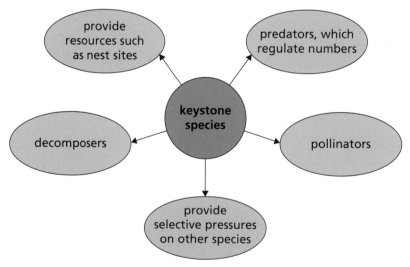

Figure 3.20 Roles of keystone species in ecosystems

Primate behaviour

Primates form the mammal group that includes monkeys, apes and humans. Primate offspring are born in a generally helpless state and have a long period of parental care. This allows time for the learning of complex social behaviours that support the social structure of the species. These behaviours include some designed to reduce conflict within the social group, such as ritualistic, display and appeasement behaviours.

The following table shows some behaviours that are important in chimpanzees.

Chimpanzee social group behaviour	Description	Function
Grooming	Includes the preening of one animal's coat by another	Reduction of tension and strengthening of alliances to increase social status in the group; strengthening of bonds between individuals
Facial expressions	Include eye closing, teeth baring, mouth opening	Act as signals to indicate position in dominance hierarchy and avoid conflict
Body postures	Include lowering of body position and bowing actions	Act as signals to emphasise position in dominance hierarchy and avoid conflict
Sexual presentation	Includes the presentation of genitalia by females to males	Acts as a signal by females to appease dominant males and avoid aggression

Factors affecting primate behaviour

External factors have a role in the evolution of primate behaviour. These include the complexity of the social structure of the species and the taxonomic group to which it belongs. The ecological niche occupied and the distribution of resources such as food and shelter are also important.

Key words

Alliance – link between individuals in a primate social group which can increase social status
Altruistic behaviour – behaviour that harms the donor but benefits the recipient
Cooperative hunting – hunting behaviour in which individuals work together to catch prey
Dominant animal – animal ranked at the top of a social hierarchy
Host – organism on or in which a parasite lives
Keystone species – species that has a central and important stabilising role in a community
Kin selection – organisms donating resources to those with whom they share genetic material
Mutualism – symbiosis in which both partners benefit from the arrangement
Parasite – symbiotic partner that damages its host but benefits itself
Parental care – activities performed by parents that increase the survival chances of their young
Primates – mammalian group that includes monkeys, apes and humans
Reciprocal altruism – when an altruistic act is returned by the original recipient to the original donor
Resistant stage – spores or other resting state of an organism that tolerates adverse conditions
Secondary host – organism involved in a stage of the life cycle of a parasite separate from the main host
Social hierarchy – grouping of individuals within a species graded by their social position
Social insects – insects that live in complex social colonies
Subordinate – animal lower in the hierarchy; below the dominant individual
Symbiosis – partnership that has coevolved between two different species
Taxonomic group – grouping of organisms used in classification
Vector – carries stages of a parasite into a host organism

Questions ?

Restricted response (structured in 1- or 2-mark parts)

1 Grey wolves live in packs in which a social hierarchy exists. The animals use cooperative hunting techniques.
   a) Give a definition of the term dominance hierarchy. (1)
   b) State **two** advantages to wolves of using cooperative hunting. (2)

2 In honey bees, worker individuals are sterile but work to ensure that offspring of their relatives are fed.
   a) Explain the altruistic behaviour of the worker bees. (2)
   b) Give the term that describes altruistic behaviour towards relatives. (1)

3 Describe what is meant by a keystone species. (2)

4 Give **two** external factors which influence the evolution of primate behaviour. (2)

Extended response (4–9 marks each)

5 Give an account of symbiosis under the following headings:
   a) parasitism (5)
   b) mutualism. (2)

   (total = 7)

6 Write notes on the evidence for the symbiotic theory of the origin of mitochondria and chloroplasts in eukaryotic cells. (4)

7 Give an account of primate behaviour under the following headings:
   a) parental care (2)
   b) behaviours for the reduction of conflict. (2)

   (total = 4)

Answers are on pages 141–142.

Key Area 3.7
Mass extinction and biodiversity

Key points !

1 Fossil evidence indicates that there have been several **mass extinction** events in the past. ☐
2 Following a mass extinction event, biodiversity is regained slowly as some survivors undergo speciation. ☐
3 The rate of extinction of species both in the past and currently is very difficult to estimate. ☐
4 The extinction of very large animals (**megafauna**) is correlated with the spread of humans. ☐
5 The increasing rate of degradation of natural ecosystems by humans has increased the rate of species extinction beyond its natural background rate. ☐
6 **Genetic diversity**, **species diversity** and **ecosystem diversity** are measurable components of overall **biodiversity**. ☐
7 Genetic diversity is represented by the number and frequency of all the alleles in a population. ☐
8 Species diversity comprises the number of different species in an ecosystem (the **species richness**) and the proportion of each species present in the ecosystem (the **relative abundance**). ☐
9 Ecosystem diversity refers to the number of distinct ecosystems within a defined area. ☐
10 A community with a dominant species has less species diversity than one with the same species richness but no particularly dominant species. ☐
11 The species diversity of a **habitat island** depends on its area and its degree of **isolation** from other habitats. ☐

Summary notes
Extinction

Living species naturally become extinct and are replaced by others. Rates of extinction are very difficult to determine but there have been times in the geological past when mass extinctions have occurred. A mass extinction occurs when very many species die out at more or less the same time. They can be indicated by fossil evidence. Figure 3.21 shows the occurrence of mass extinction events in the last 500 million years.

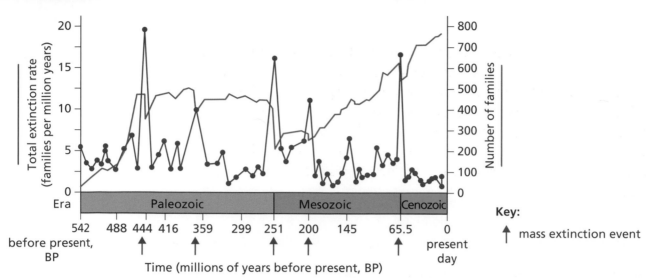

Figure 3.21 Mass extinction events

These extinctions were related to significant events in the planet's history, such as climate change or asteroid strikes, which caused indiscriminate extinction of animal groups. Following these mass extinction events, there was replacement of lost species as speciation occurred and the surviving groups diverged to fill vacant ecological niches.

Megafauna is a term usually applied to land animals larger than humans. There is a correlation between the extinction of these animals and the spread of modern humans across the planet. Megafauna are targets for human hunting because of their food potential and they are susceptible to extinction because of their slow reproduction rates and their requirements for large areas of suitable habitat.

Extinction of modern species

The increasing rate of degradation of natural ecosystems due to human activities has caused an increase in extinction rate to beyond the expected natural background rate. These activities include deforestation, burning fossil fuels and poaching. Modern megafauna are among the most endangered of all species. The following table shows some examples, with the human activities that threaten them most.

Modern megafauna species	Threats
Polar bear	Activities such as deforestation and fossil fuel burning, which lead to global warming
Siberian tiger	Low genetic diversity; poaching by humans
Black rhinoceros	Habitat destruction and poaching by humans

Measuring biodiversity

Biodiversity can be measured using components such as genetic, species and ecosystem diversity, as detailed in the following table.

Diversity component	Definition
Genetic	The number and frequency of alleles in a population
Species	The number of species (species richness) and the relative abundance of each species in an ecosystem
Ecosystem	The number of distinct ecosystems within a defined area

Habitat fragmentation and habitat islands

Biodiversity in habitats is related to the area of habitat. Biodiversity drops more quickly than the reduction of habitat size. This means that when habitats are fragmented, the impact is disproportionately high. The breaking of tracts of rainforest by logging roads or by the creation of patches of agricultural land decreases the overall biodiversity by creating small fragments known as habitat islands. The species diversity of a habitat island depends on its area and its degree of isolation from other habitats.

Key words

Biodiversity – variety and relative abundance of species
Ecosystem diversity – variety of different ecosystems in a defined area
Genetic diversity – number and frequency of alleles in a population
Habitat island – area of habitat isolated from other habitats
Isolation – situation in which genes are not able to flow
Mass extinction – disappearance of many groups of living organisms at the same point in time
Megafauna – large animals, usually bigger than humans, that need extensive habitat and breed slowly
Relative abundance – numbers of an organism compared with others in a community
Species diversity – measure of species richness and relative abundance
Species richness – number of different species in a community

Questions ?

Restricted response (structured in 1- or 2-mark parts)

1 It is thought that there have been several mass extinctions of animal families during the history of life on Earth.
   a) State what is meant by a mass extinction. (1)
   b) Describe what happens to surviving animal families following a mass extinction. (1)
   c) Give **two** examples of human activities that might be leading to a mass extinction during the present period of the Earth's history. (2)
2 State what is meant by megafauna and explain how their extinction is correlated with the spread of humans over the planet. (2)

Extended response (4–9 marks each)

3 Give an account of biodiversity and its measurement with reference to genetic diversity, species diversity and ecosystem diversity. (5)

Answers are on page 142.

Key Area 3.8
Threats to biodiversity

Key points ⚠

1 Humans have exploited certain species in the past and in some cases populations have remained large enough to recover. ☐

2 Small populations can show the **bottleneck effect**, by which they have lost so much genetic diversity that evolutionary response to environmental change is not possible. ☐

3 Small populations tend to inbreed and so their low genetic diversity leads to poor reproductive rates. ☐

4 **Habitat fragments** typically support lower species richness than larger areas of the same habitat. ☐

5 Habitat fragments suffer from degradation at their edges, which can further reduce their size. ☐

6 Edges of habitat fragments can be invaded by **edge species** adapted to habitat edges at the expense of interior species. ☐

7 Habitat fragmentation can be remedied by linking isolated fragments with **habitat corridors**, which allow species to feed, mate and eventually recolonise the fragments following local extinctions. ☐

8 **Introduced species** are non-native species that have been intentionally or accidentally moved by humans to new geographic locations. ☐

9 **Naturalised species** are introduced species that have become established in **indigenous** communities. ☐

10 **Invasive species** are naturalised species that have spread rapidly, eliminating indigenous species by out-competing them, hybridising with them or preying on them. ☐

11 Invasive species might be free of predators, parasites, pathogens or competitors that would limit their populations in their native habitats. ☐

12 **Climate change** may be caused by humans, but its impact on biodiversity is difficult to estimate. ☐

Summary notes
Exploitation

Humans exploit natural resources for food, raw materials and space. Over-exploitation, however, involves resources being consumed at a rate greater than they can be replaced. If over-exploitation is halted soon enough, populations of over-exploited species may be able to recover. An example of an over-exploited species and its potential recovery is provided by the fishing of cod. Exploitation of cod turned into over-exploitation when over-fishing caused depletion of stock. Quotas have been introduced by governments in recent years and there are some signs that cod stocks might be recovering – time will tell.

The bottleneck effect

Some populations can be reduced drastically. If the surviving population is very small, it might have lost most of its genetic variability. If the survivors are genetically similar, their inbreeding can then lead to further loss of variability and the species might be unable to adapt to environmental change in the future. This is known as the bottleneck effect. For example, the northern elephant seal, whose population was drastically reduced by over-hunting in the nineteenth century, has recovered in recent years although the genetic diversity of the modern population is very low.

Habitat fragmentation

Habitat fragmentation often occurs when humans take over an ecosystem. Forests have been cleared for agriculture and housing and to use the timber that they yield. This practice leaves behind remnants of the original habitat known as habitat fragments. Edge species that live at the edges of habitat fragments often colonise the centres of smaller fragments and can cause declines in the number of other species, reducing overall biodiversity. The collective habitat fragments support lower species richness and abundance than the original habitat.

It has been suggested that the creation of corridors of habitat between the fragments might allow species to recolonise them following local extinction. The species are able to move, feed and even mate along the corridors. This principle has been applied to hedgerows linking forest fragments on agricultural land and the creation of motorway underpasses for wildlife. However, these might not increase biodiversity because they do not provide for species that require continuous habitat with no breaks. Also, there is the suggestion that they might have a negative effect because they could allow the spread of disease between fragments.

Introduced, naturalised and invasive species

Introduced species are those that are non-native and have been moved by humans either intentionally or accidentally to new geographical locations. Some might become naturalised, which means that they become established within wild communities in their new location. Naturalised species can spread rapidly because they are free from the natural predators, parasites, pathogens or competitors that limited spread in their original habitat. They can become invasive and threaten indigenous species by preying on them, out-competing them and, in some cases, by hybridising with them.

Example

A good example of problems caused by an introduced animal becoming invasive is the cane toad, which was introduced to Australia in the 1930s as a biological control for beetles, which were damaging sugar cane crops. The toads were poisonous to predators and ate a variety of native species as well as beetles, including marsupial mammals. The toads are still increasing and threatening native biodiversity as invasive pests.

Climate change

Climate change is a natural part of the history of the planet. Anthropogenic climate change is caused by human activity. The increasing human population and rate of economic development round the world has led to increased demand for food and other resources. This in turn has led to increases in activities such as deforestation, burning of fossil fuels and certain types of agriculture, which add greenhouse gases such as carbon dioxide and methane to the atmosphere. As the layer of insulating greenhouse gas builds up, the planet gradually warms, as shown in Figure 3.22.

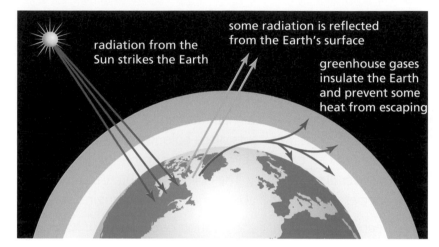

Figure 3.22 The greenhouse effect

Global warming affects the pattern of climate, bringing increases in temperature (Figure 3.23) and changes in the pattern of rainfall. These changes are expected to affect biodiversity. Already there is evidence of species changing their range and behaviour in response. Some specialised species will struggle to respond in these ways because of their very specific habitat requirements and will face extinction.

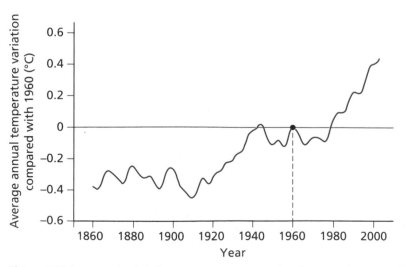

Figure 3.23 Increases in global temperatures compared with 1960, when the reference temperature was recorded and is graphed here as zero

Climate change modelling

The study of the effects of climate change on biodiversity is mainly based on computer climate modelling. This relies on human data input. Much of the input data are projected and extrapolated and therefore subject to inaccuracy. The use of modelling to predict changes in biodiversity is therefore challenging, open to different interpretation and continues to provoke disagreement among scientists.

Key words

Bottleneck effect – inability of a species to evolve due to lack of genetic diversity
Climate change – changes in climate brought about by changes in the temperature of the Earth
Edge species – species adapted to the edges of habitats
Habitat corridor – link between pieces of habitat in which species can feed, mate and pass through
Habitat fragment – very small area of isolated habitat
Indigenous species – native species occurring naturally in its ecosystem, having evolved there
Introduced species – species that has been brought by humans from one geographical location to another
Invasive species – introduced species that has become naturalised in and then harmful to its community
Naturalised species – introduced species that has taken a place in the wild community

Questions ?

Restricted response (structured in 1- or 2-mark parts)

1 Describe what is meant by the bottleneck effect. (2)
2 State what is meant by the following terms.
   a) introduced species (1)
   b) naturalised species (1)
   c) invasive species (2)
   d) indigenous species (1)

Extended response (4–9 marks each)

3 Give an account of habitat fragmentation and the measures that can be taken to minimise its effects. (5)
4 Describe how humans may contribute to climate change and how this may impact on biodiversity. (4)

Answers are on page 143.

Answers

Key Area 3.1a

Restricted response

1 population increase [1]
2 a) production of food by green plants using energy from light [1]
   b) an organism's position in a food chain [1]
3 plant a greater area of crop; use fertilisers; use pesticide; use biological control methods; grow improved/GM strains of crop plants (other answers possible) [any 3 = 2, 2/1 = 1]

4 crops are producers and livestock are consumers; energy is lost between each trophic level of a food chain [1 each = 2]

Extended response

5 a) sufficient quantities of food are produced; sufficient quality of food is produced; ability to distribute/spread food through the population [1 each = 3]
   b) knowledge required to use food properly; ability to guarantee food security; over longer periods [1 each = 2]
   [total = 5]

Answers

Key Area 3.1b

Restricted response

1 absorbed; reflected; transmitted
[all 3 = 2, 2/1 = 1]

2 absorption spectrum shows which wavelengths of light are absorbed by an isolated pigment; action spectrum shows which wavelengths of light cause most photosynthesis to occur [1 each = 2]

3 carotenoid pigments extend the wavelengths of light absorbed by photosynthesis; and pass the energy trapped onto chlorophyll [1 each = 2]

4 used in respiration; converted to starch for storage; converted to cellulose to form cell walls; passed to other biosynthetic pathways
[any 2 = 2]

5 a) (i) total plant biomass produced [1]
　　(ii) biomass of desired crop [1]
　 b) divide the dry mass of the economic yield by the dry mass of the biological yield [1]

Extended response

6 net assimilation is increase in dry mass of plant due to photosynthesis; over a period of time; minus the loss of dry mass due to respiration over the same period; per unit area of leaf surface [1 each = 4]

7 a) light energy excites electrons in pigment molecules; high-energy electrons pass through an electron transport chain; releasing energy to generate ATP; by ATP synthase; energy also used to split water into oxygen, which is released; and hydrogen, which is transferred to the coenzyme NADP [any 5 = 5]
　 b) carbon dioxide joined to RuBP by RuBisCo; to produce 3–phosphoglycerate; ATP used to phosphorylate 3–phosphoglycerate to form G3P; hydrogen from NADPH used to form G3P; G3P forms glucose; some G3P regenerates RuBP [any 4 = 4]
[total = 9]

Answers

Key Area 3.2

Restricted response

1 higher yield; higher nutritional value; resistance to pests/diseases; characteristics suited to rearing/harvesting; characteristics suitable for survival in particular habitats
[any 2 = 2]

2 cross hornless bull with (several) horned cows/cows of genotype hh; if any calves horned then bull is Hh/heterozygous *or* if all calves hornless then bull is HH/homozygous
[1 each = 2]

3 a) F_2 will contain a wide variety of genotypes; would need to be highly selected to identify valuable individuals [1 each = 2]
　 b) some of the varied F_2 may have new (combinations of) characteristics/provide a source of new varieties [1]

4 a) replication takes account of the variability within the sample and increases the reliability of the results [1]

b) randomisation eliminates bias/effects of factors other than the treatment when measuring the treatment's effects [1]

Extended response

5 inbreeding involves breeding closely related organisms together over many generations; this results in uniform/true-breeding/homozygous offspring; increases homozygosity in the stock; allows accumulation of recessive/deleterious homozygous alleles *or* produces inbreeding depression [any 3 = 3]
outbreeding involves crossing different genetic/inbred stock lines; is the natural situation for animals and most plants; produces hybrid offspring with improved/desirable characteristics/combinations of characteristics/improved vigour; avoids inbreeding depression [any 3 = 3]
[total = 6]

Answers

Key Areas 3.3 and 3.4

Restricted response

1 costs of provision; legal issues; benefits in terms of productivity; ethical questions *or* example of ethical question   [any 2 = 2]

2 a) records/results/accounts of animal behaviour studies; can be used to compare animals in natural settings with domesticated ones (other answers possible)   [1 each = 2]

   b) experiments that provide animals with controlled choices; results can help with decisions about animal welfare issues (other answers possible)   [1 each = 2]

Extended response

3 pests can multiply rapidly in agricultural communities; any two invertebrate examples from insects/molluscs/nematode worms; any two from weeds/fungi/viruses/bacteria; pesticide; any two examples from herbicide/insecticide/fungicide; can be selective or systemic; fungicide can be applied based on fungal disease forecasts   [any 4 = 4]

might be toxic to animals; might persist in the environment; might accumulate/be magnified in food chains; might lead to damage/imbalance in natural populations; might produce selection pressure on a population; might result in resistant populations   [any 5 = 5]
          [total = 9]

4 a) annual weeds grow rapidly; have short life cycles; high seed output; long-term seed viability   [any 3 = 3]

   b) perennial weeds have competitive advantages *or* example/early growth/larger size; storage organs; vegetative reproduction   [any 2 = 2]
          [total = 5]

5 use of natural predator/parasite/disease to control pest numbers; better used in enclosed situation/greenhouse; introduced organisms may be free of predators/parasites/disease themselves; could become invasive/a threat to indigenous species   [all 4 = 4]

Answers

Key Areas 3.5 and 3.6

Restricted response

1 a) dominance hierarchy is a rank order/pecking order of individuals in a social grouping of animals   [1]

   b) allows larger kills to be made; increases success rate of hunts; energy gained in food greater than that lost in hunting   [any 2 = 2]

2 a) worker bees feed the offspring of relatives because they have shared genes; the feeding helps ensure that the offspring survive   [1 each = 2]

   b) kin selection   [1]

3 a keystone species brings about stability in an ecosystem/their absence could destabilise the ecosystem; example – social insects *or* named social insect; other examples possible   [1 each = 2]

4 taxonomic group; complexity of social structure; distribution of resources; ecological niche   [any 2 = 2]

Extended response

5 a) parasites gain energy/nutrients; host is harmed by loss of these resources; parasites have more limited metabolism; cannot survive out of contact with host; are transmitted by direct contact; resistant stages or vectors; some have secondary hosts   [any 5 = 5]

   b) mutualism benefits both partners; partners are interdependent; example – bacteria in herbivore gut/photosynthetic algae in coral polyps (other answers possible)   [any 2 = 2]
          [total = 7]

⇨

6 mitochondria/chloroplasts thought to have
entered eukaryotic cells; they have double
membranes; they have genetic material/
circular chromosomes/DNA/ribosomes;
they are similar in size to prokaryotes; their
method of replication is similar to cell division
[any 4 = 4]
7 a) long period of parental care in primates;
allows opportunity to learn complex social
behaviours [1 each = 2]

b) ritualistic display *or* specific example;
appeasement behaviour *or* specific
example; general examples – grooming/
facial expression/body posture/sexual
presentation [any 2 = 2]
[total = 4]

Answers

Key Area 3.7
Restricted response
1 a) when many species die out at about the
same time [1]
b) surviving families often radiate/speciate to
regain biodiversity [1]
c) deforestation/habitat destruction; over-
hunting/fishing; greenhouse gas
emissions/burning fossil fuels [any 2 = 2]
2 megafauna are animals bigger than humans;
their extinction is related to human
colonisation; because of being hunted for
food *or* their habitat being destroyed; they
have slow reproduction rates [any 2 = 2]

Extended response
3 genetic diversity is the number of alleles in
a population; and frequencies of alleles in a
population; loss of a population can result in
loss of genetic diversity of a species
[any 2 = 2]
number of different species is species
richness; relative abundance is the proportion
of each species present [1 each = 2]
ecosystem diversity is the number of distinct
ecosystems in a defined area [1]
[total = 5]

Answers

Key Area 3.8
Restricted response
1 loss of genetic variation in small populations;
so that evolutionary responses to
environmental change cannot be
made [1 each = 2]
2 a) introduced species have been moved
intentionally from one geographic location
to another by humans [1]
b) naturalised species have become
established in wild populations in natural
communities [1]

c) invasive species are naturalised and have
spread rapidly and eliminated native/
indigenous species; they may be free of
natural predators/parasites/disease *or* they
may prey on native/indigenous species *or*
may outcompete them [1 each = 2]
d) native, naturally occurring species [1]

⇨
Extended response

3 habitat fragmentation occurs when habitat is split into small parts; fragments support lower species richness than a large area of the same habitat; fragments may be degraded at their edges; edge species may invade interiors and displace other species   [any 3 = 3]
isolated fragments can be connected by habitat corridors; species can feed/mate within corridors; recolonisation of deserted fragments can occur   [any 2 = 2]
                                                     [total = 5]

4 human activities/deforestation/fossil fuel combustion/agriculture produces greenhouse gases/carbon dioxide/methane; causing global warming; impact of changes on ecosystem diversity; difficult to measure; degree to which climate change is due to human activity; species unable to adapt face extinction; biodiversity will decrease   [any 4 = 4]

Practice course assessment: Unit 3 (50 marks)

Section A (10 marks)

1 The table below provides data relating to productivity in a field of potatoes.

Measurement	Productivity (kg dry mass per hectare per year)
Total plant biomass	9000
Potato tuber yield	3600

The harvest index of this wheat crop is

A 0.4
B 2.5
C 5400
D 12 600.

2 The following statements refer to photosynthesis:
   1 The enzyme RuBisCo fixes CO_2.
   2 Oxygen is released as a by-product.
   3 G3P is used for the synthesis of glucose.
   Which of the statements also refer correctly to the Calvin cycle?
   A 1 and 2 only
   B 1 and 3 only
   C 2 and 3 only
   D 1, 2 and 3

3 Self-pollinating plant species are less susceptible to in-breeding depression due to natural selection eliminating
   A deleterious alleles
   B dominant alleles
   C recessive alleles
   D mutated alleles.

⇨

4 A farmer used a pesticide to treat an infestation of greenfly that was damaging crops. The concentration of pesticide in the tissues of the greenfly and of the birds that ate them was measured and found to be higher in the birds which ate the greenfly than the greenfly themselves. This example shows that the plant protection chemicals can

A be systemic

B produce resistant populations

C act selectively

D accumulate in food chains.

5 Which of the following is said to occur when an interaction benefits both species in a symbiotic relationship?

A competition

B predation

C parasitism

D mutualism

6 Adult pork tapeworms live in the intestine of humans. Segments of the adult worm are released in the faeces. The tapeworm embryos that eventually develop from the segments might be eaten by pigs and develop further in their muscle tissue.

Which row in the table below correctly identifies the various roles in the tapeworm life cycle?

	Role of human	Role of embryo	Role of pigs
A	Host	Resistant stage	Secondary host
B	Host	Vector	Secondary host
C	Secondary host	Vector	Host
D	Secondary host	Resistant stage	Vector

7 Altruistic behaviour

A benefits both the donor and the recipient

B benefits the donor and harms the recipient

C harms the donor and benefits the recipient

D harms both the donor and the recipient.

8 Which of the following statements refer to advantages gained by cooperative hunting behaviour?

1 Individuals gain more energy than from hunting alone.

2 Dominant and subordinate animals both benefit.

3 Larger prey can be killed than by hunting alone.

A 1 and 2 only

B 1 and 3 only

C 2 and 3 only

D 1, 2 and 3

9 The species diversity in an ecosystem comprises

A both the genetic diversity and the ecosystem diversity

B species richness and relative abundance

C number and frequency of alleles

D number of distinct ecosystems in a defined area.

10 Over-hunting of the northern elephant seal was responsible for their dramatic decrease in numbers, which resulted in them having very low genetic variation. Present-day populations have all descended from the small number that survived.

What term is used to refer to the loss of genetic variation associated with a serious decline in population?

A founder effect

B stabilising selection

C bottleneck effect

D directional selection

Section B (40 marks)

1 As a result of the increase in human population and concern for food security there is a continuing demand for increased food production.
The table below shows the results of a field trial undertaken to investigate the effect of a fertiliser on the economic yield of grain obtained per year from an experimental plot.

Crop	Economic yield of grain (kg per hectare per year)	
	Control	Addition of NPK fertiliser
Maize	260	3200
Wheat	400	2600

  a) State the difference between the biological yield and the economic yield of a crop. (1)
  b) Calculate the expected increase in the economic yield of wheat that would be achieved by the addition of NPK fertiliser in a 50-hectare field over a 5-year period. (1)
  c) Plant field trials are often carried out in a range of environments to compare the performance of different cultivars or different treatments. Explain why the randomisation of treatments is important. (1)
  d) Apart from the addition of fertilisers, give **one** other method used in agriculture to increase crop yield. (1)

2 a) Crop breeders seek to develop crops with improved characteristics.
    Give **two** examples of improved characteristics that would be useful in terms of increasing food security. (2)
  b) Many crop plants are F_1 hybrids. Describe how these F_1 hybrids are produced and state the advantage gained by growers of these crops. (2)

3 In an investigation of the effects of different wavelengths of light on photosynthesis in green algal cells, apparatus was set up as shown in the diagram below. The glass tube containing a suspension of the cells was illuminated using filters to provide the different wavelengths of light.

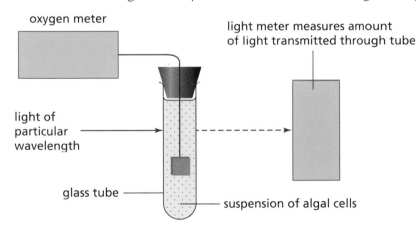

  a) Identify **two** variables that should have been kept constant each time a different filter was used during the investigation. (2)
  b) Describe a suitable control for this investigation. (1)
  c) The light meter measures transmitted light. Apart from being transmitted, state **two** other possible effects of the algal cell suspension on light striking it. (2)
  d) Describe the measurements that would need to be taken to determine the rate of photosynthesis in the algal cells at each wavelength tested. (2)

$\Rightarrow$

4 The bar chart below shows the effect of a selective breeding programme in cattle to increase milk yield over a period of 60 years. Error bars are also shown.

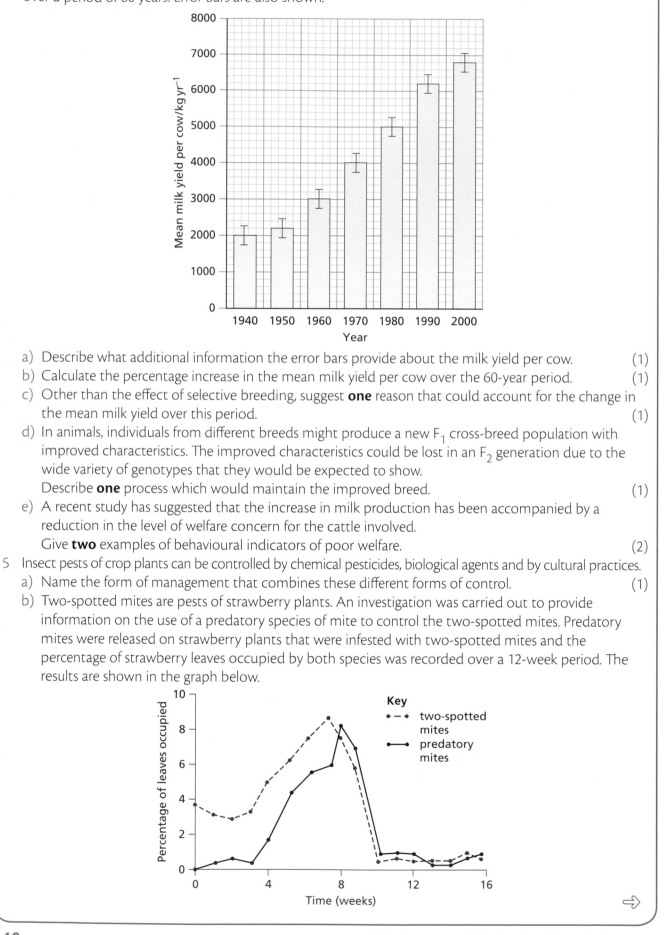

a) Describe what additional information the error bars provide about the milk yield per cow. (1)

b) Calculate the percentage increase in the mean milk yield per cow over the 60-year period. (1)

c) Other than the effect of selective breeding, suggest **one** reason that could account for the change in the mean milk yield over this period. (1)

d) In animals, individuals from different breeds might produce a new F_1 cross-breed population with improved characteristics. The improved characteristics could be lost in an F_2 generation due to the wide variety of genotypes that they would be expected to show.
Describe **one** process which would maintain the improved breed. (1)

e) A recent study has suggested that the increase in milk production has been accompanied by a reduction in the level of welfare concern for the cattle involved.
Give **two** examples of behavioural indicators of poor welfare. (2)

5 Insect pests of crop plants can be controlled by chemical pesticides, biological agents and by cultural practices.
a) Name the form of management that combines these different forms of control. (1)

b) Two-spotted mites are pests of strawberry plants. An investigation was carried out to provide information on the use of a predatory species of mite to control the two-spotted mites. Predatory mites were released on strawberry plants that were infested with two-spotted mites and the percentage of strawberry leaves occupied by both species was recorded over a 12-week period. The results are shown in the graph below.

⇨

    (i) Describe how the percentage of leaves occupied by predatory mites changed during the period of this investigation. (2)

    (ii) The investigation was repeated but a systemic pesticide was applied to the strawberry plants after 10 weeks.

    Predict the effect that the application of pesticide would have on both the two-spotted and predatory mite numbers. (1)

c) Give **one** example of a cultural control method that can be used to protect crops from pests. (1)

6 It is believed that 60% of the world's ecosystems are now degraded and that the extinction rate in taxonomic groups is now 100 to 1000 times higher than the natural background extinction rate that would be expected. Unlike the mass extinction events of geological history, the current extinction rate might be caused by human activities.

a) Give the meaning of the term mass extinction event. (1)

b) Give **one** example of a human activity that could be contributing towards increased extinction rates. (1)

c) Biodiversity can be measured by both genetic diversity and species diversity.
Describe what is meant by each of these terms. (2)

d) Explain how a loss in genetic diversity could lead to the extinction of a species. (1)

Question 7 contains a choice.

7 Either   A   Write notes on social behaviour under the following headings:

      a) altruism and kin selection (4)

      b) primate behaviour (5)

              [total = 9]

   or   B   Write notes on photosynthesis under the following headings:

      a) photolysis (4)

      b) the Calvin cycle (5)

               [total = 9]

Answers to practice assessment: Unit 3

Section A

1 A, 2 B, 3 A, 4 D, 5 D, 6 A, 7 C, 8 D, 9 B, 10 C

Section B

1 a) biological yield is total dry biomass of the crop *and* economic yield is total dry biomass of the desired product [1]

b) 550 000 kg [1]

c) to eliminate bias when measuring the effects of different environments [1]

d) using high-yielding cultivars; protecting crops from pests/disease/competition/any named example, e.g. pesticide, biological control, others [any 1 = 1]

2 a) higher yield; disease resistance; frost resistance; increased nutritional value (other answers possible) [any 2 = 2]

b) cross-breeding of different strains/cultivars/inbred lines; increase in yield *or* increase in vigour [1 each = 2]

3 a) volume of algal suspension; concentration of algal suspension; algal species; time for photosynthesis; distance of light source from algae; temperature [any 2 = 2]

b) repeat the experiment using a glass tube with no algae/distilled water [1]

c) reflected; absorbed [1 each = 2]

d) time period; volume of oxygen produced [1 each = 2]

⇨

⇨

4 a) the maximum and minimum values/range obtained for cattle in the sample; the variance of the data; values chosen to show range   [any 1 = 1]

   b) 240%   [1]

   c) better feeding; better animal welfare; genetic modification; other   [any 1 = 1]

   d) select parents from the original true-breeding stock *and* cross-breed them again *or* select F_2 individuals *and* back-cross with F_1 parents   [1]

   e) stereotypic behaviour; failure of reproduction; failure of parental behaviour; altered activity levels; misdirected behaviour   [any 2 = 2]

5 a) integrated pest management/IPM   [1]

   b) (i) increased up to eight weeks; decreased to 10 weeks *and* then remained constant   [1 each = 2]

      (ii) reduced number of/killed both species   [1]

   c) crop rotation; use of netting/scarecrows; (deep) ploughing; weeding   [any 1 = 1]

6 a) many species die out at about the same time   [1]

   b) deforestation *or* burning fossil fuels; over-hunting/fishing; pollution; habitat destruction   [any 1 = 1]

   c) Genetic diversity: frequency *and* number of alleles in a population   [1]
      Species diversity: number *and* relative abundance of different species   [1]

   d) species lacks the diversity on which natural selection can act when the environment changes   [1]

7A a) donor harmed; recipient benefits; example of altruism; roles can be reversed during reciprocal altruism   [any 2 = 2]
      kin are close relatives who share genes; kin selection is donating resources to kin; kin selection increases the chances of the donor's own genes continuing in future generations   [any 2 = 2]
                                     [max = 4]

   b) primates are monkeys, apes and humans; have long dependency period to learn complex social behaviour; ritualistic/appeasement behaviour designed to reduce conflict; examples of behaviour with description from grooming – mutual preening; facial expression/body posture/sexual presentation – acting as signals; alliances increase social status   [any 5 = 5]
                                    [total = 9]

B a) light energy excites electrons in pigments; splitting of water molecules in light-dependent stage; using energy from high-energy/excited electrons; oxygen produced, which is released; hydrogen is accepted by NADP   [any 4 = 4]

   b) carbon dioxide fixed by RuBP; RuBisCo catalyses this reaction; 3-phosphoglycerate converted to G3P; using ATP from light-dependent stage; using hydrogen from NADPH; sugars/glucose/carbohydrates made; RuBP regenerated   [any 5 = 5]
                                    [total = 9]

The questions within the Key Areas of this book all test knowledge. This section covers the skills of scientific inquiry and includes questions to test these. We have given three different approaches to working with these science skills and recommend that you use all three.

- The first approach simply provides sets of hints and tips on answering science skills questions.
- The second approach goes through the skills one by one and gives you some exam-style questions to try. There is a grid on page 156 that shows which skills are tested in the parts of each question. The answers are given on pages 165–166.
- The third approach gives an example of a scientific investigation and breaks it down into its component skills. There are questions on each skill area. The answers are on page 166.

The context of scientific skills questions will usually be unfamiliar to you but the approaches we have covered should apply to most situations. This means extra marks and improved grades.

Approach 1: hints and tips

Tips on selecting information

Note that you can be asked to deal with information that is more complex than that which you could be asked to present or process.

- Some questions might be based on passages of *text* – you could be asked to pick out information, identify evidence, explain relationships, draw conclusions and show biological knowledge. Try using a highlighter to pick out important points in the text.
- Data might be presented as a *table* – again, a highlighter is helpful.
- Figures in tables may have + or − symbols to indicate if observed values are significantly higher or lower than would have been expected by chance.
- The main types of chart you could see are **bar charts** and **pie charts**.
- You could be presented with **line graphs** or **graphs of best fit**. A line graph is used when data points are simply connected by straight lines. If data are scattered on a graph, lines can be fitted using the results of calculations on the data.
- On graphs, the variable being investigated (independent variable) is usually on the *x*-axis and what is being measured (dependent variable) is on the *y*-axis.

- You might be asked to identify variables that should be controlled – use **CID**:
  - **C**ontrolled variables should be kept **C**onstant.
  - **I**ndependent variables are being **I**nvestigated.
  - **D**ependent variables give the **D**ata that form the results.
- Sampled data, either from fieldwork or from time intervals, are often graphed on the *x*-axis but are not true variables. Watch out for this if you are asked to identify a variable.
- Watch out for graphs with a double *y*-axis – these are tricky! The two *y*-axes often have different scales to increase the difficulty. You must take care to read the question and then the graph carefully to ensure that you are reading the correct *y*-axis – there will usually be a key, which is critical.
- On bar charts and line graphs, work out the value of the smallest square on either scale before trying to read actual values.
- You might see a graph with a **semi-logarithmic scale**. These are often used when the numbers involved in a graph scale range from low to very high, such as those dealing with numbers of bacteria present in a growing culture. An example is given on page 85.
- You could see bar charts or line graphs with **error bars**. These are used to show the extent of variability of data, the level of confidence that exists regarding the data or if two sets of data differ from each other significantly. You would not be asked to draw error bars.
- If you are asked to calculate an increase or decrease between points on a graph, you should use a ruler to help accuracy – draw pencil lines on the actual graph if this helps.
- When you are asked to describe a trend it is essential that you quote the values of the appropriate points and use the exact labels given on the axes in your answer. You must use the correct units in your description.
- Sometimes there will be two sources of data, for example a graph and a table. Make sure you study the two sources carefully – there will be something that links them and it is this link that you will be asked to use.
- You could be asked to deal with statistical measures such as **mean**, **range** and **standard deviation**. The mean is an arithmetic average of the data and the range is the difference between the highest and lowest values in a group. The standard deviation is a measure of how varied the data are. You would not be expected to calculate standard deviation values.
- **Box plots** are used to show differences between groups of data – they are graphical ways to display the data so that groups can be compared visually. A group of data is put into rank order. The rank is split into four quartiles, each of which contains 25% of the items of data. The

value at the boundary of the second and third quartile is called the median value. The box plot for a group of unspecified data values is constructed as shown below.

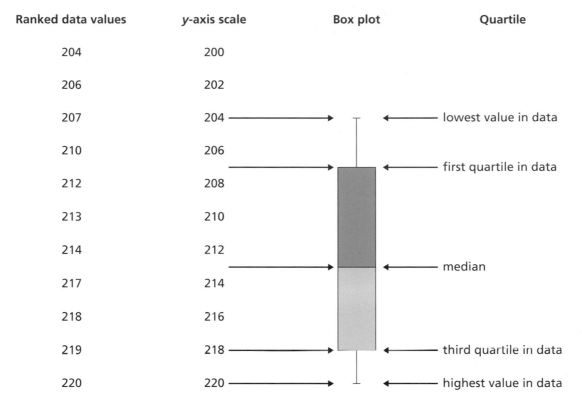

Ranked data values	y-axis scale	Box plot	Quartile
204	200		
206	202		
207	204		lowest value in data
210	206		
212	208		first quartile in data
213	210		
214	212		
217	214		median
218	216		
219	218		third quartile in data
220	220		highest value in data

- You could see box plots in a question but you would not be asked to draw one. There is an example of a box plot question on pages 160–161.
- **Keys** are used to identify and, usually, name an organism using features of its body as clues.

Tips on presenting information

- The most common question in this area requires students to present information that has been provided in a table as a graph – usually a line graph or sometimes a chart (usually a bar chart), although it is possible that you could be asked for a simple diagram or to draw a key.
- Check the question to see if it is a line graph or a bar chart that is required – the question will usually tell you.
- Marks are given for providing scales, labelling the axes correctly and plotting the data points. Line graphs require points to be joined with straight lines using a ruler. Bar charts need to have the bars drawn precisely, using a ruler.
- Ensure that you can identify the dependent and independent variables.
- The graph labels should be identical to the table headings and units. Copy them exactly, leaving nothing out.
- You need to decide which variable is to be plotted on each axis. The data for the variable under investigation (independent variable) is placed in a left column of a data table and should be scaled on the x-axis. The right column in a data table provides the label and data for the y-axis – the dependent variable. You will lose a mark if these are reversed.

- You must select suitable scales. Choose scales that use at least half of the graph grid provided, otherwise a mark will be deducted. The values of the divisions on the scales you choose should allow you to plot all points accurately.
- Make sure that your scales include zero if appropriate and extend beyond the highest data points.
- The scales must rise in regular steps. At Higher level the examiners will often test you on this by deliberately skipping one of the values that they have given you to plot in the table.
- Be careful to include one or both zeros on the origin if appropriate. It is acceptable for a scale to start with another value other than zero if this suits the data.
- Take great care to plot the points accurately using crosses or dots and then connect them exactly using a ruler.
- Do not plot zero or connect the points back to the origin unless zero is actually included in the data table. If 0 is there, you must plot it.
- When drawing a bar graph, ensure that the bars are the same width. Remember to include a key if the data require it.
- If you make a mistake in a graph, a spare piece of graph paper is provided at the end of your exam paper.

Tips on processing information

General points

- You can be asked to do calculations involving whole numbers, decimals or fractions. Answers might be whole numbers or decimals.
- Decimal answers should be rounded to the appropriate degree of accuracy, which will generally be to the nearest two decimal places or to three significant figures.
- You can be asked to convert between units, such as those for mass (μg, mg, g and kg) or for distance (μm, mm, m and km).
- You might be asked to do calculations involving negative numbers or using scientific notation.
- You might be asked to put values into a given equation and calculate an unknown.

Tackling the common calculations

Percentages: expressing a number as a %

The number required as a percentage is divided by the total and then multiplied by 100, as shown:

$$\frac{\text{number wanted as a \%}}{\text{total}} \times 100$$

Percentage change: increase or decrease

First, calculate the increase or decrease to find the change. Then, express this value as a percentage:

$$\frac{\text{change}}{\text{original starting value}} \times 100$$

Ratios

These questions usually require you to express the values given or being compared as a simple whole number ratio.

First you need to obtain the values for the ratio from the data provided in the table or graph. Take care that you present the ratio values in the order they are stated in the question. Then simplify them, first by dividing the larger number by the smaller one then dividing the smaller one by itself. However, if this does not give a whole number then you need to find another number that will divide into both of them. For example, 21:14 cannot be simplified by dividing 21 by 14 since this would not give a whole number. You must then look for another number to divide into both, in this case 7. This would simplify the ratio to 3:2, which cannot be simplified any further.

Mean

This is one type of average – the others are the median (used in box plots and indicating the middle value of a set of data) and the mode (the most common value in a set of data).

Add up the values provided and then divide the total by the number of values given. Make sure you include all values even if one or more is actually a zero value – they still count.

You might be asked to calculate the mean increase per unit time in a value over a period. If so, calculate the total increase, then divide by the number of units of time in the period given.

Range

This refers to the difference between the lowest and the highest values in a set of data. Find the lowest and the highest – subtract one from the other.

Tips on experimental skills of planning, designing and evaluating

Experimental aims

The aim of an experiment or investigation is usually stated at the start of a question – make sure you read the stem carefully because you cannot give a conclusion without knowing the aim.

Hypothesis formation

When an observation is made, the suggested scientific explanation for it is called a hypothesis. You may be given an observation and asked to construct a hypothesis.

Variables

You should be able to identify the independent and dependent variables in an investigation or experiment.

- The **i**ndependent variable is the **i**nput variable – it usually appears in the first column of a data table and is plotted on the *x*-axis of a graph.
- The **d**ependent variable refers to the **d**ata (results) produced – it usually appears in the second column of a data table and is plotted on the *y*-axis of a graph.

Validity

To achieve validity, only the independent variable should be altered while the other variables should be kept constant. Examples of the variables that might need to be controlled and kept constant to ensure results are valid include temperature, pH, concentration, mass, volume, length, number, surface area and type of tissue, depending on the experiment.

The control should be identical to the original experiment apart from the one factor being investigated. If you are asked to describe a suitable control, make sure that you describe it in full. A control experiment allows a comparison to be made and allows you to relate the dependent variable to the independent one.

Experimental procedure

- If the effect of temperature on enzyme activity is being investigated, it is good practice to allow solutions of enzyme and substrate to reach the required temperature before mixing them, to ensure that the reaction starts at the experimental temperature.
- It is good experimental practice to use percentage change when you are comparing results. A percentage change allows a fair comparison to be made when the starting values in an investigation are different.
- Watch out for questions that refer to dry mass. Since the water content of tissues is variable and can change from day to day, dry mass is often used when comparing masses of tissues that are expected to change under experimental conditions.
- Precautions to minimise errors include washing apparatus such as beakers or syringes or using different ones if the experiment involves different chemicals or different concentrations. This prevents cross contamination.
- Questions regarding procedures that ask why the experiment was left for a certain time require you to state that this is to allow enough time for particular events to occur. These events could include the following:
  - diffusion or absorption of substances into tissue
  - growth taking place
  - the effect of substances being visible
  - a reaction occurring.

Observations and measurements

When observing and measuring you need to ensure reliable results. To improve the reliability of experiments and the results obtained, the experiment should be repeated.

Remember **ROAR**: **r**epeat and **o**btain an **a**verage, which increases **r**eliability.

Modifications needed in light of experience

You will probably be asked to suggest a modification to an experimental procedure to test different variables. If you are asked about this, think about how to alter the different variables while keeping the original variable constant. For example, when investigating enzyme action, temperature is often varied. If temperature were kept constant then pH level could be investigated as long as all other variables were kept the same.

Concluding, predicting and generalising

When **concluding**, you must provide a reference to the experimental aim, which is likely to be stated in the stem of the question. You could be asked to:

- summarise experimental results, including describing patterns, trends or rates of change
- look at supplied information and **predict** results or outcomes of experiments
- make **generalisations** about, state relationships between, or suggest rules about biological processes.

Approach 2: skill by skill

The basic skills that can be tested in your exam are listed in the table below. We have provided four practice questions (1–4), one from each Unit and a data display question, which cover all the skill areas between them. The table shows the parts of the practice questions where you can find each skill tested. It is probably better to try the whole of each question in turn. If you find particular difficulty with any part of a question, you can use the table to identify the skill area that needs further work. Use the other material in this chapter to work on each skill, either in turn or as you come across difficulties.

Skill area	Category within skill area	Practice questions			
		1: Unit 1 data	2: Unit 2 practical	3: Unit 3 data	4: Data display
1 Selecting information...	...from a line graph or bar chart	e	–	–	e, f
	...from a table	–	–	–	a
2 Presenting information...	...as a line graph	–	b	a	d
3 Processing information...	...as a ratio	–	–	eii	–
	...as an average	–	g	–	–
	...as a percentage	–	–	c	–
	...by general calculation (addition, subtraction, multiplying, dividing)	c	–	–	–
4 Planning and designing	Planning: aim, hypothesis, dependent and independent variables	–	c	b	g
	Designing: apparatus, replicates, other variables, controls	–	a, d, f	–	–
5 Predicting and generalising	Predicting	–	i	d	–
	Generalising	d	–	–	–
6 Concluding and explaining	Concluding	a, b	h	ei	–
	Explaining	–	–	–	h
7 Evaluating	Identifying source(s) of error	–	–	–	c
	Suggesting improvement(s)	–	e	–	b

Unit 1 DNA and the genome

Question 1 Data question ?

Chemical analysis of the nucleotide bases present in DNA samples from various sources was carried out. The number of thymine, guanine and cytosine bases present in a sample was divided by the number of adenine bases present.

The results are shown in Table 1.

Table 1

Source of DNA sample	Number of each base present divided by the number of adenine bases in the sample		
	Thymine	Guanine	Cytosine
Human	1.00	1.50	1.50
Cattle	1.00	1.30	1.30
Domestic hen	1.00	1.45	1.45
Wheat plants	1.01	1.42	1.41
Yeast	1.00	1.67	1.67

a) Describe the evidence in Table 1 that suggests the following conclusions:
   (i) Adenine pairs with thymine in DNA. (1)
   (ii) There may have been experimental error in the analysis of the sample from wheat plants. (1)
b) Explain why the ratios of adenine to guanine and adenine to cytosine in Table 1 are almost identical. (1)
c) Using information in Table 1, copy the table below and complete it to show the numbers of guanine, cytosine and thymine bases in the human DNA sample. (3)

Base name	Number of molecules present in sample
Adenine	2800
Guanine	
Cytosine	
Thymine	

d) Explain why the ratios of adenine to guanine are different in different groups of living organisms. (2)
e) DNA strands are separated by melting. The melting temperature (T_m) is proportional to the percentage of guanine to cytosine bonds (% G–C) present in the molecule, as shown in the graph below.

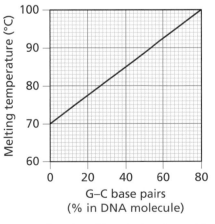

(i) Give the % of G–C base pairs in a molecule of DNA that has a T_m of 80°C. (1)
(ii) Give the T_m for a DNA sample in which 20% of the bases are guanine. (1)
(iii) Use information in Table 1 and the graph to predict the T_m for the human DNA sample. (1)

Answers are on page 165.

Unit 2 Metabolism and survival

Question 2   Practical question ?

Hydrogen peroxide is a toxic substance produced during metabolism.

Catalase is an enzyme that breaks down hydrogen peroxide, as shown below:

$$\text{hydrogen peroxide} \xrightarrow{\text{catalase}} \text{water} + \text{oxygen}$$

An experiment was carried out to investigate the effect of a competitive inhibitor on the action of catalase.

Raw potato containing catalase was chopped finely and added to 5 cm³ of 5% hydrogen peroxide solution in a tube. The tube was kept at 20°C and the volume of oxygen released was measured every minute over a period of 6 minutes, as shown in the diagram below.

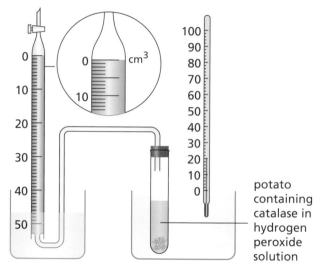

The experiment was repeated with the competitive inhibitor hydroxylamine hydrochloride added to the tube. The results are shown in the table below.

Time (minutes)	Volume of oxygen produced (cm³)	
	Without inhibitor	With inhibitor
0	0.0	0.0
1	7.8	3.4
2	8.6	5.8
3	9.0	6.6
4	9.3	8.6
5	9.5	9.3
6	9.6	9.6

a) Suggest why the potato was chopped finely before being added to the hydrogen peroxide.   (1)
b) On a sheet of graph paper, draw a line graph of time against volume of oxygen produced when the inhibitor was absent.   (2)
c) Identify the independent variable in this investigation.   (1)
d) Identify **two** variables not already described that should be kept constant to ensure the validity of the results.   (2)
e) Describe how the reliability of the experiment could be increased.   (1)
f) Explain how the tube with no inhibitor acted as a control in this experiment.   (1)

⇨

g) Calculate the average volume of oxygen produced per minute over the first 3 minutes in the tube without the inhibitor. (1)
h) State the effect of the inhibitor on the activity of catalase. (1)
i) Predict the volume of oxygen that would have been produced after 7 minutes in the tube without the inhibitor. (1)

Answers are on page 165.

Unit 3 Sustainability and interdependence

Question 3   Data question ?

Leg deformities in the Pennsylvania wood frog *Lithobates sylvaticus* have been linked to infection by parasitic worms and to a weakening of the immune system caused by exposure to pesticides.

Samples of 50 frogs, each with a different number of parasitic worms, were examined and the percentage of each sample showing leg deformities was calculated.

Table 1 shows the results of this investigation.

Table 1

Average number of parasitic worms per frog	Frogs in sample with deformed legs (%)
0	14
1	12
2	20
3	28
4	36
5	44

a) On a piece of graph paper, draw a line graph to show the average number of parasitic worms per frog against the percentage of frogs in the sample with deformed legs. (2)
b) One hypothesis was that the limb deformities that occur in frogs are caused by infection with the parasitic worm.
  (i) Give evidence from the table that supports this hypothesis. (1)
  (ii) Give evidence from the table that does **not** support this hypothesis. (1)
c) Calculate the number of frogs with three parasitic worms that had leg deformities. (1)
d) Predict the percentage of frogs in a sample with six parasitic worms that would be expected to have leg deformities. (1)
e) In a further investigation, groups of uninfected tadpoles were placed in containers with a fine screen that prevented the parasite from entering, and other groups into containers with a larger-mesh screen that allowed the parasites to enter and infect the tadpoles. Some containers were placed into ponds with pesticide contamination and some into pesticide-free ponds, as shown in Table 2. The tadpoles were allowed to develop into frogs and the percentage of frogs in each container that had leg deformities was measured.

Table 2

| | Frogs with leg deformities (%) | | | | | |
	Pond with pesticide contamination			Pond free of pesticide		
Pond number	1	2	3	4	5	6
Containers allowing parasite entry	24	23	28	5	4	6
Containers preventing parasite entry	0	0	0	0	0	0

(i) Give **two** conclusions that can be drawn from the data provided in Table 2. (2)

(ii) Express, as a simple whole number ratio, the average percentage of frogs with leg deformities in the ponds containing pesticide to the average percentage of frogs with leg deformities in the ponds with no pesticide. (1)

Answers are on page 165.

Question 4 Data display question ?

In an investigation that aimed to show changes in the body mass of willow warblers (*Phyloscopus trochilus*) in Scotland, a sample of 15 birds was trapped during their breeding season in June and a further sample of 15 birds about to start their autumn migration in October. The birds were weighed to the nearest gram and the masses were arranged in order, as shown in the table below. The mean values were plotted on the chart below and error bars added. The data were processed and box plots drawn, as shown in the chart below.

Table

Bird	Masses of individual willow warblers in sample (g)	
	June sample	October sample
1	7	7
2	7	9
3	7	10
4	8	11
5	8	11
6	8	11
7	8	11
8	9	11
9	9	12
10	10	13
11	10	14
12	11	14
13	11	15
14	12	15
15	12	16
Mean	9	12

Chart

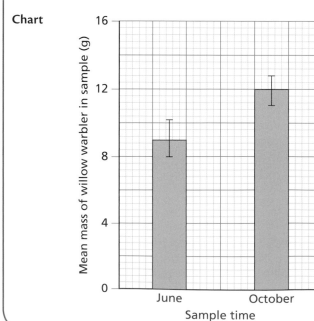

Box plots

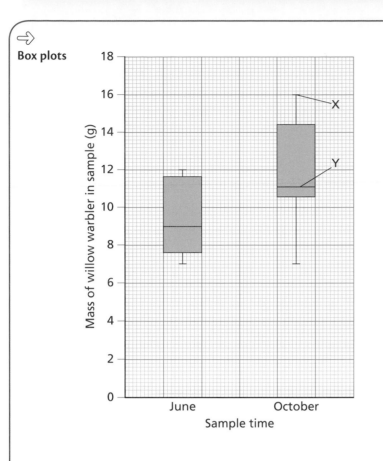

a) Using information in the table, give the range of values in the October sample. (1)
b) Describe how the reliability of the results of the investigation could be improved. (1)
c) Identify an error that might influence the results and suggest a method of avoiding it. (1)
d) Give **one** reason for the inclusion of error bars when presenting data. (1)
e) The list below shows terms that describe values in data.

median   mean   maximum   minimum   standard deviation

Identify the terms that could be applied to the data represented by lines X and Y on the October box plot. (2)
f) Describe the advantage of producing box plots to assist the drawing of conclusions rather than using data in the table alone. (1)
g) Suggest a hypothesis that might be confirmed by the results of the investigation. (1)
h) Suggest a reason for the increase in mean mass in willow warblers immediately before they migrate. (1)

Answers are on pages 165–166.

Approach 3: through an example

Investigating the effects of different antibiotic concentrations on the growth of *E. coli*

Read through the information about the experiment below and then work through the skill areas listed, commenting on the questions in each category.

Introduction

Bacteria can grow into colonies on nutrient agar. Antibiotic multidiscs are blotting papers that have circular areas that have been soaked in antibiotic. Colonies are not able to grow in areas of agar into which antibiotic substances have diffused and so clear areas are created, as shown in the diagram below.

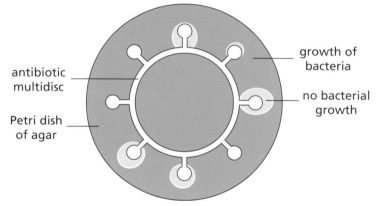

In an experiment that aimed to investigate the effects of increasing the concentration of an antibiotic on the growth of the bacterium *Escherichia coli* (*E. coli*), the following method was used. *E. coli* is an easily obtained, fast growing bacterium which is of great interest in medicine because it lives naturally in the human gut.

Method

1 Five Petri dishes were set up, each containing 10 ml of sterile nutrient agar.
2 An antibiotic multidisc with different concentrations of an antibiotic was added to the surface of the agar in each, pressed down and left for 24 hours.
3 Using a sterile pipette, 0.5 ml of broth containing a suspension of 10^5 *E. coli* per ml was removed from a culture bottle and squeezed onto the surface of each agar plate.
4 The culture was carefully spread across the agar surfaces using a glass spreader, which was sterilised between uses.
5 The dishes were kept in an oven at 30 °C for 48 hours, then removed, and the diameters of any clear zones that were visible around the antibiotic measured using a ruler.

Results

The mean diameters of the clear zones that developed around each antibiotic concentration are shown in the table below.

Antibiotic concentration (%)	Mean diameter (mm)
Control	0.0
0.5	0.1
1.0	3.3
1.5	4.1
2.0	4.6
2.5	6.1
3.0	6.6
3.5	6.7

Planning experiments and designing experiments

This is about confirming the aim of an experiment and suggesting a likely hypothesis, choosing apparatus, thinking about the dependent variable and deciding what to measure. Designing is closely related to planning but involves details of how often to measure, which variables need to be controlled and how to do this. It also involves anticipating possible errors and trouble-shooting these.

Q1   Suggest what the aim of the experiment was.

Q2   Suggest a hypothesis that would go with this aim.

Q3   Why is *E. coli* used?

Q4   What should be done to minimise the risks linked to using *E. coli* in the experiment?

Q5   What is the purpose of the control arm on each multidisc?

Q6   Why is nutrient agar used? (Hint: think about the conditions for bacterial growth.)

Q7   Why is the multidisc pressed into the agar and left for 24 hours?

Q8   Why is sterility important in this investigation? (Hint: many species of bacteria and fungi are present in air and on surfaces.)

Q9   Why is the plate left in the oven at 30 °C for 48 hours?

Q10   Why is the *E. coli* culture spread evenly on the agar?

Q11   Which variables have been controlled in this procedure?

Q12   Which is the dependent variable and which the independent variable?

Q13   Why was the experiment repeated five times?

Selecting information

This is about using a source such as a table or line graph to extract particular pieces of information. This can be simply reading off a value. The skill requires knowledge about labels, scales and units.

Q14   How could the results be expressed in a different numerical form?

Q15   Which concentration of antibiotic had the most effect on the *E. coli*?

Presenting information

This is about taking some information and presenting it in a different and more useful form. A common type of presentation might be to take information from a table and present it as a line graph. The skill requires knowledge of labels, scales and units, as well as careful drawing using a ruler and accurate plotting.

Q16 On a sheet of graph paper, draw a line graph to show the effect of antibiotic concentration on the growth of *E. coli*.

Processing information

This is often about working with numerical data and using calculations to convert a lot of data in a simple form.

Q17 What is the ratio of the diameter of the clear zone produced by antibiotic at 1% compared with that produced by antibiotic at 3%?

Q18 What is the mean diameter of the clear zones around the different antibiotic concentrations?

Q19 What is the percentage increase in the diameter of the clear zone at 0.5% antibiotic compared with 2.5%?

Q20 What is the range of diameters of clear zones in the investigation?

Q21 How many bacterial cells were in 0.5 ml of the culture liquid?

Q22 How could 0.5 ml of a culture with only 50% of this number be obtained?

Predicting and generalising

Predicting is about taking an experimental result and imagining what would happen if a variable changed. Generalising is about looking at experimental results and trying to find a rule that would hold true in all situations.

Q23 Predict the effect on the diameter of the clear zone produced if a concentration of the antibiotic at 4% was used.

Q24 How would you expect the results to compare if a different species of bacterium was used?

Q25 How could the diameters of the clear zones be increased without changing the concentration of antibiotic in the disc?

Q26 How could the diameters of the clear zones be decreased without changing the concentration of antibiotic in the disc?

Concluding and explaining

Concluding involves making a statement about the relationship between variables in an experiment. Explaining is about using knowledge to understand why a result has been obtained.

Q27 What is causing the clear zones?

Q28 What is the general conclusion that can be drawn from the results? (Hint: remember to look at the aim of the experiment.)

Evaluating

Evaluating is looking critically at an experiment and deciding if it is likely to be valid and if its result can be relied on; it is about looking for potential sources of error. Evaluating also involves suggesting improvements to an experiment that might remove sources of error in future experimental repeats.

Q29 What sources of error might be present?

Q30 How could the reliability of the results be improved?

Q31 How could this experiment be improved?

Q32 Which other substances that might affect bacterial growth could be investigated using a multidisc approach? How could you adapt the experimental set-up to investigate one of these?

Answers are on page 166.

Scientific inquiry skills answers

Skill by skill

1 a) (i) number of adenine molecules divided by number of thymine molecules equals 1.0 *or* ratio of adenine to thymine is 1:1 [1]

(ii) the answer/value obtained for adenine divided by thymine is very slightly more than 1.0 *or* ratio of adenine to guanine very slightly different from ratio of adenine to cytosine [1]

b) number of cytosine should equal the number of guanine (because they pair) [1]

c) guanine 4200; cytosine 4200; thymine 2800
[1 each = 3]

d) different groups have different proteins; and so different genetic codes in their DNA [1 each = 2]

e) (i) 26–27% [1]

(ii) 77–78°C [1]

(iii) 92–93°C [1]

2 a) to maximise/improve the release of catalase into the solution [1]

b) scales and labels with units; plotted correctly and connected with straight lines [2]

c) presence of inhibitor/hydroxylamine hydrochloride [1]

d) mass of potato; variety of potato; pH; volume of inhibitor; concentration of inhibitor [any 2 = 2]

e) repeat the investigation with and without the inhibitor [1]

f) showed that it was the inhibitor that was causing the effect [1]

g) 3.0 cm³ [1]

h) slows down/decreases the rate of enzyme activity over the first 5 minutes of the experiment [1]

i) 9.6–9.7 cm³ [1]

3 a) scales and labels with units; plotted correctly and connected with straight lines [1 each = 2]

b) (i) as the number of parasitic worms increased the % of frogs with deformed legs increased [1]

(ii) deformities are caused even with no parasitic worms present [1]

c) 14 frogs [1]

d) 52% [1]

e) (i) pesticide increases % of frogs with leg deformities; deformities do not occur if there are no parasites present [1 each = 2]

(ii) 5:1 [1]

4 a) 7–16 g [1]

b) catch and weigh more birds at each season [1]

c) not weighing birds accurately enough; weigh birds accurately and use mass values to (at least) one decimal place (other answers possible) [1]

d) to give information about the spread of the data; to show the confidence levels linked to the data; to indicate significant differences between sets of data [any 1]

e) X – maximum
Y – median [1 each = 2]

f) show the distribution/spread/variability of the data more clearly; allow sets of data to be compared more easily [any 1]

⇨

⇨

g) willow warblers increase body mass just before migrating [1]

h) birds require stored food reserves for flight [1]

Through an example

Q1   To show the effects of increasing antibiotic concentration on the growth of *E. coli*

Q2   Increasing the concentration of antibiotic would increase the inhibition of growth of *E. coli* or converse or increasing the concentration of antibiotic would have no effect [any 1]

Q3   Easily obtained bacterium which grows rapidly in culture

Q4   A risk assessment should be carried out to identify and minimise the impact of hazards using sterile/aseptic techniques

Q5   To show that any effect recorded is due to presence of antibiotic

Q6   Provides food and other requirements for the culture of *E. coli*

Q7   To allow the substance to diffuse into the agar

Q8   To prevent entry of other microorganisms that might compete with *E. coli* and affect results or that are hazardous

Q9   To provide optimum conditions for enzymes involved in growth of *E. coli*

Q10   So that any colonies develop evenly on the agar and are easier to see

Q11   Volume of nutrient agar; volume of *E. coli* culture; concentration of *E. coli* culture; temperature; time dishes were left for; type of antibiotic; area of disc in contact with agar

Q12   independent – concentration of antibiotic; dependent – diameter of clear zones

Q13   To increase the reliability of the results

Q14   Area/radius of clear zones

Q15   3.5%

Q16   Scales, labels and units *and* points plotted accurately and joined with straight lines

Q17   1:2

Q18   4.5

Q19   6000%

Q20   6.6 mm

Q21   50 000 *or* 5×10^4

Q22   Mix the culture with an equal volume of distilled water

Q23   6.7–6.8 mm

Q24   Might be expected to have similar effects

Q25   Leave dishes longer at start to allow more antibiotic to diffuse into agar

Q26   Do not leave dishes for 24 hours at the start of the experiment

Q27   Antibiotic prevents growth of bacteria, so no colonies develop

Q28   That increasing the concentration of antibiotic increases inhibition of the growth of *E. coli*

Q29   Potential for contamination; failure to have multidisc evenly pressed down; failure to spread bacteria evenly; errors in measuring diameters of clear areas

Q30   Reliability could be increased by repeating with more dishes

Q31   More dishes; more accurate measurement of clear zones

Q32   Different types of antibiotic; nutrients; precursors; inducers; hormones; pesticides; others; repeat experiment with discs containing appropriate substances but keeping all other variables constant

The assignment is an open-book task, which is based on a research investigation that you have carried out, mainly in class time. *You choose the topic* to be studied and then investigate or research the underlying biology and any impact it may have on society or the environment.

The assignment will assess the application of skills of scientific inquiry and related biology knowledge and understanding that you have developed throughout the course.

The investigation is supervised by teachers. You will have to write up the work in the form of a report of 800–1200 words, or equivalent, under *controlled assessment conditions* at a later stage. During your write up you will have access to your investigation notes.

The report will be *marked out of 20 marks* with 15 of the marks being for scientific inquiry skills and 5 marks for the application of knowledge. It is marked by the SQA and contributes 17% to the overall grade for your course.

Outline of the stages in the assignment

Research stage
1 Selection of a topic

The topic must relate to a key area of the Higher Biology course. Once you have chosen your topic, you need to decide on the specific aspect that you want to research. This will become the aim of your assignment. The aim might change during the research stage of your assignment, depending on the information you find.

Your teacher will probably give you some ideas to choose from. Make sure you choose something you are interested in and that you understand. The lists below show some suggested topics from the three Units – don't feel you need to use any of these.

Unit 1 DNA and the genome
- Case study on the bacterial transformation experiments of Griffiths.
- Case study on identification of DNA as the transforming principle by Avery *et al.*
- Case study on phage experiments of Hershey and Chase.
- Case study on Meselson and Stahl experiments on DNA replication.
- Case study on the use of PCR.

- Investigating plant evolution using chloroplast DNA and PCR.
- Tissue culture of plant material.
- Case study on use of stem cells in repair of diseased or damaged organs (e.g. skin grafts, bone marrow transplantation and cornea repair).
- Case study on ethics of stem cell research and sources of stem cells.
- Research the rarity of polyploidy in animals.
- Sexual selection in brine shrimp or other organisms.
- Case study on hybrid zones.
- Research the importance of the *Fugu* genome.

Unit 2 Metabolism and survival

- Case study on the toxic effects of venoms, toxins and poisons on metabolic pathways.
- Research different use of substrates during exercise and starvation.
- Case study on adaptations to survive low-oxygen niches.
- Case study on the response of a conformer to a change in an environmental factor.
- Comparisons of marine and estuarine invertebrates and their response to variation in salinity.
- Research aspects of surviving adverse conditions.
- Research the genetic control of migratory behaviour in studies of populations of the blackcap.
- Research different types of extremophile.
- Research the use of H_2 in methanogenic bacteria and H_2S in sulfur bacteria.
- Research industrial processes that use microorganisms. Suitable processes include the production of citric acid, glutamic acid, penicillin and therapeutic proteins such as insulin, human growth hormone and erythropoietin.
- Case study on bacterial transformation.
- Research the development of a microbiological product from discovery to market.

Unit 3 Sustainability and interdependence

- Case study on the challenge of providing food for the global human population.
- Contribution of biological science to interdisciplinary approaches to food security.
- Case histories of plant mutations in breeding programmes.
- Genetic transformations in plant breeding.
- Case study on the control of weeds, pests and/or diseases of agricultural crops by cultural and chemical means.
- Case studies on, for example, control of glasshouse whitefly with the parasitic wasp *Encarsia*, control of glasshouse red spider mite with the predatory mite *Phytoseiulus* and/or control of butterfly caterpillars with the bacterium *Bacillus thuringiensis*.
- Investigate the chemical and biological control of red spider mite.

- Research the five freedoms for animal welfare.
- Research the links between symbioses and anthropogenic climate change.
- Case study on primate behaviour.
- Research the Permian, Cretaceous and Holocene mass extinction events.
- Analyse data on the exploitation of whale or fish populations.
- Research the impact of naturally low genetic diversity within cheetah populations.
- Research the impact of habitat fragmentation and the benefits of habitat corridors for tiger populations.
- Case study on invasive species.
- Analyse data on crop planting density, biological yield and economic yield using leaf area index, crop growth rates and harvest index.
- Evaluate crop trials to draw conclusions on crop suitability, commenting on validity and reliability of trial design and the treatment of variability in results.
- Case studies on the development of particular crop cultivars and livestock breeds.
- Research self-pollinating plants – naturally inbreeding and less susceptible to inbreeding depression due to the elimination of deleterious alleles by natural selection.

2 Planning the investigation

Think carefully about your task – what do you already know? Where can you find out more? Focus on any applications and on the impact the content of your chosen topic has on society or the environment.

Ensure that you have a clear aim for the assignment and are sure of the reason you chose your topic. Be clear about the process you will adopt and how you might finally present your findings, including any data or results that you collect.

3 Identifying resources

You can use books, magazines, journals, monographs, the internet, resource packs, personal interviews, visits to appropriate facilities or any other suitable approach that your teacher agrees with. Choose media that you have easy access to. Your school library and librarian might be able to help.

4 Carrying out the investigation

As you work through various sources and extract relevant information, you will want to record anything of potential value. How will you record this material?

Downloading directly from the internet or copying directly from books might suggest that you have not understood the biology involved. This can be considered as plagiarism unless you acknowledge the sources carefully. It is always best to put things in your own words to make sure you really understand them.

Be aware of the need to provide a balanced evaluation in terms of the impact the topic you have studied might have on society or the environment.

You must select sufficient sources of information/data that are relevant, reliable and useful for your topic. These could include raw data from an experiment/practical activity, as well as extracted tables, graphs, diagrams and text. They can have similar or different perspectives and they can agree or disagree with each other.

If you are working in a group to gather data/information, you must take an active part in this and choose your own sources of data/information.

If you use an experiment/practical activity as one of the sources of information/data, your assessor will give you instructions for this. The experiment/practical activity will not be assessed and you may carry it out as part of a group.

Record the sources you have used with enough detail to allow someone else to find them again. If one of the sources is an experiment/practical activity, then you need to record the title and the aim.

This stage should be carried out mainly in class time and you will be allowed to take some of the material produced during this stage for use in the controlled assessment stage – *make sure you know what you will be taking in!*

Checkpoint

This is the point at which you inform your teacher that you have finished the research stage.

5 Selecting and gathering relevant information

You will go through a process of selecting the most relevant and appropriate material from the research stage to include in your final report. How will you organise your report?

Communication stage

6 Writing up your assignment report

You will have to write up your assignment under controlled, supervised conditions, with access to your notes (which cannot include a prepared draft report). As a guide, your report should be 800–1200 words, excluding tables, charts and diagrams.

It is also expected that your work will show literacy and numeracy skills. Here is a short checklist:
- Topic and aim clear
- Spelling and grammar correct
- Word count appropriate

- Explanation of how the underlying biology relates to the topic
- Divided up into coherent sections
- Relevant material only
- Graphs and tables neatly presented with labels, headings and units
- Statistical calculations (averages, percentages and ratios) accurate and clear
- Conclusion(s) justified
- Impact on society or environment clearly stated
- References with sources given

The table below shows how many marks are available for each aspect of your report.

Skills, knowledge and understanding	Mark allocation
Aim	1
Applying knowledge and understanding of biology	5
Selecting information	2
Processing and presenting data/information	4
Analysing data/information	2
Conclusion	1
Evaluation	3
Presentation	2

Before submitting your assignment report, check that you have included everything that is required – there is a grid on page xi to help with this.

Your exam

General exam revision: 20 top tips

These are very general tips and would apply to all your exams.

1 **Start revising in good time.**

   Don't leave it until the last minute – this will make you panic and it will be impossible to learn. Make a revision timetable that counts down the weeks to go.

2 **Work to a study plan.**

   Set up sessions of work spread through the weeks ahead. Make sure each session has a focus and a clear purpose. What will you study, when and why?

3 **Make sure you know exactly when your exams are.**

   Get your exam dates from the SQA website and use the timetable builder tool to make up your own exam timetable. You will also get a personalised timetable from your school but this might not be until close to the exam period.

4 **Make sure that you know the topics that make up each course.**

   Studying is easier if material is in chunks – why not use the SQA chunks? Ask your teacher for help on this if you are not sure.

5 **Break the chunks up into even smaller bits.**

   The small chunks should be easier to cope with. Remember that they fit together to make larger ideas. Even the process of chunking down will help!

6 **Ask yourself these key questions for each course.**

   Are all topics compulsory or are there choices? Which topics seem to come up time and time again? Which topics are your strongest and which are your weakest?

7 **Make sure you know what to expect in the exam.**

   How is the paper structured? How much time is there for each question? What types of question are involved – multiple choice, restricted response, extended response?

8 **There is no substitute for past papers – they are simply essential!**

   The last four years' papers for all Courses are on the SQA website – look for the past paper finder and download as PDF files. There are answers and mark schemes too.

9 Use study methods that work well for you.

People study and learn in different ways. Reading and looking at diagrams suits some people. Others prefer to listen and hear material – what about reading out loud or getting a friend or family member to do this for you? You could also record and play back material.

10 There are only three ways to put material into your long-term memory:
- practice – e.g. rehearsal, repeating
- organisation – e.g. making drawings, lists, diagrams, tables, memory aids
- elaborating – e.g. winding the material into a story or an imagined journey

11 Learn actively.

Most people prefer to learn actively – for example, making notes, highlighting, redrawing and redrafting, making up memory aids, writing past paper answers.

12 Be an expert.

Be sure to have a few areas in which you feel you are an expert. This often works because at least some of them will come up, which can boost confidence.

13 Try some visual methods.

Use symbols, diagrams, charts, flashcards, post-it notes etc. The brain takes in chunked images more easily than loads of text.

14 Remember – practice makes perfect.

Work on difficult areas again and again. Look and read – then test yourself. You cannot do this too much.

15 Try past papers against the clock.

Practise writing answers in a set time. As a rough guide, you should be able to score a mark per minute.

16 Collaborate with friends.

Test each other and talk about the material – this can really help. Two brains are better than one! It is amazing how talking about a problem can help you solve it.

17 Know your weaknesses.

Ask your teacher for help to identify what you don't know. If you are having trouble, it is probably with a difficult topic so your teacher will already be aware of this – most students will find it tough.

18 Have your materials organised and ready.

Know what is needed for each exam. Do you need a calculator or a ruler? Should you have pencils as well as pens? Will you need water or paper tissues?

19 Make full use of school resources.

Are there study classes available? Is the library open? When is the best time to ask for extra help? Can you borrow textbooks, study guides, past papers, etc.? Is school open for Easter revision?

20 Keep fit and healthy!

Mix study with relaxation, drink plenty of water, eat sensibly, and get fresh air and exercise – all these things will help more than you could imagine. If you are tired, sluggish or dehydrated, it is difficult to see how concentration is even possible.

Higher Biology exam tips

These tips apply specifically to Higher Biology. Remember that your assignment is worth 20 marks – the other 100 marks come from the examination.

Section A: multiple choice (20 marks)

- Do not spend more than *30 minutes* on this section.
- Answer on the grid within the question paper.
- *Do not leave blanks* – complete the grid for each question as you work through.
- Try to answer each question in your head *without* looking at the options. If your answer is there, you are home and dry!
- If not certain, choose the answer that seemed most attractive on *first* reading the answer options.
- If you are guessing, try to eliminate options before making your guess. If you can eliminate three, you are left with the correct answer even if you do not recognise it!

Section B: restricted and extended response (80 marks)

- Spend about *120 minutes* on this section.
- Answer on the question paper. Try to write neatly and keep your answers on the support lines if possible – these are designed to take the full answer.
- Another clue to answer length is the mark allocation. Most questions are restricted to 1 mark and the answer can be quite short; if there are 2 or 3 marks available, your answer will need to be extended and may well have two, three or even four parts.
- The questions are usually laid out in unit sequence but remember that some questions are *designed* to cover more than one unit.
- Grade C (less demanding) questions usually start with 'State', 'Give' or 'Name'.

- Grade A (more demanding) questions begin with 'Explain' and 'Describe' and are likely to have more than one part to the full answer.
- Abbreviations like DNA and ATP are fine, as is referring to the nucleotide bases as A, T, G and C.
- Don't worry that some questions are in unfamiliar contexts. This is deliberate. Just keep calm and read the questions carefully.
- If a question contains a choice, be sure to spend enough time making the right choice.
- Remember to *use values from the graph* if you are asked to do so.
- Draw graphs using a ruler and use the data table headings for the axes labels.
- Look out for graphs with two *y*-axes – these need extra concentration as they can easily lead to mistakes.
- Answers to calculations will not usually have more than two decimal places.
- If there is a space for calculation given it is very likely that you will need to use it.
- Do not leave blanks. Have a go, using the language in the question if you can.

Glossary

The terms included here appear in the SQA Course Assessment Specification for Higher Biology. The Key Area in which a term first appears is given in the brackets after each term.

Where a term has an unusual singular or plural, this is given in brackets with the definition.

You could make flashcards with the term on one side and the meaning on the other – a great resource for revision!

3′–5′ (1.2)   strand of nucleic acid running from a sugar to a phosphate

3′-phosphoglycerate (3.1b)   intermediate compound produced when RuBisCo fixes carbon dioxide by attaching it to RuBP

Absorption spectrum (3.1b)   graph showing wavelengths of light absorbed by a pigment

Accumulate (3.3)   build up or magnify

Acetyl group (2.2)   produced by breakdown of pyruvate; joins with oxaloacetate in the citric acid cycle

Action spectrum (3.1b)   graph showing the wavelengths of light involved in photosynthesis

Activation energy (2.1b)   input of energy required to start a chemical reaction

Active site (2.1b)   region on an enzyme molecule where the substrate binds

Adenine (A) (1.1)   base that pairs with thymine in DNA or uracil in RNA

Aestivation (2.5)   reaction of an organism to tolerate extreme drought

Agriculture (3.1a)   human practice of growing crops and keeping livestock to maintain food security

Alliance (3.6)   link between individuals in a primate social group which can increase social status

Allopatric speciation (1.7)   speciation in which gene flow is prevented by a geographical barrier

Alternative respiratory substrate (2.2)   substrate used for respiration other than carbohydrate

Altruistic behaviour (3.5)   behaviour that harms the donor but benefits the recipient

Alveoli (2.3)   microscopic parts of the gas exchange system in vertebrate lungs (*sing*: alveolus)

Amino acid (1.3)   unit of polypeptide structure

Anabolic (2.1a)   metabolic activity that requires energy input and builds up complex molecules

Annual weed (3.3)   weed plant that completes its life cycle in 1 year

Anticodon (1.3)   sequence of three bases on tRNA that specifies an amino acid

Antiparallel (1.1)   parallel strands in DNA running in opposite directions

Archaea (1.8)   a domain of life

ATP (2.2)   molecule used for energy transfer in cells

ATP synthase (3.1b)   membrane-bound enzyme that synthesises ATP

Atrium (2.3)   receiving blood entering a chamber vertebrate heart

Back-cross (3.2)   crossing an F_1 hybrid organism with a parental type to maintain characteristics of a new breed

Bacteria (1.8)   a domain of life

Base (1.1)   nitrogenous substance that is a component of a DNA nucleotide

Beef extract (2.6)   complex growth medium for microorganisms

Behavioural barrier (1.7)   barrier to gene flow caused by behavioural differences between individuals

Biodiversity (3.7)   variety and relative abundance of species

Bioinformatics (1.8)   use of computers and statistics in analysis of sequence data

Biological control (3.3)   method of controlling pests using natural predators, parasites or diseases

Biological species (1.7)   group of similar organisms interbreeding to produce fertile young

Biological yield (3.1b)   total dry mass increase

Bottleneck effect (3.8)   inability of a species to evolve due to lack of genetic diversity

Calvin cycle (3.1b)   carbon fixation stage of photosynthesis

Carotenoids (3.1b)   orange and yellow accessory pigments in plants

Catabolic (2.1a)   metabolic activity that releases energy in breakdown reactions

Cellular respiration (2.2)   release of energy from respiratory substrates

Cellulose (3.1b)   structural carbohydrate in plant cell walls derived from photosynthesis

Chlorophyll (3.1b)   green pigment molecule in plants that absorbs red and blue light for photosynthesis

Chloroplast (1.1)   organelle in which the chemical reactions of photosynthesis occur

Chromosome (1.1)   structure that contains the genetic material of an organism encoded into DNA

Citrate (2.2)   citric acid; first substance produced in the citric acid cycle

Citric acid cycle (2.2)   second stage of aerobic respiration, occurring in the matrix of mitochondria

Climate change (3.8)   changes in climate brought about by changes in the temperature of the Earth's surface

Codon (1.3)   sequence of three bases on mRNA that specifies an amino acid

Coenzyme A (2.2)   substance that carries an acetyl group into the citric acid cycle

Coenzyme NADP (3.1b)   hydrogen carrier in photosynthesis

Compartment (2.1a)   small membrane-bound region of a cell

Competition (3.1a)   struggle for existence between two organisms

Competitive inhibition (2.1b)   the slowing of reaction rate due to the presence of a substance resembling the substrate

Complete double circulation (2.3)   double circulation with complete separation of oxygenated and deoxygenated blood (e.g. in birds and mammals)

Conformer (2.4)   animal whose internal environment is dependent on its environment

Consequential dormancy (2.5)   dormancy that occurs in response to the onset of adverse conditions

Cooperative hunting (3.6)   hunting behaviour in which individuals work together to catch prey

Crop pest (3.3)   organism that reduces the yield of crops

Cross-breeding (3.2)   breeding organisms of different genotype together

Cultivar (3.1a)   variety of cultivated crop

Cultural (3.3)   based on human behaviours and activities

Cytosine (C) (1.1)   base that pairs with guanine

Death phase (2.6)   phase of microorganism growth in which death rate of cells exceeds rate of cell division

Dehydrogenase (2.2)   enzyme which removes hydrogen from its substrate; important in the citric acid cycle

Deleterious sequence (1.7)   DNA sequence that lowers survival rate

Deletion of genes (1.6)   chromosome mutation in which a sequence of genes is lost from a chromosome

Deletion of nucleotides (1.6)   single gene mutation involving removal of a nucleotide from a sequence

Deoxyribose (1.1)   pentose sugar that is a component of a DNA nucleotide

Differentiation (1.4)   changes to cells involving switching on certain genes and switching off others

Directional selection (1.7)   natural selection that tends to favour an extreme value of a varied characteristic

Disruptive selection (1.7)   natural selection that favours two different values of a varied characteristic

DNA (1.1)   deoxyribonucleic acid; a molecule that holds the genetic code in living organisms

DNA polymerase (1.2)   enzyme that adds free complementary DNA nucleotides during replication of DNA

Dominant (3.2)   allele that always shows up in the phenotype of an organism

Dominant animal (3.6)   animal ranked at the top of a social hierarchy

Dormancy (2.5)   response made by organisms to tolerate adverse conditions (e.g. hibernation, aestivation)

Double circulation (2.3)   blood flows through the heart twice during a full circulation of the body

Double helix (1.1)   three-dimensional shape of a DNA molecule

Duplication (1.6)   chromosome mutation in which a sequence of genes is repeated on a chromosome

Ecological barrier (1.7)   barrier to gene flow caused by ecological preference differences between individuals

Ecological niche (2.4)   the way of life and the role of an organism in its community

Economic yield (3.1b)   dry mass of desired product from a crop

Ecosystem (3.3)   interaction between communities and their habitats

Ecosystem diversity (3.7)   variety of different ecosystems in a defined area

Edge species (3.8)   species adapted to the edges of habitats

Electron transport chain (2.2)   group of proteins embedded in membranes of mitochondria and chloroplasts

Embryonic stem cell (1.4)   stem cell from an embryo that can divide and become any type of cell

Ethical issue (2.7)   issue affecting human attitudes and decisions regarding various choices

Ethology (3.4)   the observation and study of animal behaviour

Eukaryotic (1.1)   cell with a discrete nucleus

Evolution (1.7)   changes to organisms over time that are mainly caused by natural selection

Exon (1.3)   sequence of DNA that codes for a protein

Exponential growth (2.6)   growth phase of microorganisms involving a rapid geometric increase in numbers

Extremophile (2.5)   organism that lives in an environment with extreme abiotic conditions

F_1 generation (3.2)   first generation of offspring from a genetic cross

F_2 generation (3.2)   offspring of an F_1 generation

FAD (2.2)   hydrogen carrier important in the citric acid cycle

Feedback inhibition (2.1b)   enzyme inhibition caused by the presence of an end product of a metabolic pathway acting as an inhibitor of the pathway

Fermentation (2.2)   progression of pyruvate in the absence of oxygen

Fertiliser (3.1a)   chemical addition to soil to increase plant growth

Field trial (3.2)   non-laboratory test on the performance of a crop in various environmental conditions

Food chain (3.4)   diagram to show the flow of energy in an ecosystem

Food security (3.1a)   measure of the human ability to produce and use food

Fossil evidence (1.8)   information derived from the remains of extinct organisms

Fungicide (3.3)   chemical substance that kills fungal pest species

Gene expression (1.3)   transcription and translation

Generation time (2.6)   time taken for a microorganism cell to divide

Genetic diversity (3.7)   number and frequency of alleles present in a population

Genetic drift (1.7)   random changes to DNA sequences

Genetic transformation (3.2)   changes made to the genetic material of a cell by the addition of DNA from another cell

Genetic vector (2.7)   used to carry genetic material from one cell to another

Genome (1.5)   total genetic material present in an organism

Genome sequencing (3.2)   procedure to produce the nucleotide sequence of an entire genome

Geographical barrier (1.7)   physical barrier to gene flow, such as a mountain or river

Glyceraldehyde-3-phosphate (G3P) (3.1b)   compound in the Calvin cycle that can be converted to glucose or used to regenerate RuBP

Glycolysis (2.2)   first stage in cellular respiration

GM crop (3.2)   genetically modified crop that contains a gene from other species

Growth medium (2.6)   substance in which microorganisms are encouraged to grow

Guanine (G) (1.1)   base that pairs with cytosine

Habitat corridor (3.8)   link between pieces of habitat in which species can feed, mate and pass through

Habitat fragment (3.8)   very small area of isolated habitat

Habitat island (3.7)   area of habitat isolated from other habitats

Harvest index (3.1b)   value obtained by dividing dry mass of economic yield by dry mass of biological yield

Hazard (2.7)   a danger derived from an activity

Heat-tolerant DNA polymerase (1.2)   enzyme from hot-spring bacteria, used in PCR

Heterozygous (3.2)   having two different alleles of the same gene and so not breeding true

Hibernation (2.5)   response of an animal to avoid adverse conditions by reduction of metabolic rate

High-energy electron (2.2)   electron that can yield energy as it passes through an electron transport chain

Homeostasis (2.4)   maintenance of a steady state in the cells of a living organism

Homozygous (3.2)   having two identical alleles of the same gene and so breeding true

Horizontal inheritance (1.7)   inheritance of genetic material within a generation

Host (3.5)   organism on or in which a parasite lives

Hybrid zone (1.7)   region in which frequent interbreeding between two species occurs

Hydrogen bond (1.1)   weak chemical link joining complementary base pairs in DNA

Hypothalamus (2.4)   region of the mammalian brain in which blood temperature is monitored

Inbreeding (3.2) crossing organisms of the same or similar genotype

Inbreeding depression (3.2) accumulation of homozygous recessive alleles that lower biological fitness

Incomplete double circulation (2.3) double circulation with some mixing of oxygenated and deoxygenated blood (e.g. in amphibians and some reptiles)

Indigenous species (3.8) native species occurring naturally in its ecosystem, having evolved there

Induced fit (2.1b) change to an enzyme's active site brought about by its substrate

Inducer (2.6) substance that causes a gene to be expressed, often leading to production of an enzyme

Innate behaviour (2.5) unlearned instinctive behaviour

Insertion (1.6) single gene mutation in which an additional nucleotide is placed into a sequence

Integrated pest management (3.3) IPM; use of chemical, biological and cultural means to control pests

Intermediate (2.2) substance in a metabolic pathway between the original substrate and the end product

Introduced species (3.8) species that has been brought by humans from one geographical location to another

Intron (1.3) non-coding sequence of DNA

Invasive species (3.8) introduced species that has become naturalised in and then harmful to its community

Inversion (1.6) chromosome mutation in which a set of genes rotates through 180°

Isolation (3.7) situation in which genes are not able to flow

Keystone species (3.5) species that has a central and important stabilising role in a community

Kin selection (3.5) organisms donating resources to those with whom they share genetic material

Lactate (2.2) produced by the anaerobic conversion of pyruvate in mammalian muscle cells

Lag phase (2.6) earliest growth stage in microorganisms

Lagging strand (1.2) DNA strand that is replicated in fragments

Lead strand (1.2) DNA strand that is replicated continuously

Learned behaviour (2.5) behaviour of an individual organism not common to all members of its species and which is acquired by experience

Ligase (1.2) enzyme that joins DNA fragments to make the lagging strand

Light energy (3.1b) radiant energy used in photosynthesis

Livestock (3.1a) agricultural animals

Log phase (2.6) exponential phase of microorganism growth

Low-oxygen niche (2.3) way of life in a habitat with little oxygen present, such as at high altitude or in a deep ocean

Mass extinction (3.7)   disappearance of many groups of living organisms at the same point in time

Mature messenger RNA (mRNA) (1.3)   carries a copy of the DNA code to a ribosome

Megafauna (3.7)   large animals, usually bigger than humans, that need extensive habitat and breed slowly

Meristem (1.4)   regions in a plant in which mitosis occurs

Metabolic pathway (2.1a)   enzyme-controlled sequence of chemical reactions in cells

Metabolic rate (2.3)   rate of consumption of energy by an organism

Metabolism (2.1a)   total of all metabolic pathways in an organism

Migration (2.5)   response by an organism to avoid adverse circumstances

Misdirected behaviour (3.4)   normal behaviour that has been directed inappropriately, such as over-grooming

Mitochondria (1.1)   cell organelles in which the aerobic stages of respiration occur (*sing.* mitochondrion)

Molecular clock (1.8)   graph that shows differences in sequence data for a protein against time

Molecular interactions (1.3)   various chemical links joining amino acids and giving protein molecules their shape

Mutagenesis (2.7)   stimulation of mutations in a species

Mutations (1.6)   random changes to DNA sequences

Mutualism (3.5)   symbiosis in which both partners benefit from the arrangement

NAD (2.2)   hydrogen carrier important in the citric acid cycle

Natural selection (1.7)   process that ensures survival of the fittest

Naturalised species (3.8)   introduced species that has taken a place in the wild community

Negative feedback (2.4)   system of maintaining homeostasis in regulator organisms

Net assimilation (3.1b)   total dry mass increase through photosynthesis minus the loss from respiration

Non-coding sequence (1.5)   DNA sequence that does not encode protein

Non-competitive inhibition (2.1b)   enzyme inhibition by a substance that permanently alters the active site of an enzyme

Nucleotide (1.1)   component of DNA consisting of a deoxyribose sugar, a phosphate group and a base

Outbreeding (3.2)   breeding of organisms of different genotypes

Oxaloacetate (2.2)   substance that combines with the acetyl group in the citric acid cycle to form citrate

Parasite (3.5)   symbiotic partner that damages its host but benefits itself

Parental care (3.6)   activities performed by parents that increase the survival chances of their young

Peptide bonds (1.3) strong chemical links in the primary structure of polypeptides

Perennial weed (3.3) weed that persists in the community by continuing to grow year after year

Persistent (3.3) unable to be broken down by enzymes

Personalised medicine (1.8) possible future development in which treatment is based on an individual's genome

Pest (3.1a) organism that damages agricultural produce and reduces food security

Pesticide (3.3) chemical that kills pests

Phenotype (1.3) outward appearance of an organism

Phosphate (1.1) component of a DNA nucleotide that is derived from phosphoric acid, H_2PO_4

Phosphate (Pi) (2.2) inorganic phosphate used to phosphorylate ADP

Phospholipid membrane (2.1a) membrane of a cell made from fluid phospholipid molecules and proteins

Phosphorylation (2.2) addition of phosphate to a substance

Photolysis (3.1b) breakdown of water molecules using energy from light

Photosynthesis (3.1a) production of carbohydrate by a plant using the energy of light

Phylogenetics (1.8) study of evolutionary relatedness of species

Pigment (3.1b) coloured substance that absorbs light for photosynthesis

Plant and animal breeding (3.2) methods of crossing domestic animals and plants

Plasmid (1.1) circular loop of genetic material found in prokaryotic organisms and some yeasts

Polymerase chain reaction (PCR) (1.2) method of amplifying sequences of DNA

Polypeptide (1.3) short strand of amino acids

Polyploidy (1.6) possession of extra sets of chromosomes

Pore (2.1a) small gap in a membrane created by a channel-forming protein

Post-translational modification (1.3) changes made to polypeptides following translation

Precursor (2.6) substance needed to start a metabolic pathway

Predictive dormancy (2.5) dormancy that occurs before the onset of adverse conditions

Preference test (3.4) experiment in which animals are given choices to guide the planning of their welfare

Primary transcript (1.3) molecule made when DNA is transcribed

Primates (3.6) mammalian group that includes monkeys, apes and humans

Primer (1.2) short complementary strand of DNA

Product (2.1b) substance resulting from an enzyme-catalysed reaction

Productivity (3.1b) measure of the performance of a plant

Prokaryotic (1.1) cell that has no discrete nucleus

Protein (1.1) large molecule made up from a chain of amino acids linked by peptide bonds

Pump (2.1a)　protein in a phospholipid membrane that carries substances across it by active transport

Pyruvate (2.2)　end product of glycolysis

Randomised (3.2)　applies to values that have been arrived at by chance

Recessive (3.2)　allele that only shows in the phenotype when homozygous

Reciprocal altruism (3.5)　when an altruistic act is returned by the original recipient to the original donor

Recombinant DNA technology (2.7)　activities in which DNA is moved from one species to another

Reflection (3.1b)　when light that strikes a leaf, for example, passes away from its surface back to the atmosphere

Regulator (2.4)　animal that can adjust its metabolic rate to maintain a steady internal state

Relative abundance (3.7)　numbers of an organism compared with others in a community

Replicate (3.2)　repeat experiment in an investigation

Replication (1.2)　formation of identical copies of DNA molecules

Resistant stage (3.5)　spores or other resting state of an organism that tolerates adverse conditions

Restriction endonuclease (2.7)　enzyme that cuts genetic material from a chromosome or is used to open a plasmid

Ribosomal RNA (rRNA) (1.3)　type of RNA that makes up ribosomes

Ribosome (1.3)　site of protein synthesis; composed of rRNA and protein

Ribulose bisphosphate (RuBP) (3.1b)　acceptor of carbon dioxide in the Calvin cycle

Risk (2.7)　calculated chance of a potential hazard arising

RNA (1.3)　ribonucleic acid, which occurs in several forms in cells

RNA polymerase (1.3)　enzyme involved in synthesis of primary transcripts from DNA

RNA splicing (1.3)　joining of exons following the removal of introns from a primary transcript

RuBisCo (3.1b)　ribulose bisphosphate carboxylase; fixes carbon dioxide in the Calvin cycle

Secondary host (3.5)　organism involved in a stage of the life cycle of a parasite separate from the main host

Secondary metabolite (2.6)　substance produced during the stationary phase of growth of a culture of microorganisms (e.g. antibiotic)

Selective (3.3)　applies to pesticides whose action is targeted

Self-pollinating (3.2)　passing pollen within the flowers of a single individual

Sequence data (1.8)　information concerning amino acid or nucleotide base sequences

Sexual selection (1.7)　natural selection of characteristics that increase reproductive success

Single circulatory system (2.3)　blood flows through the heart once during a full circulation of the body (e.g. in fish)

Social hierarchy (3.6)   grouping of individuals within a species graded by their social position

Social insects (3.5)   insects that live in complex social colonies

Speciation (1.7)   evolutionary process by which new species are formed

Species diversity (3.7)   measure of species richness and relative abundance

Species richness (3.7)   number of different species in a community

Splice-site mutation (1.6)   mutation at a point where coding and non-coding regions meet in a section of DNA

Stabilising selection (1.7)   natural selection that favours a middle value of a varied characteristic

Starch (3.1b)   storage carbohydrate in plants

Stationary phase (2.6)   phase of microorganism growth during which secondary substances can be made

Stem cell (1.4)   cell that can divide and then differentiate in animals

Stereotypic behaviour (3.4)   repetitive movements, such as apparently aimless pacing

Sterile (2.6)   not containing contaminating microorganisms

Subordinate (3.6)   animal lower in the hierarchy; below the dominant individual

Substitution (1.6)   single gene mutation in which one nucleotide is replaced by another

Substrate (2.1b)   substance on which an enzyme acts

Sugar–phosphate backbone (1.1)   strongly bonded strand of DNA

Symbiosis (3.5)   partnership that has coevolved between two different species

Sympatric barrier (1.7)   behavioural or ecological barrier to the flow of genes

Sympatric speciation (1.7)   speciation in which gene flow is prevented by ecological or reproductive barriers

Systemic (3.3)   affecting all tissues of an organism's body

Taxonomic group (3.6)   grouping of organisms used in classification

Template strand (1.2)   DNA strand on which a complementary copy is made

Test cross (3.2)   cross between an organism of unknown genotype and a homozygous recessive organism

Therapeutic (1.4)   used as part of medical therapy

Thermophilic bacteria (2.5)   bacteria that live in hot springs or seabed vents

Thermoreceptor (2.4)   heat-sensitive cell in the hypothalamus of mammals

Thermoregulation (2.4)   use of negative feedback in regulation of body temperature in mammals

Thymine (T) (1.1)   base that pairs with adenine

Tissue (adult) stem cell (1.4)   stem cell from tissue that can divide and differentiate to become cells of that tissue

Torpor (2.5)   state of reduced metabolic activity in response to adverse conditions

Total cell count (2.6)   total number of cells in a culture including viable (live) cells and dead cells

Transcription (1.3)   copying of a DNA sequence to make a primary transcript

Transfer RNA (tRNA) (1.3)   transfers specific amino acids to the mRNA on the ribosomes

Translation (1.3)   production of a polypeptide using sequences of mRNA

Translocation (1.6)   mutation in which part of a chromosome becomes attached to another

Transmission (3.1b)   physical process of passing light energy through a surface

Trophic level (3.1a)   feeding level in a food chain

True breeding (3.2)   homozygous

Uracil (1.3)   RNA base not found in DNA

Vector (3.5)   carries stages of a parasite into a host organism

Ventricle (2.3)   chamber of a vertebrate heart that distributes blood

Vertical inheritance (1.7)   inheritance of genetic material from parents by offspring

Viable cell count (2.6)   number of live cells in a total cell count

Virus (1.7)   genetic material enclosed in a protein coat

VO_2 max (2.3)   maximum volume of oxygen that can be absorbed by an organism in a period of time

Welfare of animals (3.4)   relating to activities designed to be humane to livestock while maximising their yield